THE SINGER

PATRICK DUFF

Had i the heavens' embroidered cloths,
Enwrought with golden and silver light,
The blue and the dim and the dark cloths
Of night and light and the half-light,
I would spread the cloths under your feet:
But i, being poor, have only my dreams;
I have spread my dreams under your feet;
Tread softly because you tread on my dreams

WB YEATS

THANKS TO

JO NICHOLLS

JANET BELL MBE
...AND ALL AT GLASTONBURY ABBEY
ALL MY FAMILY
STRANGELOVE
CERNE & VICKY CANNING
ANDY ROSS RIP & HELEN POTTER
THOMAS BROOMAN CBE & MANDY
DODGE HOLME RIP
GIL GILLESPIE
DAVID FRANCOLINI
RICH BEALE
PAUL WILSON
DAMIEN 'SCAMP' MALONEY
JAY WILLIAMS
SIENA BARNES
LUC NICHOLLS
ALESSIA ZONA
RICHARD JONES
SOL WILKINSON
NEIL, SIA& WOODY TAYLOR
FR BEDE AND FR ANSLEM
FR DOMINIC
SISTER FEE
ANYONE ELSE WHO IS MENTIONED
BY NAME IN THIS BOOK.
ALL MY STUDENTS EVER.
BILL AND BOB ET AL
TINKER AND BUNDLE

Tangent Books

The Singer
First published 2022 by Tangent Books

Tangent Books
Unit 5.16 Paintworks, Bristol BS4 3EH
0117 972 0645
www.tangentbooks.co.uk
richard@tangentbooks.co.uk

ISBN 978-1-914345-25-8

Author: Patrick Duff

Publisher: Richard Jones

Production: Sol Wilkinson

Design: Joe Burt

A CIP record of this book is available at the British Library.

Printed on paper from a sustainable source
Print management Akcent Media

Pictures: Thanks to Dorian Holbrook for finding the Moon picture. Strangelove press pictures courtesy of Warner Music – thanks to Dave Reilly, Kathy Kelly, Gavin O'Neill and Nigel Reeve. We have attempted to trace the owners of all images. If we have used an image without permission please contact Tangent Books via the website. Thanks to Gordanna, Chilli and Georgie Jesson for the picture of Rayner.

Also, thanks to Drew Morgan, Annie Gardiner, Guy Metcalfe, Mike Youe and Andy Guosh.

Index

CHAPTER ONE

HOW DOES REMEMBERING WORK?

T he rows of beds were piled three-storeys high and ran along the central
section of the coach with an aisle down the middle. There were 18 of
them all in all. Each with its own electric light and a short black curtain
which helped you to shut out the rest of the world. Your own little bed
that you could crawl into while travelling along. Other bands had dreamed
the same dreams away on these sweat-stained pillows and there were grey
woollen blankets too, like the ones in police cells.

Once inside, there was just enough room to lie flat on your back, like
a coffin. They said it was best to sleep with your feet going in the direction
of travel so that if we crashed, you'd be less likely to break your neck. I'd
always liked being in bed and, over the next few weeks, would develop black
bruises all over my forehead, suffering nightmares and waking so startled
that I'd regularly smash my face into the ceiling only inches above.

This particular night was Strangelove's first on a sleeper bus. Springtime
1995 and our first big tour of Europe, as the support act to Suede, driving
towards gig number one in Strasbourg the following evening.

At the back of the same coach was a horseshoe of seats in a lounge area,
which reeked of stale tobacco. A television, a CD and video player, as well
as a fridge for putting the drink in. I couldn't get any of it to work and sat
there in silence as we trundled on; head pounding with the thud of this first
rude awakening.

It was past three in the morning and nervous of sobering up and being left alone with myself for too long, I grabbed the last bottle of hypermarket wine and stumbled all the way down to the front of the coach to meet our new driver, whose name was Steve. Welsh Steve from South Wales. A wasted looking drifter in his early forties with a flushed face and straggly brown hair.

"Alright, man?" I said, but he just shrugged back at me and carried on staring ahead. Reactalight spectacles framing his road-watery eyes.

We'd never met before this evening and for some reason my arrival in the seat next to him was creating an unsettling atmosphere. Maybe it wasn't the done thing for someone in the band to sit up next to the driver on the first night. I pushed in the cork and took a series of glugs yet still couldn't think of anything else to say.

He eventually put on a CD and *Up From The Skies* by Jimi Hendrix came dripping out from the overhead speakers in the cabin, but the volume was down so low you couldn't get into it properly and I continued to rack my brains. Somebody needed to say *something*.

Not a single word passed between us till the album reached *If 6 Was 9* and, despite my best efforts, it was him who finally found a mouth for it.

"Hendrix was a Sagittaaaarius. Keith Richards was a Sagittaaarius," pausing for effect, "And I'mmm a Sagitaaaarius," he croaked in a valley boy's drawl.

Removing his bloodshot eyes from the road and glancing over for a reaction. But all that came out of me was a half-choked giggle as my mind raced to cover it up with some other response. Was he seriously soliciting some kind of credit for this brag?

Mercifully, however, something in that nervous laugh had been enough to break through to him and he suddenly turned the music up, turned his head towards me grinning, and soon had me rolling up for him, as he began to recall stories about the singer/songwriter John Martyn, who he'd chauffeured around for years in a pink Chevrolet van. How John had 'heroically' (he implied) carried on drinking, snorting, and smoking spliff every waking moment despite the warnings of everyone around him, and then how he'd carried on going even after he'd lost his leg.

Rock music runs on these stories. You hear them from the drivers, road crews, lighting men, promoters, managers, producers, engineers, and even the tea boys in the studios. Everywhere you go, someone's sounding off an eyewitness account about somebody whose music you loved or didn't love, as the case may be. In the end that didn't matter so much. The stories were what mattered and they ran everywhere, serving as a bloodstream for the entire scene, and you quickly learned they were the one way of being accepted by the people you met. Often anecdotes you didn't read about in the music press at the time. This was insider information. Passed around so often, these stories had been smoothed to perfection by all the hands, and sometimes you heard the same ones miles away in different countries told to you by different roadies on different tours, who nevertheless used exactly the same phrases leading to exactly the same punchlines. You listened endlessly, totally believing it was all true, and there never seemed to be enough of these legends to satiate the fascination. Above all, you secretly hoped that one day there'd be stories about you and that rock 'n' roll's slave army would sooner or later salute you by keeping your name alive with amusing and clammy anecdotes about your failings.

So, over the years, as we shakingly climbed the ladder, it became more and more important to me that our drivers and crews did not find me aloof. I was the singer and, in listening to more and more of these stories, I'd gathered that we were the self-obsessed, prima donna ones. The drummers, bass players, and even guitarists, seemed to come out in a better light.

At the start of a tour, during the crew introductions, you could sometimes sense that they already held you in contempt simply because that's who you were. You were the singer. I wanted to prove that this wasn't the truth in my case. I was going to be a man of the people. So, for many years in Strangelove, once we'd moved on from our windowless van, I sat up front with the drivers asking them all sorts of spirited questions and open-heartedly soaking up their insane lives.

We sped along into the night. Once in a while, after I'd run out of drunken enquiries, they'd stop talking. It would all go quiet and you could properly listen to the music. Out of my mind, but with enough drink left to guarantee a loose yet vigilant ride till morning. The Doors, Bowie, The Beatles, Dylan, Syd Barrett, The Velvets, Leonard Cohen, Captain Beefheart, Iggy and the Stooges, and the foreign black roads swallowing through you. Staring at the white lines and the yellow motorway lights arriving with a comforting regularity, pouring across and illuminating the huge, greasy front windows of the coach over and over until you were hypnotised. Something was starting to happen and you were finally getting somewhere. Gazing at the same spot of disappearing road horizon for hours and wiggling your toes with self-gratification.

All at once, whooping out to the music with the sheer indulgence of being young, still alive for now and in a rock band on the road. Really hearing the bass bit over that drum fill for what seemed like the first time ever. Garnering insights into the lyrics so fathomless you would never be able to grasp these realisations again. Maybe it must have been a bit like this for Jim? It was almost sacrilegious to be allowing such thoughts, but in inebriated secrecy you could begin to dare. If sales went well (and who cared about that) you might make it properly big one day, and maybe you already had. You'd never ever, ever have to get a straight job. You could see yourself at some charity event at Wembley Stadium. In the dressing room sharing a cheeky line with David before you went on. You could see the faces of the kids at school. Yeah, what are you saying about me now then you wankers. Look at my girlfriend compared to yours. See mum, see dad, I was *right*!

The road went on and on and there was plenty of time for dreaming. The night thickened and there was an even better place further along where the dreaming ended, a place of deeper intoxication where you realised that none of it mattered anyway. None of it. The whole thing was just dust, man. A total joke. Then, all of a sudden down some French motorway, you were free and in absolute cooperation with the inevitable. Let it roll, baby, roll.

This particular all-night-long, we were joined up front by Gary the Geezer, our new tour manager. Geez was a tall, well-built man from Canvey Island with a crew cut. A reformed ex-mod/skinhead with a lingering allegiance to Fred Perry and a surprising gentle-heartedness that slowly revealed itself as the days spun round. He once beat the living daylights out of some scally in Manchester who dared to try and steal one of our guitars, but at the same time managed to remain a certifiably good bloke, transmitting an unsettling calm even when he was coked up.

That night, we three unlikely companions sat together at the front for the very first time. Welsh Steve, Geez, and me.

Another great thing about the road were the huge panels of lights 'inside' the coach, running along the driver's dashboard. They went on when it got dark outside and as the night deepened and we hurtled along in the smoky cabin these lights appeared increasingly evocative and consoling. Their existence meant that someone, who had something to do with us, knew what we were doing and was in charge of all this chaos. You could pass over even the vaguest concerns of personal responsibility and just slip into pretending to be the co-captain of some weird futuristic spaceship.

Or imagine if Stone Age man was sitting here now in my place on the same coach, speeding through this landscape of flickering neon and cat's eyes with the music blaring. He'd be convinced he was travelling through the borderlands of the Gods.

With this new bus it got even better. On Steve's left-hand side, separating the driver and passenger seat was a fake wooden panel, containing lights the likes of which I'd never seen before. There were probably about six of them; each one a bit smaller than a tea light and these ones were square. You could see straight away that they were for pressing. One shining yellow, one red, one green, one orange, one blue, one purple. They looked so cool and I'd been losing myself staring at them for a while now. Slipping deeper and deeper into a trance. So intriguing how they just waited for you, waited for you, waited for you.

Then, suddenly, I pressed the red one. I had a vague sense within me, which I'd been wrestling with for some time, that it was not the right thing to do. It was actually that sense, the sense that pressing this light was the wrong thing to do, that made me do it. Also, in some weird way I dreamily imagined that maybe it might make people like me more, but I don't know where that came from and there was no reason I can recall attached to this particular notion at the time.

And although I fully admit I'd been staring at it for quite a while, in my cloudy defence, when finally pressing that shiny red square, it wasn't really a decision at all. It was a completely impulsive act.

Welsh Steve didn't act immediately, he just kind of froze, but I still had enough sensitivity left in me, even that late into the evening's chemistry, to be able to sense his discomfort and apprehension straight away. I found out that they don't have normal gear sticks on these kinds of coaches and you change gears by pressing the lights. I'd put the bus in reverse. He fumbled around trying to do what he could to re-reverse my actions as the engine made grumbling noises and we began to decelerate at an unimaginably reluctant rate. Almost coming to a stop after about 10 minutes.

I don't know how it happened but as we slowed the others woke up and were suddenly arriving at the front of the bus. It was late and there was a kind of hush in the air as we waited to see what was going to happen next. The only thing that broke that silence was when a new person arrived up front and the whole story about what had happened had to be retold. Alex, Joe, and Julian. John, our drummer, and the roadies too. Then, it all went quiet again. Every time I heard that story it made me wish a bit more that I hadn't done it. It was too embarrassing to even ask for a cigarette or have another increasingly necessary slug of wine because it wasn't actually my bottle. In a way, it was even worse that no one was having a go at me.

Thankfully, everyone in Strangelove was too thoughtful, and intuitively understood I wouldn't have been able to cope. As usual it was just the silence of the whirring inside their brains that I was left to deal with. After we got close to stand-still, the coach seemed to miraculously throw off this episode and started to accelerate away again. The motorway coming back at us quicker and quicker. A cigarette alight. The hush in the air (sort of) over. Slowly but surely, people returned bleary eyed to their bunks. Somebody said something about 'singers' and Geez said he thought it might be a good idea for me to try and get some sleep so I slunk away into my coffin and closed the curtain. I lay there awake for a long while but it wasn't till years later that it came to me. Just as things were looking up and we were finally getting somewhere and the band was careering through France on our first major European tour, for some inexplicable reason, I put the whole thing into reverse.

CHAPTER TWO

58 WELLFIELD AVENUE

In 1920, aged 19, my grandfather, whose name was Jim Duff, left his home in Dingle on the west coast of Ireland and went out looking for work. He walked and hitchhiked east across the whole country surviving on odd jobs and handouts until he reached the port of Dun Laoghaire. From there he found passage on a boat to South Wales, settled in Neath and secured permanent employment at the mines.

On long, rambling nights, I heard stories recalling his adventures from my dad's eldest brother Bill, who lived in Porthcawl. As a teenager, I'd been sent away to live with Uncle Bill because no one in my family knew what to do with me anymore and *he'd* promised to sort me out. I'd sit in his snug, little lounge, listening as he passed on these legends to me. Three sheets to the wind on gin every night, Bill also insisted my grandfather had made the whole of that journey without shoes. But, after I was ordered back home, my dad rolled his eyes and said, "Rubbish! Of course he had shoes."

However, they did agree on many of the other tales and these stories painted clear pictures in my mind, which appeared strangely familiar. Grandad had seen out his education in the wide-open air, at makeshift schools in muddy fields where Catholic priests dug a ditch near the side of the road. Children sat with their feet in the ditch whilst the Fathers read to them from the bible. It was those priests who'd taught him how to read and write and my grandfather cultivated a lifelong love of words. Especially poetry. W.B. Yeats and Dylan Thomas were his favourites.

Throughout his life grandad remained a reserved man who would read for hours every day and, by chance, he came to stay in Porthcawl when I was living there because grandma was rushed into hospital with gallstones. On his suggestion, we relocated to the pub every lunchtime to drink at an easy going pace and in virtual silence. Still only 18 at the time, I didn't realise what was actually happening and how in later years that same silence would return to me again and again.

Seeing him back at Bill's house in the afternoons sitting on a chair in the front room reading verse from some old volume. Clear, blue eyes peering through his black framed specs. Watching him stop with his finger in the text to stare out the window at the sky. Whistling a vague, unconscious melody.

I believe those melodies are still arriving in me now from a never-ending spring.

****

Years before my stay in Porthcawl, when I was a child of six or seven, we'd go across to stay at my grandparent's council house in Neath. Even then, I can recall the retiring atmosphere around him and the sense that if you disturbed his concentration something precious might break.

Grandad woke every morning at five o'clock to rekindle the fire in the living room grate and then sat to witness the sunrise colours dissolving through his kitchen window. Whatever the weather, dressed smartly in a white shirt, a tie, a dark green jumper, and a threadbare suit. Thin as a rake, he kissed you good morning with the stubborn smell of coal and offered you his seat. The radio, incomprehensibly quiet, spitting away in the background. The back door opened and the birdsong and the cold air and the waft of the chimneys.

On first arriving in Neath, he'd fallen in love with my grandmother Mary Kenneally, whose family had emigrated from Fethard in Tipperary, and after marrying they lived out their lives at number 58 Wellfield Avenue where grandma gave birth to five children in the bedroom at the top of the stairs. On 3rd May 1936, out came number three, my dad Gerard. But everyone calls him Gerry.

Mary was a fiery redhead and held charge over the running of the family with an unquestionable authority. As well as raising all those children through the rationing of the Second World War, her charitable works continued to reach so far into the community that in 1972 she was recognised by Pope Paul VI, who granted her the Benemerenti. A medal in the shape of a fat silver cross awarded to priests and occasionally to laity for services to the Catholic church. It sat pride of place on her mantelpiece and when she was in another room, or out somewhere, I heard them whispering that she was always doing something for somebody else.

****

In the final year of grandma's life, my mum and dad drove me to see her in an old people's home in Neath. I was in my 20s then and singing for Strangelove. Just back off that first sleeper bus tour. This wasn't my kind of thing, man. Ushered into a house of flowery wallpaper that was poached in the steam of decades of boiling vegetables. 30 grey, old people arranged in chairs around the outskirts of a warm, mouldering front room, muttering into the middle distances of a blaringly loud TV set.

Mary was upstairs in a bedroom – too far gone even for the TV room – and didn't recognise me or anyone, sitting on the bed oblivious, slightly grinning. One of the nurses gushed on, shifting grandma's long-lost belongings into neater piles and nervously cooing about how she still seemed to enjoy the semolina. Eventually, my mum and dad went outside to talk to the nurse more privately and left us alone in the room.

I stared into her pale blue eyes.

"Grandma, grandma. It's Patrick. It's Patrick."

Silence.

"It's Patrick. I love you Grandma!"

Silence.

Grinning.

I kept searching into her eyes. There was nobody there behind her eyes who you could say recognised you. No one anywhere in the way. No judgement of me. She didn't want anything. Yes, it was unsettling, but I also came to see how blessed I was. To be there and to look into her eyes. Two cool blue motorways that led to the stars. Two cool blue motorways that led nowhere. Unadulterated life. Grinning myself now. We drifted into a kind of ecstasy together. She was already gone, but at the same time more 'grandma' than ever. She and I smiling at each other in this weird hell hole. The clock honestly did strike 'one' in agreement. You could hear the TV, chattering away its emptiness downstairs. My mum and dad on the landing, discussing practical details. Being 'reassured'. None of it mattered. Grandma held me high above it all, suspended in her bright silence.

Then, all at once, the others returned from the stairs and I fell back down into my chair. Our strange communion had ended just as suddenly as it had begun and there was no time to think. I was dumbfounded when dad said we had to go and I couldn't explain to them why I wanted to stay.

As we drove away along the M4 and back onto the next Strangelove tour bus I carried on thinking about her. Fading away, alone in her room, where soon afterwards she died. Transmitting boundless blue love out into the world. At the time I had a notion that, if we only knew how, she could have been wired up and kept all the light shows in Las Vegas running. Or stressed businessmen, or in fact any kind of businessmen or politicians or record company executives could be made to go to her and look into her eyes for several hours before they made any of their 'decisions'. Wondering how many more old people were out there. Staring into the depths. Infinity pouring out of their eyes. Disappearing into the walls of some rest home. With all their answers out of sight.

****

My dad clearly remembers the 1940s. Grandad showed him Swansea docks burning in the distance after a night of German bombing. Together they'd built an Anderson air raid shelter in the back garden, but according to the warden it was too close to the house so they were forced to use the public ones. The blitz was at its height and my dad witnessed the locals playing gramophone records and dancing in the shelters.

Dad's a great storyteller and with a few drinks on board he can do a pretty good impersonation of a Messerschmidt too. Regarding the war years of his childhood, maintaining that he'd no sense of the gravitas of the situation and how he and his friends would race around the streets shortly after the raids shouting and laughing, causing mischief and looking for a prize of fresh shrapnel.

In a failing attempt to keep them in line, the grown-ups around Wellfield Avenue would often try to frighten his gang of little tearaways, calling out the front doors as they sprinted by.

"Watch out you boys, the Germans are going to get you if you're not careful!" Prisoners had escaped from the POW camp in nearby Porthcawl and were rumoured to be on the run in the area.

One night the whole family gathered once again in the air raid shelter, but this time grandma had forgotten to bring salt from the kitchen. Against the rules, she uncharacteristically took the risk to run back, but shortly afterwards returned saltless. One of the escaped prisoners had broken into their house and was upstairs in the bedroom, staring out of the window. Eventually, on her insistence, my grandad was ordered to go out there and investigate.

Minutes later he popped his poker face back into the shelter. The 'apparition' my grandmother had seen was, "Not a German prisoner", he said in his quiet Irish brogue. "Not a German at all." But a large white barn owl which had landed on the upstairs windowsill. Everyone in the shelter was laughing now, even grandma, and that teasing was to continue for years because the barn owl returned almost every night after that incident for the rest of the war. Perching on the same sill to survey the wasteland behind Wellfield Avenue, before flying on over the park and down to the nearby slaughterhouse looking for scraps of meat.

****

When I was growing up as a child on Saturday nights my dad would bring his friends back from the local pub and tell stories. That's how I know about all this. They would get boisterously drunk and then my dad would play guitar into the small hours and sing Irish songs that grandad had taught him. Even though I didn't realise it at the time, this is when I fell in love with music.

At the beginning of these sing-songs the house was rowdy and the tables in the kitchen and front room crammed with bottles of Irish whiskey and huge metal tins of beer called Jackpots. The laughter was so contagious that despite the fact you were young and didn't quite understand, you found yourself joining in anyway. Then later on, if they were so drunk that they let you stay up really late, you got to listen to the sad ones too. It was out of this world. Their faces grew long in the veils of tobacco smoke that twisted and curled in the lounge lamplight. Even as a child, you could sense something was happening. Spirits rising up from the foundations of the house. Ghosts who weren't happy. We were in another country and there was some kind of injustice going on right in front of our eyes that we kept forgetting about. The world we lived in was not our own. And there was something else too. We were all going to die. The songs told you about that too. My dad's friends would sit so still as some old lady sang a warbling tune. Her twinkling eyes staring into distances far beyond the living room. A place that I didn't know about yet. But this was the beginning of a lifetime of finding myself drawn towards the melancholy in music and art.

Then they'd drink down what they had left and shake off those sad songs, pour another and launch back into some rebel yell and everyone would be cheery again.

When they sang and the whiskey flowed the whole atmosphere of our house changed. The troubling unease of the weekdays was gone. There were no more rules. My dad transformed into a different person. Wild and free like the Transfiguration. His blue eyes filled with white fire. Everybody loved him.

I now realise how lucky I was to have experienced this as a child. Something came down the bloodline to me through those songs. That's why later on I could do it myself without even having to try. Of course, as I got older and deeper into music, and as a teenager discovered and assimilated many new musical heroes, I never stopped to think much about my dad and his drunken mates still singing away downstairs on a Saturday night. I can see my room as a teenager now. Wasted, hollow-eyed rock 'n' roll faces staring back at me from the posters on the walls. Most of them already dead, or not feeling very well. I thought those people were so cool and in many ways I still do. But as the years have gone by, I now realise what a greater influence my dad and his friends had upon me.

They never worried about looking cool when they were singing. They never thought of getting paid or expected any criticism either positive or negative for their efforts. There weren't any phones to film them. The *NME* were not present. Neither were *Q* or *Melody Maker*. Neither were any apparently interested labels or agents. Or eccentric girls who'd flown in from Hong Kong. My dad didn't make music with any kind of ambition whatsoever. He and his friends whipped up their maelstrom just because that's what you do to get through life and have a good time on the weekend.

Now after all these years, I aspire to give concerts that reflect what I grew up with. Concerts that come from a place of uncalculated, free-spirited expression. Which to me is a kind of purity. Freedom to make music without any affectation. My dad played totally acoustic, never knew what kind of reverb to put on a high hat. I never heard him use the word 'compression'. But the atmosphere of his songs and those spontaneous performances are still alive in me and remain an inspiration. More than any of the hours of analysing I've heard chatted about music, over more recent years especially. My dad knew what good lyrics were, what a proper story was, and how to sing a song in a way that could make black snakes start coming up out of the carpet without even knowing it. To me that's the most important thing about music. That it is a vehicle to keep a kind of spirit alive. That spirit gets passed down through the generations and it needs music to exist.

'We shall not cease from exploration and the end of all our exploring will be to arrive at the place we started and know the place for the first time.'
T.S Eliot

CHAPTER THREE

PORTHMAI

M y mother's name is Margaret and she was born on August 9th 1939 in a small farmhouse called Porthmai, which sits on top of a steep hill, part of the Gregynog estate near the village of Tregynon in Mid Wales. Mum was out feeding chickens by the age of two and there's a famous old black-and-white photograph treasured by my family that shows her in a nappy scattering grain to a brood of hens around her feet. Throughout her childhood she worked hard with numerous chores, helping my grandmother Flo churn the butter and cheese and tend to the goat and pig. Washing the sheets and blankets in the river and running errands to the surrounding villages on a clattery bicycle.

My grandfather, John Evans, rented Porthmai from Gwendoline and Margaret Davies, two sisters who lived for many years as sole residents at Gregynog Hall, a black-and-white concrete mansion house at the centre of the sprawling estate. These two spinsters had been gifted the mansion, the estate and a great fortune by their father, the Welsh entrepreneur Lord David Davies, who'd made millions from the mines and also built the railways across Wales.

Both Gwendoline and Margaret had a lively interest in art and music and, after their father died, spent their lives collecting. Most notably a Rodin bust, a Cezanne, a number of Monets and Van Goghs, which hung in the numerous drawing rooms alongside all manner of other illustrious paintings. All through those years the mansion was full of music and poetry readings. George Bernard Shaw and Gustav Holst were among the regular visitors who attended parties there.

As well as scratching a living from the farm, where my mum and her three brothers and three sisters were born, my grandfather, full-time gardener to the Davies, carried the gun for the estate and often trapped rabbits and pigeons to feed their esteemed guests. Grandad John was a quiet man with calluses on his hands, who woke at dawn and worked all day long till it grew too dark to carry on. A man of the hillsides, who still practised the ancient ways and spent his mornings and evenings with the dogs and the flocks up in the high fields. With the moon in his eyes (they'd say) as he came in through the back door at the end of the day. Occasionally cradling an orphaned lamb in his arms.

His wife, my grandmother, was hardworking and down to earth too. But talkative and full of humour, gossip, and teasing, as she whistled up the kettle for yet another pot of tea. Granny had a wide smile and in her later years always kept a boiled sweet or two in her apron for us children.

****

After the Davies died, Gregynog estate was bequeathed to the University of Wales and today you can stroll the grounds. A short walk away from Gregynog Hall, along a tree-lined path towards the garden cottages, you can stare across the valley to view Porthmai on top of the hill. You can see the giant ash tree beneath which my mother spent much of her free time as a child, arranging her dollies in lines. You can hear the cries of buzzards and red kites swooping in circles high above. There are cattle and sheep and horses grazing along the Werne Bottom. There are rabbits and weasels and mice in the undergrowth. Hornets' and wasps' nests in the eaves of the garden cottages, and on the forest path behind the old wash houses, I have from time to time come across snakes. At night with no light pollution, the sky over the farm turns pitch black and is scattered with bright stars and the air comes alive with the calls of owls and the whisperings of the Tylwyth Teg.

As a young woman my mother possessed a striking beauty. Long dark hair and dark eyes which sparkled with the song of those remote Welsh hillsides. When summer term was over, she'd drive us back 'home' on holiday, instilling in me and my three sisters a quiet sense of place and belonging. High up on those hills of hers. Picnicking in the clouds. Where heaven was wet against your face and hands and washed you clear of all the dreary classrooms of the previous year. With the knowledge in her blood that it is not in complications that truth arises but in simplicity. Because my mother always pointed us to the wonder of the world and lived by it all of her life. The wonder that is present to us all wherever we are. But that does not appear to be known to many individuals in the particular time we live in.

****

Even now we return each year on a pilgrimage to the graves to bring flowers. My grandparents, John and Florence, are buried on the side of a hill in the village of Berriew and my great grandparents lie at rest in a churchyard in the nearby village of Manafon. The same church built of river stone where R. S. Thomas, the great Welsh poet, was rector from 1942-1954. From where he wrote his first three volumes and from where, as a girl, my mother listened to him preach from the pulpit on Sunday mornings throughout this time.

We also go to the grave of mum's eldest sister Joyce, who died of tuberculosis in 1947 aged just 23. Despite the fact we've never met, I have a particular connection to Aunty Joyce and have lived with a sketch of her face for many years. As always, she is looking at me now as I write. Joyce worked as a nurse in the hospital wards that tended to the soldiers returning from the Second World War and it was as a result of this care that she contracted the illness that led to her untimely death.

Her loss was rarely discussed in my family, but as a boy I once remember my mother describing Joyce as something of an angel and the only person she has ever known who never had a bad word to say about anyone. For some reason, that brief description left a lasting impression on my young heart and Joyce's unlived life has always called to me. She remains as a presence in many of my songs, buried under the sycamore trees in a far corner of the churchyard in the village of Tregynon.

The dark wilderness of that particular hillside and the wind that blows almost constantly over her stone have become one of the mainstays of my life. My mother's ancestors lived for generations within the few square miles of those hills and it was through this land and my connection to it that I would one day come to realise my own place and to recognise the murmuring of the upland streams flowing through my own veins.

My roots come from Ireland and my roots come from Wales and far beneath the earth they meet together somewhere in the middle of the Irish Sea.

CHAPTER FOUR

STRASBOURG

The next morning, we arrived in Strasbourg. I must have fallen asleep because the engine was quiet. The bus parked up. I slowly pulled open the black curtain to my bunk, stuck my head into the aisle and peered down to the back of the coach. It was daylight but no one else was up yet. Last night's alcohol and drugs had pretty much worn off and my stomach was twisting in cramps. There would be no way to face anybody without a drink and I would have to get off that bus – quick.

Frantically searching around for my shoes, the jarring physical symptoms and the mess the intoxicants were making of my thoughts jostled for pole position in awareness like a delay pedal set on the merciless screaming-monkeys setting. This morning, as on most others, there was one more incident to add to the hundreds I was already trying to forget. Oh my God, I'd pressed that red light and put the bus into reverse, reverse, reverse, reverse, reverse.

I'm not writing the lyrics. I'm not writing the lyrics. I'm not writing…

Without help, when it comes to someone like me, drinking and taking drugs are your full-time career and it's tricky to fit in any other stuff around that. We were overdue to put out our second album. The others had come up with pieces of music all ready to go and everyone from the band to the management to the record company were waiting for me.

They're not going to wait forever. They're not going to wait forever. They're not going to…

We were supposed to be finalising ideas on the road ready to go into the studio when we returned to London. Every morning for months I'd been awoken by the same mounting pressure I'd been trying to drink away the previous day; looking for ways to steady myself in order to work out what to do about all this rock 'n' roll responsibility. It wasn't like this in the music biographies I'd read. You had to do a lot more than just get out of it, get in the papers, and rely on your talent. Sitting down and writing the lyrics of course was too simple a solution. I'd got it into my head that the problem was something altogether more complicated.

I'd reasoned it was when I was out of my mind that the best ideas came through, but that I was just too mashed up then to bring any of them back to the so-called real world. Already knowing by the numerous notebooks filled with doodles, and short phrases like 'I Can't Go On' written over and over again, that pens clearly weren't working, I'd recently invested in a Dictaphone. In fact, I'd got it together to go to Phillips the day before we went on tour. So I wasn't that useless. The plan was that when those wasted inspirations arose, I would just have to press play and record, open my mouth to the gates of hell, and Bob's your uncle! I'd have all the lyrics we needed and probably more.

First things first though, we had a gig that night and I'd have to start getting well. Creeping off the bus and quietly closing the door behind me. Outside it was a bright springtime morning with clear blue skies. The shadows in the streets were long and it remained chilly though the sun was shining strong. Maybe six o'clock? That evening's venue was a sinister looking affair of tinted glass with girders and the surrounding streets were dusty and offered three almost identically unpromising directions. Fingers crossed, I walked up the one I concluded to be the least threatening, hoping to buy a bottle of wine with the French money Geez had handed me the night before – just before I'd pressed the red one, red one, red one. All the shops had Arabic writing on the front with metal shutters pulled down, but there was somewhere further along with tables of fruit outside.

Halfway up the road, I was suddenly stopped in my tracks. Floating out from inside that grocery was some of the most haunting singing I'd ever heard. A woman's voice acapella holding pure notes and then cascading through Arabic cadences with a terrifying sense of loss and longing. Even in my desperate state I stood motionless in the middle of the road in a kind of rapture. At one with her sweet voice in the now sweet early morning anticipation.

I had a Dictaphone. I could record this. I ran towards the shop fumbling to pull it from my jacket. Storming in and holding it aloft in the air. However, at that very moment the singing ceased and her mesmerising voice mutated into the sound of some man speaking loudly in Arabic.

In my imagination this singing had originated from a woman who was present, either inside the shop or out back. I was wrong, because it now became clear that the graceful voice had in fact come from a radio station, and the announcer was gabbling away with the same lame-brained urgency most of those presenter-people seem to think necessary. His jarring enthusiasm, although incomprehensible, wrestled me out of my musical high and returned me slam dunked to the shop floor. Standing in an Algerian grocery store in Strasbourg at six in the morning, pale as a ghost in a dark-brown flared suit, platform heels and last night's smudged eyeliner.

The two burly middle-aged men and the tiny old lady who ran the shop stared back, turning down the radio so that the store became decidedly eerie.

"I'm sorry," I blurted out.

"I'm sorry. I heard the music. I'm sorry. It was the woman's voice. I mean it was beautiful. I didn't mean to. I wanted to record it on this thing."

My hand was still in the air holding the Dictaphone.

"I'm sorry."

They continued to stare frostily. It wasn't till later I recognised that this was France, in an Arabic store, and they probably didn't understand a word of this unprovoked apology. In my frazzled mind however, I knew their silence meant only one thing. I had somehow insulted these people by mistake. The paranoid, cold jitters of daylight clearly translating the distaste in their expressions.

"I'm sorry."

I said one more time before stumbling out. Half walking, half running to get away. Turning back to see a little boy of about six or seven darting out into the street behind me. I don't know where he'd been before that.

He was pointing at me and shouting back into the shop to his elders in Arabic and I kept turning my head to look at him whilst continuing up the road. He was standing outside the store and pointing at me again and shouting to his elders with even greater agitation.

A little boy with black hair, dark skin, and a white shirt, jumping up and down like he was witnessing the swan song of some idiot sideshow freak. His voice echoed behind me as I turned a corner into another corner. The shabby roads were narrow and confusing and plunged in shadows and sunshine. It was a run-down area with beggars in your face demanding money, fascinated by my presence and crowding round and shuffling along beside me in my bewilderment. I kept turning into street after street to get away from the one I was on. There were more and more of these beggars. There was a poor man in a doorway with deformed legs on a piece of cardboard reaching out his hand for help. I didn't know where I was, or where the bus was, or which way to turn with no friendly direction. I found myself returning into those same cobbled streets and seeing the same haunted faces puzzling over me against the lousy smell of the overflowing rubbish bins. A blackbird pecking at a circle of oil that some dilapidated Renault had leaked onto the side of the curb. Pouring with sweat, I ran into the road and alongside a line of parked cars all the way out of the neighbourhood.

On crashing into the physical barrier where you can no longer run, I stood catching my breath. It was quieter. There was no one around and further along this street I saw the spire of a church. On reaching its stone wall, I stopped once more in front of a black wooden door that was partially open. Having not set foot inside the house of God for many years, there was still a marked reluctance. However, this morning it seemed that perhaps there was something like safety in there. Something left over from my childhood. I crossed the road, out of the sunlight and into the cool stone hush. The sweat, suddenly cold on my forehead. Momentarily lost as my eyes readjusted to the sombre light. It had been many years and yet it was all too familiar. The gaping hollow of the roof and the stillness in comparison to my racing heart. I shuffled towards one of the smaller side chapels to escape the towering emptiness. Towards a stained-glass window of Mary standing with her head bowed and her hands reaching out in supplication. The blue of her dress in the stained glass with the sun shining through. The image seemed to pull me in. My grandmother, her Benemerenti. Floundering towards the light of that dress and the sanctuary of that blue colour. Before I could prevent myself, I fell down on my knees in the chapel and screamed.

Help me! Help me! Help me!

CHAPTER FIVE

REST ON THE FLIGHT
INTO EGYPT

My mum and dad met at a dance in the nurse's refectory of the General Hospital near Bristol's city centre. A series of grey Georgian buildings on the harbourside. My dad's friend said to him,

"Why don't you go and dance with Stripey?"

Because that evening my mum was wearing her striped dress.

They were married close to the Welsh border in Oswestry and a year later I was born on 30th June, 1966 in a red-brick hospital on the top of Blackboy Hill, Redland in Bristol. It was a long and painful labour for my mother lasting almost two days and the doctors eventually had to employ forceps. Leaving little scars around my eyes to this day.

Only hours after they'd dragged me out, my mum was still lying on the bed when an uninvited man arrived at the hospital and sent up a message saying he was down at reception with a gift. But this was a man my parents only vaguely knew and someone my dad considered to be a bit eccentric. So, with the stress of the birth still pressing they ignored the gesture. However, the strange man kept sending through his request, insisting to the nurses that he be allowed upstairs to hand over his present; adamant to the point that my dad grew frustrated enough to go downstairs and find out what was going on.

On arriving on the ground floor, the man handed over a brown paper parcel and said, "This is for the new baby," and disappeared without further explanation. In fact, they never saw him again.

Back upstairs, the gift was opened and they discovered a print in a thin gold frame. *Rest On The Flight Into Egypt* by the Flemish painter Gerard David painted in 1510. A picture of the Madonna and child captured in a moment's rest from fleeing Herod's persecutions in Israel. Mary sits on a rock in a blue dress with her head slightly bowed and her eyes lowered, holding the infant Jesus, who is sitting on her lap and picking from a bunch of grapes. In the background, against a backdrop of green forests and rolling hills, Joseph raises a great wooden cane over his head, caught in the act of trying to knock chestnuts down from a nearby tree, while a donkey stands waiting in the left-hand side of the frame. At the bottom of Mary's blue dress you glimpse that she's wearing an undergarment of red.

That same picture hung in a place of honour above my parents' bed throughout my childhood.

****

Those early years were spent growing up with three younger sisters. Catherine, Jacqueline, and Bridget. Four of us, born between the years 1966 and 1970. My mum had her hands full from the start and every nine months or so another Catholic hit the streets.

We all attended a convent school in Henleaze called St Ursula's and for the first four years of my schooling I was taught by nuns who floated around in black habits with wrinkly faces and twinkly eyes. They each had a decided faith, which they conveyed to us through simple stories, and despite what I've heard from others I never experienced anything but kindness from them.

Wandering between classrooms, I can still recall the dark corridors and the alcoves in the walls with candles in blue glass burning in front of statues of the saints. The convent was connected through to a church called the Sacred Heart, where a single candle glowed inside a red glass. The nuns told us that this red glow signified God, who though invisible, was always present in the church, and on many occasions at playtimes I would forget my friends, tiptoe into a pew, and gaze into the eyes of Mary's statue for what seemed like hours.

The nuns taught us about a Jesus who was gentle and mild. They promised he loved us, especially if we were good, and that this love was the most important thing in our lives. I soon learned that if you repeated this simple formula back it made them happy. Because for some reason from the very beginning I wanted to make people happy. But this wasn't as easy as it sounded, and the desire burned so brightly inside me that it often hurt. Grown-ups were complicated and somewhere in my own heart I began to sense that the nuns were more right than ever. We needed God's help and every night for years as a child, I prayed one hundred Hail Marys for my family and friends and teachers before being able to get to sleep.

When it came to my first confession, aged about four or five, this early schooling had made such an impression that however seriously I considered my young life, I could not recall anything I'd actually done wrong. This was surprisingly worrying because they'd all assured me a first confession was an important step, and right down to the gun going off I had nothing.

The shadowy priest behind the screen hunched forward in expectation as I entered the confessional box.

"Bless me father, for I have sinned. This is my first confession."

Still hardly knowing what to say, I opened my mouth and began to invent sins to satisfy him, fabricating stories of throwing stones through the windows of my own house and upsetting my parents. Then, throwing sticks through some of the other windows too. My head, racing. I'd been disobedient. I'd disobeyed the teachers. I hated them. I wanted to run away. None of it was true but the more carried away I became by the sway of my voice, the more this rebellious alter ego appeared heroic to me. I was also beginning to sense that the priest was impressed too because his overcast presence seemed to lighten to a further and further degree as I beamed on through my long and winding tales of mumbo jumbo, and I felt him relax enough to slump back into his seat as the familiar and comforting odour of whiskey fumes perforated through the hatch between us.

****

Towards my final term at St Ursula's, I started to experience blinding headaches. A pain that meant I had to stop playing, draw the curtains, and get into bed under the blankets. When I closed my eyes all you could see in my dark were these weird, swirling star shapes. It was meningitis. I was driven by ambulance to the BRI hospital in Bristol to spend an antiseptic springtime in one of the isolation rooms. Lying there with no idea that I may have been close to death. Thank God for my dad's visits, and Uncle Bill too, who kept up my spirits with dot-to-dot puzzle books and stories about Welsh and Irish sporting events.

There was a colour TV in the hospital room and we only had a black-and-white at home. One morning, without a word of warning, a cross-eyed boy of about my age appeared with a sad face. They'd tucked him into the other isolation room across the corridor. There were large windows between us and we had to watch the same TV set. My dad said that the sound was pumped into his room through special speakers. The sad boy looked through the glass in his room and through the glass in my room and into the glassy-eyed screen. It was unsettling trying to accustom myself to his magnetism and I could sense black holes tunnelling into the back of my head as we watched *Basil Brush* and *The Generation Game* on Saturday evenings.

Between programmes, when the TV went momentarily blank, you could see his reflection reappearing in the dark screen. That first shadowy presence was me but that other smaller shadowy presence was him. This was mostly how we got to know each other because he never returned my smile when I turned around. So, I stopped trying to be friendly and soon couldn't enjoy the TV anymore either because I never knew whether I'd picked the channel he wanted.

Who was he? Why did he never smile? What made him happy? Where were his mum and dad? Why did he never seem to get any visitors? Why did his eyes look in different directions like they'd fallen out after a disagreement and were both too proud to change their point of view? When the TV was off there wasn't much else to think about and one morning I finally found the courage to look round again and he'd disappeared. Uncle Bill said he'd gone somewhere else, refusing to elaborate, and the sad boy's fate remained with me as a vague and somehow nagging preoccupation.

One afternoon, towards the end of that stay of illness, my dad ushered me along an empty corridor to a window which gazed out over the hospital car park. I hadn't been out of my room for weeks. Way below on the black concrete standing between the white lines were my mum and three little sisters waving up. My mum in her red coat and a white Alice band in her black hair. My sisters in their floral Bizzy Lizzie dresses. I waved back till they all started slipping and sliding around. Suddenly, there were 12 of them and fat tears were pouring down my face. The picture of that hospital car park and everything I loved so dearly burned deeply into my memory by the furnace at the centre of the earth.

****

After six or seven lumber punches, they drained some kind of fluid out of my spine and I went home.

Just after coming out of hospital, on reaching the age of seven, like every other Catholic boy in the region I took the summer exam for St Brendan's College; a large secondary school run by the Congregation of Christian Brothers. Despite that hospital malaise, I managed to win a free place and mum and dad were delighted. In the first few terms, I was spotted as having a talent for music and story writing and after the parents' evening they returned home with half-cut smiles. As a result of this encouragement, and my desire to please, I began to write stories every weekend. Sitting at the dining room table, listening to the sound of my family watching TV in the lounge, as my imagination took complete possession of my body. Not turning on the light as the sun went down so that I could write on, in the darkness, with just the yellow glare of the nearby streetlamps across the page. The reflections of raindrops on exercise books on the windowsill. I could feel myself lifting out of my body as the pencil raced over the paper and the words poured out of my hands all by themselves.

Those faraway stories were later read out on Friday afternoons by our English teacher, Mr Pullin. The other boys appeared to enjoy them too as it was also a chance for us to get out of the more usual monotony of copying stuff off a blackboard.

However, something about all this attention and enthusiasm for my primitive creations did not go down well with certain other teachers and as the years went by there was a price to pay for that early promise. Aged 10, I was told by our alcoholic music teacher Brother Gleeson that my singing was too 'boisterous'. Then, at the age of 12, an English teacher Mr Martin, who was in his 40s and rumoured to be living with his mother, informed me that my writing was 'immature'.

In truth, I was a sensitive soul, and not well equipped for criticism that wasn't delivered with a little kindness. Because, on reflection, it wasn't actually the words themselves that did it, more the fact that on each of these occasions they'd also taken a delight in humiliating me in front of the rest of the class. The 70s was a strange time for schooling and Mr Martin went so far as to slap the exercise book in which I'd written that story across my face – to the howling amusement of the rest of the boys. Immediately afterwards I dried up. All the writing and all the singing stopped there and my creative spirit disappeared underground for years.

CHAPTER SIX

THE QUIET ONE

As the 70s drew to their close and into the 80s, there was a proliferation of youth gangs. Punks, mods, skins, bikers, goths, rockabillies. As a young person, you quickly began to learn that a hair-raising antagonism existed between these gangs and also between youths who lived in different districts of Bristol. In fact, these border disputes could unite otherwise opposing cults for the honour of the area they shared. For one night only, the hatred of your neighbours allowing you to forget your differences and form pacts to try and kick the shit out of Henbury or Southmead or Lockleaze or Sea Mills. Avonmouth or Bedminster or Brislington or Eastville. Redcliffe or Hartcliffe or Withywood or Hengrove. Lawrence Hill, Barton Hill, Lawrence Weston, Knowle.

Our family had recently moved to a snoozy little suburb, surrounded by council estates, and walking the streets was now terrifying. On several occasions, I was punched and kicked and headbutted in the face and soon the sense of violence erupting at any moment was on me even if no one else was around. You heard stories of fights with knives and baseball bats and pieces of wood with nails driven through. The fear became such a preoccupation that I began to dread the long journey to and from school and preferred to stay home at weekends.

However, my dad wasn't scared of any of them. I can clearly remember him running at a gang of about 20 skinheads shouting at the top of his voice in a Welsh accent,

"Come on then you cheeky bastards. Come on then you."

They'd cat called something back down the street after we'd walked by and the whole lot of them scarpered in all directions. I simply couldn't understand where he got his bottle from.

****

To travel back and forth from St Brendan's every weekday was a 90-minute bus ride across town. One morning, I was standing at the stop near our house just after seven a.m. The grey sky drizzled with a fine rain; it was gloomy and ominous. The number 29 was almost always late and that left you just standing there. Suddenly, over the brow of the hill, sitting fully upright on a cow-handle-barred push bike and riding the streets like he owned them, came a real life psychobilly. I'd only ever heard of these before. A mutation of punk, skinhead, and rockabilly. With bands like The Meteors to unite them. Bands who celebrated unnatural acts of mental illness, violence, and lurid sex. My sister Catherine, who swallowed and then spat out every youth movement, already had a few singles by them.

Head completely shaved apart from two dyed red horns of hair pointing vertically up out of his forehead. You could tell he was on one by the way he chewed his gum. Instinctively 'my' head dropped. I'd already learned that they don't like it if you look at them. Even a curious glance is disrespectful enough to be taken as a challenge. They honestly then believed that it was 'you' who'd started it.

I stood at the bus stop staring at the pavement. The sound of bike tyres whizzing through the rain splintering over the spokes as they carried him towards me over the smooth, rock hard tarmac. Time stretches and disappears. I could not hold it a moment longer and my head popped up just as he arrived in front of me. I caught his eye and he spat in my face. Sailing by up the road. My head went back down again. Hands trembling, breathing in and out. Again, the sound of tyres through the rain. Too scared to even wipe his gob from my face in case he looked back and took offence. A glance up. The back of a studded leather jacket scooting up the road. I closed my eyes and clenched my fists. It took every ounce of willpower I had at that time to keep my mouth shut and stop myself from shouting up the street after him – the word "Sorry".

At this time, my Aunty Ethne and her son Edward came to live with us. Ethne was my dad's sister and her husband Uncle Michael had recently died of a stroke when they were on holiday. Tragically, over the next few months my aunty's health deteriorated to such an extent that she took to her bed and a few months later died in my sister's bedroom. I will never forget the night dad came into the lounge to break the earth-shattering news.

Edward, who was only six at the time, ran upstairs to his mother's side and we all followed him into the room where she lay. Our local priest Father Ryan was reading the last rites and my grandparents Mary and Jim sat on chairs with their rosaries. We stood in the dim light of the bedside lamp listening to the priest's voice muttering the Latin. It was the one and only time I ever witnessed my dad cry. For perhaps a second or two. The room was cloudy with incense and I could sense the doors between the worlds as they opened.

Throughout the rest of the evening my perception of that opening grew and by the time we went to bed it seemed to occupy the whole house. Senses wide, I couldn't sleep and left my bedroom door ajar onto the landing to take comfort from the electric light. Deep into the small hours I began to discern voices. Bright singing radiating through from the other world. What I came to fancy was a choir of angels announcing Ethne's entrance into heaven. Listening, with my eyes open, staring at the ceiling of the tiny bedroom where I slept with the hairs on my arms and legs and the back of my neck standing up. The singing was sweet and distant but it also seemed to reverberate around on the landing in a circle. A holy transparency at the top of the stairs. I wanted to run through it, into my parent's room, to ask if they could hear the voices too but I was in awe and afraid to move.

The next morning the memory of those voices remained clear. Almost as if they were still singing. I couldn't hold myself in and blurted it out to my mother who didn't appear to be surprised and immediately suggested we should tell Uncle Ger, who was arriving to help us come to terms with our loss. Uncle Ger was my grandfather's brother and a Cistercian monk who'd lived 40 years in a silent order at Sancta Maria Abbey in Nunraw, Scotland. He was coming at the weekend, breaking his vow of silence and travelling down from the abbey to conduct Ethne's funeral at The Sacred Heart church in Henleaze.

Sitting at the wooden table in our kitchen Uncle Ger listened with his head bowed and, encouraged by my mother, I revealed all I could of the sense of that heavenly singing. He wore the black and white habit of a Cistercian and although just a spindly man with a bald head and friendly eyes, his listening was so deep and so still and so unfamiliar to me that it was unnerving talking to him because of that great silence that happened to be listening alongside him. When I'd finished he allowed that silence to hang as he considered my words and then spoke back with a strong southern Irish accent. A voice which to my young ears sounded so slow and rich and incredibly low.

"God does not reveal himself and his truths to many people in this way Patrick. You can only look upon what happened to you as a gift from Our Lord."

****

I served as his altar boy at the funeral and, after returning to the abbey, Uncle Ger began a written correspondence with me. They often suggested I might go to visit him on a holiday and I sensed that behind the scenes it was perhaps being considered that one day I might join the Cistercians myself as a result of having heard the music. Perhaps if I'd been able to listen a little more deeply, I might have lived a very different life and saved myself and my family from the almighty suffering I was about to enter into. But aged only 13, it was difficult to read Uncle Ger's archaic handwriting and the news about the abbey and the everyday joys of his garden were hard for me to appreciate back then. To my regret, I only ever replied a few times to his weekly letters and they eventually dried up.

****

After Ethne's death, Edward remained with us and became our dearly loved brother. We all swapped rooms and I moved upstairs into the attic and retreated further into myself. At night I now began to suffer sleepless migraines that seemed to be the shadows of the meningitis I had contracted as a child. When the pain died away, I'd lie in bed with every jangling nerve awake. A fizzy sensation that seemed to stretch tendrils out into the night – to invoke something beyond my will.

The first time it happened it was three a.m. and it came out of nowhere. A distant droning noise that slowly began to gobble up all my other thoughts and feelings, eventually becoming so loud that it blotted out every other sound except for the sense of my heart pumping faster. An awareness I'd never experienced before that slithered out of the darkness and swallowed my 13-year-old world whole. A scream looking for a mouth. Like everything that lives, it wanted to survive and it needed me for that. At first a pure sensation that entered through my solar plexus, but once inside swarmed down my arms and legs and up into the ends of my hair. Sweat on my forehead and in between my fingers and toes. Under my armpits. Gagging with panic and breathing fast and shallow till it ultimately settled down and made its home in my stomach and began to talk. An unfamiliar voice that whispered unfamiliar phrases.

"Everything they've told you about God is a lie."

"None of it's true."

"They're afraid."

"Because that's it when we die."

"There's nothing more afterwards."

At night the voice started eating everything. It ate the bible and all the stories. It ate Jesus and Sunday afternoons with my sisters. It ate football and rugby and fruit machines and the green of the grass on summer days. Until all that was left inside me was the voice – and it was my voice now.

"I hadn't heard that music. I'd just imagined it."

"When life was all over. I would never see my mum or my dad or my sisters or my brother again."

"I'd never know anything again."

"What would nothing be like?"

I was growing away from my Catholic childhood and at the very centre of this newly emerging young man was a terrifying sense of mortality. Lying awake at night listening to the push of blood rushing through veins. The intestines and the stomach. The internal organs I'd learned about in biology that were working away regardless of me in the mushy darkness of my body. Wormlike contractions inside a hard calcified skeleton. Right now, a grinning Yorick who would one day be released when the maggots ate my skin. Ate my eyes. Ate my lips and my brain.

The secular age had found its way in and many times the fear became unbearable. I'd take off my pyjamas and open the curtains and lie under the light of the moon, crying to the moon and asking her to help me. Praying the old prayers I used to believe. Creeping downstairs in the dark to my parents' bedroom and swaying before their door, wanting to knock and break down in front of them and tell them how terribly afraid I was. But I could never do it. Maybe I was too scared of what they'd think. Maybe I'd be in trouble for being this weird and freaked out. Maybe I was going mad. Maybe I sensed I was on my own with this one. Nobody could help. Nobody?

****

Two years later, aged 15, it was alcohol and drugs that saved me.

The first night we got drunk, we went out to do it with a purpose, having passed around some book about The Stones and all the boozing and the drugs they'd taken. My friends Paul and Rich and a load of other budding misfits drank bottles of cider in the street. Like teenagers do. Our shouts became raucous and as the excitement grew we ran around the roads breaking the rules. Eventually, I sprinted along over the bonnets and roofs of a long line of parked cars with my arms in the air shouting,

"Freedom!"

The fear had disappeared and I was able to look up from the pavement. Now that I was drunk, the constant threat of violence and my dark preoccupation with existence faded away into the background and I could be a relatively normal person.

His dad was often out, so we piled round to Marco's house where we were allowed to be a bit loud and I found myself making my friends laugh in the living room. It was the first time I'd ever known a sense of connection with the people from school. The first time I'd ever really made people laugh. Somehow being drunk you could just think of clever things to say without even having to try. Now that might not sound much to most people, but to a shy teenage boy who'd spent years feeling like a mute it was everything. That same creativity which had disappeared underground for years was emerging again as madcap humour and jumping up and down dancing.

Later that evening, in the midst of all our shrieking and craziness and blaring music the whole gang turned on me. They'd pilfered from the drinks cabinet and began pouring neat spirits from all kinds of bottles down my throat as I lay, surrendering on the sofa – gagging. Gangs of wild kids have a strange primal intuition to them and somehow on that first night it seems they'd already grasped my fate.

We ran amok in the streets again, but I was fading fast and had to be half carried. Someone threw a brick through one of the classrooms in Bristol Grammar School and we ran up into the gardens of Cabot Tower to escape the police. In a black out, I tumbled face down into one of the ponds. My friends told me later that they'd dragged me out and probably saved my life because they could see bubbles coming up onto the surface of the water.

The next day in school the stories were already legendary and despite a dry mouth and an aching head I was buzzing with a new sense of belonging, revelling in all the laughter and the exaggerating. Because I was part of something now. In fact, The Star of the Show. Later that evening back home in my room, I sensed something had changed forever. The realisation I'd finally found something that worked. No wonder the grown-ups loved this stuff so much.

Alcohol knew me better than I knew myself. Reached its hands down my throat and touched the place where the fear lived and soothed it away like magic. The same fear I'd never told anyone about. The same fear I'd hidden away from them all – and had no clue how to conquer. No amount of willpower had made any difference until now. I couldn't tell how alcohol understood me so well and how it knew exactly what to do about me. But all you had to do was swallow and you didn't care anymore – so I drank and took drugs at every opportunity from that moment onwards.

Because there was no rite of passage into adulthood for people like us, the ritual you underwent to go from a child to a young man was all about getting out of it and smoking cigarettes and flailing about to The Stooges. That's how you made it through. That's how you proved to yourself and everyone else that you weren't a kid anymore.

∗∗∗∗

Inspired by the blooming of this new version of myself, instead of doing homework, I began to teach myself guitar on a nylon-string acoustic that belonged to my sister Jacqueline. Reclaiming that natural streak the teachers had stolen away and closing my eyes into a world of sound that belonged to 'me' again. They couldn't take it away this time because it wasn't anything to do with them. I spent hours upstairs lying on my bed playing.

Allowing the vibrations to come down the strings and into your fingers and through your nerve endings and on into the place inside your heart where you understood things in a totally different way. Allowing that music to flow through your veins whilst watching yourself take the places of your heroes on huge stages in an imaginary world where, despite the fact you could barely play a handful of chords, you were already a star.

Through absorbing lyrics on records I was listening to and skimming through rock biographies, I began to learn something else too. If you wanted to be cool you needed to be a rebel. So many of those lyrics made sense to me in a way no other teacher ever had. Because rock singers were young and pale and skinny like me. They were imaginative, funny, and venomous too. Jim Morrison, Lou Reed, and Iggy handed me their sunglasses and after I'd borrowed them for a while, I could see what was really going on. Who I was and who I wanted to be. The Quiet One was becoming 'somebody' at last.

This new me didn't care so much about making people happy. It was so much easier being out of it. My parents had me in a bow and arrow pointing at university but I began to turn myself in a different direction. Towards the rebels, towards the misfits, towards the outsiders – the crazy ones who seemed to burn brighter than the rest.

Man, it was exciting but it was unsettling too. Because all through those wasted years that lay ahead, there were many times in the mornings when I sensed I didn't have the courage it took to be that rebel. The rebel who put soap in his hair and dyed it black and wore scruffy drainpipes and long black coats and returned the abuse hurled at him by builders from white vans. The rebel who smoked and told his dad to fuck off and didn't believe in anything that wasn't coming out of a bottle or a pill or a powder or a record player. Secretly, I couldn't be him unless I was out of my head and I hid that away from the start. Deep down I always knew the truth. Every time I sobered up I was frightened again and tongue-tied and went straight back to being The Quiet One.

CHAPTER SEVEN

THE SCREAM

Help me! Help me! Help meeeee!

Over the years, I've reflected many times on this moment. When as a 28-year-old rock singer and atheist, I fell to my knees and screamed out early one morning in a church in Strasbourg. I've come to believe that everyone has a scream like that somewhere within themselves. Some people may never have to cry it out. Perhaps life (on the whole) has been kind to them, or perhaps they are stronger or more reasonable. Perhaps pure reason is sufficient to guide them more assuredly through the certain trials and low spots of living. Or perhaps life has been so cruel that they've had to shut down emotions to such an extent that their sensitivity has hardened into another kind of silence. Or perhaps there's some other way of coping with the world that I know nothing about.

But for whatever reason at that precise moment in Strasbourg, I'd finally cracked and found that scream waiting for me. It's there, underneath it all, waiting for anyone who needs it. Regardless of your upbringing or your genes. A scream whose nature it is to cry out to something greater than itself. A cri de coeur that is a part of what makes us human and what makes this particular cry different from others I'd yelled out in blind-drunken rages at the traffic. In times of despair. This scream was different. It wasn't angry. It wasn't judgemental. It wasn't pointing the finger or making demands. It was a scream crying out into the void for help. Help from something that at the same time I neither knew nor believed was there. But it cried itself out anyway. Because after all my reflection I eventually came to believe – that scream screamed itself.

The reverberations died, swallowed within the chasm of the stones. I remained on my knees in the side chapel in front of the stained glass window of Mary. But everything had changed. Suddenly, some great vastness was looking out of my eyes and the heart of all this vastness was a deep, curious love. The neurotic freaked out singer I'd known myself to be from a teenager onwards had suddenly been pushed to one side like a puppet and this timeless immensity was now staring through me and I knew a profound sense of light and peace that I could never have imagined even existed.

'Everything's got a crack in it, that's how the light gets in'.
Leonard Cohen

CHAPTER EIGHT

TURNING POINT

1984: I was 17 years of age and still attending St Brendan's College for boys and, more recently, girls too. Sitting in the large, airy wooden-floored examination hall for my first A Level. Chemistry.

Chemistry. Chemistry, chemistry, chemistry, chemistry. By repetition you could drain all meaning out of the word and start to float away on the sound like a magic carpet ride. I couldn't pick up the pen. Even after the invigilator called,

"Turn over your papers. You may begin writing."

I can clearly recall looking round that hall in 1984. The huge windows that plunged from the ceiling to the floor. You could stare out into a bleak courtyard where no one ever went, apart from the weirdos, because the teachers could see you there. Stunted brown shrubs grew out of concrete troughs, landscaped into a labyrinth of low walls that muddled their way through a dreary and neglected square. Maybe it looked good on architectural paper, but in real life it was always in shadow and I'd never seen any green shoots. Not in all my years at this puzzle house of a school.

Inside the hall, everybody was feverishly writing away. You could sense the smooth, scratchy ooze of hundreds of ink pens scribbling you out under the examination silence. Your fellow pupils with whom you'd just squandered years in gloomy classrooms where you'd been dragooned into sitting at a desk for the past decade. When your whole body was seething with life and all you really wanted to do was run and run and run and run around playing football. Geography, French, and mathematics. History and physics. Baffling Egyptian hieroglyphics that tumbled out of the teachers mouths year after year as your childhood drained away. You'd seen these classmates almost every drab day of your life and it had all led up to this. There they were again. Those odd misshapen heads with their disobedient hair and helpless, often zit-infested faces that, unbeknownst to you at the time, had branded themselves into your consciousness for ever.

All those faces, whose names after all these years you can still pull like rabbits from a hat. Sean Madelana, Kerry Satterswaithe, James Hurford, Joe Tully, Ann Briody, Paddy Broderick, Sipper, Brendan MacDonald, Dave Oldfield, Nigel Fletcher, Paul Flook. Names and faces like tattoos on the inside of your skull that you got done in a blackout in the port of Amsterdam. Rubber stamping you forever onto your formative years like some sad old Teddy Boy with his long-lost girlfriends fading across his arm. Or like stones in your shoes that have hurt for so long you've forgotten they are there. Living rent free in your head.

People who'd bullied you. People you'd once called your best friend. People you'd knocked over crosses to who'd scored, still now, unimaginably important headers. People whose far-fetched sexual activities you'd always be trying to forget. People you'd told all 'your' secrets to who'd badly let you down. Girls you'd fancied to the point of considering suicide after they laughed at you. People in whose houses you'd once played mini snooker. Whom you'd briefly thought were friends too. You were just finding out about those people. The ones who, for some reason, you just don't have any business with in this lifetime. Their posh English mums were too kind and their dads too distant – preoccupied with something you would never know anything about. Large, creepy houses haunted by unfamiliar ghosts who did not want you there. You never went back and never spoke to those people again without even noticing it.

There they were, one and all, in the examination hall. Mostly frowning and looking unsure. Especially the bullies and the so-called cool kids. Their cocksureness was twisting up through the ceiling of that room like holy smoke. Grant 'Robbo' Robson's days were numbered. It was the quieter, geeky ones who were coming into their own now after years of being on the ropes. Pale, ugly, ungainly-looking kids with glasses, whose mums made them sandwiches because their stomachs wouldn't agree with the greasy school lunches. Who'd never even had a smoke. Who huddled together because they got spat on. Oh my God! They'd actually listened to the teachers and they were going to be the ones with the expense accounts. The ones with the big, creepy houses. The ones in charge.

My hand was frozen. My body was refusing to respond. I could not even turn over the exam paper to see what it said. About half an hour passed as I vacantly perused that room with my 17 year old eyes and all I could see was a kind of slavery. Slaves in a weird temple to the God of the rational mind.

Because instead of revising, I'd been starting to drop acid in the months running up to this turning point. Looking back, maybe that was something to do with it. And as I continued to look around that hall, a strange new world kept whispering away to me from somewhere deep inside.

"You have to completely change your life."

"Duff, pick up your pen!" came a voice from behind me. "Pick up your pen and start writing now, boy!"

They always called you by your surname and I never got used to it right up till the end. They also called you boy when they didn't like you. A woodwork teacher called Mr Savage was leaning over my shoulder and fiercely whispering speckles of saliva across the side of my neck. But I still couldn't pick up the pen. It wasn't even a rebellious act. I just simply could not go on with it.

The years of being told what to do and what not to do and what to think and the threats of what would happen if you didn't toe the line. The beatings I'd received from teachers with leather straps, conductors' batons; wooden blackboard dusters thrown at my head, daps across the backside. A teacher called Derek Chiles who'd thrashed me with a leather belt in a biology lab till I broke down and wept and begged him to stop. The insults they hurled and the contempt they appeared to hold you in. I'd just accepted it. Never questioning whether what they were doing was wrong. Never caring about any punishment for long. In fact, on the surface, better to get a beating and get it over with than the monotony of hundreds of lines. 'I must not misbehave on the school minibus'. And anyway, the bullies seemed to leave you alone for a bit if the teachers were strapping you for them.

Of course, some of the teachers were kind and almost inspiring. But most weren't. Looking back, I don't believe many of them wanted to be there and they'd have been about the same age as I am now. That chills me when I think of what some of them did. Because on this day in 1984, something had changed and I wasn't taking it anymore.

"Do you hear me? Pick up your pen!" repeated Mr Savage

I finally let out a shriek there in the examination hall that had been germinating inside me for years.

"Noooooooooooooooooooooooo!"

Not a scream howled out to some hitherto unsensed higher being but a scream that was fuelled by a big *Fuck You*. Its adolescent vitality echoed round the ceiling and everyone looked up from their papers. Finally, I was the centre of attention. I stood up and shocked myself by walking out shouting obscenities.

An hour or so later, the on-duty teachers found me lying on my back outside the common room smoking a Benson and Hedges and staring at the clouds. I wasn't even in trouble. You could immediately tell it was somehow deeper than that. I had to go to the headmaster's office, but was allowed to finish my cigarette. Like a firing squad. The one and only time 'they' waited for 'me'.

There was quite a posse standing in that office. The headmaster, the educational psychologist I'd been assigned over the past few years, my form tutor, and my parents, who'd already been called in. I swallowed hard because I loved my mum and dad and was a bit scared of them too and certainly didn't want them to be embarrassed in front of these people. Because who were these people anyway?

The Christian Brothers had left St Brendan's in disgrace a year or two earlier when the previous headmaster, Brother Coleman – supposedly a celibate – was discovered to be having an affair with the wife of one of the governors. That was the end of the whole lot of them, and after that we became a comprehensive school. This new headmaster, Dr Davies, wasn't from a religious order. He wore a brown tweed suit and smoked a pipe. I'd never seen him up close before. This was the clean-shaven early 80s and he had a salt-and-pepper beard. The remaining skin on his face was dry and pink and wrinkled and behind his eyes he appeared to be contemplating complex sociological graphs that you'd never be able to comprehend.

Instead of dragging me across the room by my hair and throwing me over his desk kicking and beating me with a leather strap as Brother Coleman had done a few semesters previously, this guy had a totally different approach. He slowly patrolled my eyes like a horse whisperer and spoke calmly and softly.

"Why did you walk out of the examination hall?"

"I don't know, sir."

"What do you think you were accomplishing by your actions?"

"I don't know, sir."

"What's your purpose?"

Silence.

"Do you want to leave education? Do you not believe in education?"

Silence.

"Are you a nihilist?"

"I don't know, sir."

He continued to ask questions I had no answers to, using long words I didn't understand back then. It was a bit like the interviews with certain music journalists I would one day end up having to endure.

"I don't know, sir."

For some strange reason, on entering the office I'd been offered the headmaster's swivel chair and found myself sitting in the middle of the room. The adults all standing around me in a perplexed circle of cross examination. On reflection, it appeared for the first time ever they'd become interested in who I might be and in the vast distance that had opened up between us and now they wanted to understand. But I had absolutely no explanations for them or anyone else from their planet or even for myself, for that matter.

Eventually, Dr Davies said (and they were all saying it), "Well what do you think you are going to do now then?"

It was just another one of those sorts of questions people like this always asked. Annoying stuff that I didn't want to think about. I'd already walked out of their world. Didn't they realise I wasn't ever coming back?

Out of frustration, and also a vague sense of newly found liberation, I unconsciously twisted my feet out to the side, hooked them around the metal cross that formed the base of the headmaster's chair and spun around at Waltzer spinning speed with my legs tucked back and under. Whoosh! I could see their temporal middle-aged faces all going round and round me in a blur, the high-pitched creaking joints of the metal chair as it went pirouetting round, and somewhere far away the sound of my voice.

"I don't knowwwwwwwwww!"

CHAPTER NINE

BUSKING

After leaving school you didn't have to do much (if you didn't want to) and that didn't take too much getting used to for me. In fact, there was no adjustment period whatsoever. I found myself slipping into doing nothing like a consummate professional who'd successfully done nothing all his life.

My dad, hardworking and steeped in the gruff ethic of a South Wales mining community, thought I should 'get a bloody job', but increasingly regular doses of hallucinogenic drugs told me he was wrong. Whilst lecturing me, with a good deal of passion at times, I learned to be able to tune into a high-frequency drone that was way above our capacity to hear with actual ears. When concentrating upon this ultra-high transmission, I could still see his lips moving and his expression becoming animated as he talked on and I could look at him and pretend to be humbly engaging, but all I could really hear was the drone that appeared in sound as the colour violet, and in my imagination was transmitted here by intelligences on a distant galaxy. A celestial communication which allowed me to not have to listen or accept his down-to-earth wisdom in any way whatsoever.

Though he never knew about those violet drones, the more visible space cadet traits inhabiting my personality at the time put a distance between us that caused uneasiness in our household. This was an apprehensive and volatile time for our family. Especially if I couldn't get out of bed before he arrived home from work at 7 p.m.

As a young man, my dad had risen to life's challenges and remained financially responsible for us all. It was fair enough that I should get out if I didn't want to go along with the rules of society but, as he so often pointed out, still wanted to partake of the fruits of someone else's labours. And in those later teenage years I did leave, although I kept crawling back. My life collapsed over and over again. I'd appear on my parent's doorstep one more time penniless and hoping to be taken back on a mercy plea. For a period, they relented despite being thoroughly fed up with me, but eventually they had to say no.

At the best of times though, it really did feel like some kind of liberation, after all that dreary schooling, to be laughing and staggering around in circles, living a life of undiluted hedonism. Admittedly, it wasn't long before that laughter started to sound suspiciously like the kind of laughter you hear coming from someone who is about to have a nervous breakdown. Endless days swallowed up in parks and graveyards and the rundown rough cider houses of Bristol with my new slacker friends Dodge, Gil, John the Greek, Chas, and Domdee.

****

I started busking on my sister's acoustic with a piece of string around my neck for a strap. Singing spontaneous compositions in a subway called the Bear Pit. The walkway beneath a large city centre roundabout.

Day after day, a relentless soul-sucking wind blew along the concrete tunnels as I stood playing minor chords and chanting one gloomy line over and over again, waiting for a kind of primitive poetry to flow from my mouth. Because somewhere along the hours of that underpass, I began to recognise that when the moment came it was a case of stepping aside to allow something else to do the singing for you. Some kind of carefree spirit that would borrow your mouth for a bit. I called them *Sky Songs* because they seemed to come from another world and as a result of that spirit, I began to experience a real sense of release and purpose when busking. Especially during those purple patches when the coins flowed in and, on really good days, the occasional silent contribution was thrown down onto my coat. Frozen hands and blood all over the guitar from getting carried away and thrashing at the strings. Without knowing it, these were my earliest lessons in the arts of songwriting and performance.

However, I was also forced into straight-up begging too because it was easy to lose acoustic guitars when you were always out of it. This was back in the early 80s when the only other beggars were old tramps and as a result, the 'normal' people were often intrigued as to why we were on the streets in torn clothes asking for money; shocked at being confronted with young people who seemed so far from their understanding of how things should be. You'd have to explain yourself to some pompous old man who couldn't understand why you didn't have a job and wanted to 'know' why.

****

My friend Gil and I begged outside the 10 o'clock shop off-licence in Clifton, claiming that we were out-of-work fashion models. Clifton was a posh area and there were rich pickings, especially if you had an angelic face. Gil, however, was a useless beggar because he lacked in any portion whatsoever the kind of beaten-down apologetic lowliness that it is essential to embody for a successful vagrant. He was never as scruffy as the rest of us either and instead looked like David Bowie when he went through his *Let's Dance,* white-teeth, smart phase. Gil hated the general public anyway and what emerged in our disagreements was his scathing contempt for what he considered most people's lack of intelligence.

I, on the other hand, made friends with the older homeless people who were attracted to our vibrant drunken energy, sharing our booze with them without a second thought.

Gil insisted that we shouldn't do that because of:

A) Diseases…

B) It was a waste of his share of the drink and…

C) Because we were better than they were and he didn't like to be associated with other dossers.

"Fuck off and leave him alone, you fucking wankers," he'd suddenly blurt out all slurry and venomous; whereas I thought they were cool because I liked their sad stories.

Whilst drunk, Gil and I argued between ourselves a lot and the truth was that he would probably have been happier snorting cocaine as part of some media event in a fancy hotel in London rather than being a useless beggar with me. He didn't appear to be battling with the same kinds of self-esteem issues and in my estimation also made a bit too much of the 'unemployed models' angle, which was originally 'my' joke idea anyway. I was getting the increasingly weird feeling that he was actually starting to believe it. He was often rude to the stuck-up people who ignored us and even more anti-social in putting them to rights as they walked away. In that way, he put off other nearby punters who may have indeed given. When I tried to point this out to him, he became even more belligerent and one day we ended up having a kind of imbecile fight outside the offy, where I almost knocked him out by mistake with a half empty bottle of Scotsmac.

But despite all this nonsense, the truth was that we loved each other like brothers.

Unlike some of my other friends, Gil got out alive and ended up earning a living as a music journalist and self-professed political analyst. He married a beautiful woman called Lucy who gave birth to their son. He never did get any modelling work though. Whereas funnily enough, in later years, I did.

****

The thing about the full-time drinking game was that even though your whole life was going down the drain right in front of your eyes, at some point each day we would reconvene to some sticky cider house with our various piles of coins and soon be crawling around laughing till it hurt.

Drink lied. It said everything was all right when it wasn't all right and in the final analysis, I wanted to believe that lie more than I wanted to face the truth.

My friend Dodge and I became deeply embroiled for a long stretch in something called the 'Mick and Keith joke'. That game revealed itself to us under the influence of LSD over a number of weeks. Acid was cheap and easy to score. Threadbare hippies with nervous tics sold it to you out of their tobacco tins from the gardens of run-down pubs. The joke that emerged from those tins was so complicated and obscure that for a few years no one else could quite understand what we were talking about. As far as I remember, it was something to do with us actually being the 'real' Rolling Stones (who hadn't sold out) with a manager called Roy, who was behind the scenes and manipulating everything that happened.

"Roy was taking the piss? Why was he sending that police car past now? This is freaking us out, Roy! You're supposed to be looking after us. Sort it out, man!"

We were able to communicate with Roy using imaginary transmitters and receivers in our right hands.

At the same time, we were trying to materialise a mysterious finale called 'The Crown'. It's hard to explain 'The Crown'. It was something like the philosopher's stone of rock 'n' roll. You could experience it, especially when listening to Jimi Hendrix or Syd Barrett, but it couldn't be grasped by talking about it or trying to work it out.

However, what *was* clear was that if and when we ever managed to successfully materialise 'The Crown', everything would go back to the 60s and we'd be famous. Marnie's dad, who was called Bob, would not be able to break up the party and we would be widely recognised by everyone as the 'real' Mick and Keith – and that was what I was hanging on for.

We used to hang out in Marnie's bedroom a lot. She'd hung blackout curtains across her windows, which remained permanently drawn, living her whole life in candlelight, listening to Vaughan Williams, Leonard Cohen, The Velvet Underground, and Suicide. Marnie was quiet and sexy and her face was sad and thoughtful like some pre-Raphaelite painting and she'd grown the longest brown hair in the world. She was loosely my girlfriend at the time, having got to know her because she'd attended the same school as Dodge – Henbury Comprehensive. Marnie didn't approve of the daytime or small talk and so her house became all about smoking drugs and really absorbing the music on a kind of cellular level.

I went on some reveries lying on my back on her bedroom floor that have most probably left parts of my psyche all over the cosmos. It wasn't long till Dodge and I ended up there just about every night. Unlike other people, she'd put up with us for hours and sometimes even laugh at the wheels within wheels of our endless rock 'n' roll dadaism.

However, I'll never forget late one night witnessing the uncharacteristic angst in her voice when she finally cracked,

"For God's sake Dodge will you STOP staring at my tits!"

****

It was never decided which one of us was Mick or which one was Keith (that wasn't so important anyway), but we spoke in mockney accents for well over two years and rarely came out of character. Pretending to be someone else so much that you actually started to become them was plainly better than being the actual us. I loved Dodge like a brother too, and our complicated drug-and-alcohol-fuelled understanding through those years brought us dangerously close.

We sat together in The Bell on Stokes Croft. This time, we really had taken too much acid and even though it was my turn, Dodge had to go to the bar because I was too scared. He was back at the table now with two pints of Guinness. We hung our heads in speechless paranoia. It was early evening, perhaps six o'clock. There was no one else in there. Instead, the whole place was full of echoes and the stark and terrifying sound of pint glasses being removed from a dishwasher. Suddenly, the phone rang from behind the bar. We both looked up at the sullen barmaid who picked up the receiver and spoke briefly. The intensity was unimaginable. You couldn't hear through the murmuring of her voice but at the end of the call just before replacing the handset she glanced across, checked us both out and nodded.

There was a brief moment of silence and then Dodge spoke up.

"That was Roy," he said gloomily, "Just checking up that we're all right."

I spat my mouthful of Guinness across the table. The beginning of the longest fit of laughter of my lifetime. We could not stop for 20 minutes and were drawing unwanted attention to ourselves as the early evening punters floated in. Eventually, the giggling got so overwhelming, we had to leave the pub and abandon our pints unfinished. It was that bad.

****

Only a few days later, we were shepherded onto a minibus with a load of other wasters to attend a day at the races as part of a government scheme for the long-term unemployed called JobStart. That afternoon we guessed all the winners at the Cheltenham Gold Cup by simply choosing the ones with the most curious sounding names and won hundreds of pounds.

Despite all the drugs there really was a strange kind of magic in the air.

Roy spoke in a coded language of great depth and insight through random strangers or taxi drivers. Sometimes the profound implications of their initially innocent-seeming words would not hit till hours, or even days, later. But then the deeper meanings would roll over us like a truck. Everything was connected in the most impenetrable way and I can remember on numerous occasions friends and girlfriends walking away baffled. Summed up quite succinctly by our mate James Goodland who once said to me,

"What the fuck are you and Dodge talking about, Patrick?"

Thankfully, the intricacies are lost to me now. Buried somewhere deep in the imagination of that time. An imagination which I retreated into almost exclusively throughout those formative years. Other than that, it was those close friendships that sustained me and I remain grateful for them to this day.

****

Sometimes there was nowhere to go. I slept in car parks and school playgrounds and came across myself waking up underneath bushes, or half-on/half-off park benches, or spreadeagled face down in graveyards. Lying on damp discarded mattresses in the street on Stokes Croft, or being escorted by security guards off the grass outside student halls of residence where I lay unconscious in the early morning dew. It was beginning to dawn on me that I was not living up to the potential of the boy who had once been described (by my dad's drinking friend Uncle John) as 'university material'.

Alternatively, there were people in bedsits who watched *Neighbours* and *EastEnders*. You had to sit there too because there was no more money and there was nowhere else to go. Those dreary characters in soap operas spilling their guts as you sat unwelcome in some poor bastard's rented room still haunts me. The uncomfortable silences between programmes and the embarrassing intimacy of not being able to leave or get out of the way when they had to deal with family or bills, landlords or irritated girlfriends. Life was not easy for them either and in all honesty why else would they have let you be there? I sat all day and all evening pretending to watch the TV shows but secretly trying to garner up enough courage to ask to borrow money for alcohol. The internal battle of conflicting voices was outrageous. I'd usually concluded that I just couldn't do it. But then all of a sudden, I'd hear myself blurt it out.

"Hey man. My giro's coming next week and… Blah, blah, blah…"

It was usually to no avail. Then, you had to sit there in the foetid atmosphere your question had wafted into the room. The rotten smell of your self-serving words hanging in the air. Trying to pretend the stench wasn't you when everyone else knew it was. As if a place to stay and food wasn't enough.

It went on like this for a few years. Sometimes the shame got so unbearable that I would walk around all night instead. Alone in the freezing cold, staring at the ground just in case someone had dropped money; playing weird counting games against the paving stones for hours on end. If I could stay off all the cracks to the end of Cheltenham Road, 'everything' was going to be 'alright'. The aroma from the late-night chip shops became so overwhelming because of the hunger that you'd have to walk out of town into the suburbs where it felt somehow safer but actually wasn't. If you started running it would make it go away for a bit. Or you'd give up and be back on someone's doorstep saying, "I'm sorry. I'm so hungry. Please. Please help me." The truth was that despite all the drunken bravado, I wasn't tough or streetwise in any way whatsoever.

CHAPTER 10

ELIN

Behind my back, life had transformed itself into a huge incomprehensible weight and I'd no idea how it would ever drop off my shoulders when at 22 I met a young woman of the same age called Elin. She was an abstract artist and painstakingly talented and intellectual but she also had brooding, wild Welsh blood. Her hair was black and her skin was pale and she had luminous pale blue eyes like some ancient prophet priestess from Lapland. Elin was scruffy, talked in a clever mumbling voice, and read complicated books about politics and philosophy. She didn't wear make-up and that was something to do with men. In fact, she appeared to nurse a host of grievances towards men in general, drank red wine, and became passionate about art. She would rattle on angrily about Kandinsky or something like that and I couldn't understand most of what she was talking about. She challenged and unsettled me and I soon came to believe that she was the one thing in the world that mattered more than alcohol, drugs, my friends, and even Nick Cave and The Bad Seeds.

I'd first met Elin at a 'drinking cheap wine and cider in the afternoon party' on The Downs. A wobbly stretch of grass, meadowland, and landscaped trees, on top of the hills surrounding central Bristol.

I'd already sensed her presence as I rolled in with Dodge and Gil – our little gang that we had jokingly christened The Big Three. Later on, as the sun began to set, I overheard her saying to another girl that she was never going to get a job or drive a car or contribute to the insanity of the world in any way whatsoever; that she was quite happy to be living a quiet life with her mum, signing on the dole, and painting in her bedroom; that everybody should have the right to opt out if they wanted to; that universities were a joke; that she didn't care about fame or notoriety or money and the whole political system was a mess too. I sat there, eavesdropping with my back towards her and butterflies in my stomach. It wasn't just the cool things she was saying. There was something about the way she spoke. Something incredibly comforting and familiar in the tone of her voice. Unbeknownst to me at the time overhearing that conversation was the beginning of the end for The Big Three.

I was in love.

I suppose being in love is in the post for everyone who gets born, if you're lucky enough not to mentally collapse beforehand under the catastrophes that hit us all at some point in varying degrees. When it happens, as it surely must for most of us, and you're in love for that first time, everything suddenly turns real for a while. Love takes on a shape and my love from that day on was Elin shaped. For a while, you lost that confusing sense of separation. You felt connected again. To someone and through someone back into the whole world.

Old couples walking down the street, who I previously would have ignored, suddenly appeared incredibly touching to me and the innocence and vulnerability I perceived in their togetherness brought tears welling up into my eyes. The trees outside the shops were greener, you could hear the birds singing again, even the traffic was singing, the sun was singing, so was the rain and everything along with it. A symphony of some vast agreement. The sense of a great absence which had haunted me for years was disappearing and I didn't know who I was anymore without it.

We began by meeting every few days in The Old England pub but I felt lost without my friends around to bounce off. I couldn't say anything at all till I'd drunk about three pints. She came across as cool and smart and wasn't particularly impressed by the jokes I pretended to make up on the spot but were actually things The Big Three had said before. In truth, I couldn't quite believe that she actually wanted to be there and desperately wanted to impress her but didn't know how to. She was complicated and when we were together my whole body writhed with snakes. I couldn't be myself. So, most of the time I listened instead and soon looked up to her more than I wanted to admit to. It was love, but it hurt too.

I moved in almost straight away. She lived with her mum, Jane, in an area of Bristol called Montpelier. It's a kind of hipster zone now but back in the 1980s it was run down. Sometimes through our bedroom window you could hear Irish tramps playing harmonicas for money on the street below and Elin would go out 'doing stuff' while I lay in bed listening.

Don't play me the latest track you wrote on a computer in your home studio with a pretty young singer-songwriter from London who you think might have a chance of being signed because it's difficult for me to really understand that kind of thing.

You see, I heard Irish tramps who are now dead playing harps in a state of total desperation. Their music floated into me through an open window when I was young and desperate myself and it went right into my bleeding heart and stayed there. The gravitas is still in me now as I write, even though that music is lost forever and those particular kinds of guys don't exist anymore. I listened for hours in a state of half-terror, knowing in my blood it was being played for me in particular by some ancestral spirit; channelled through a dying homeless drunk who'd built the motorways and still wore a suit and slept in a skip and didn't even know I was there above him hanging on his every breath.

The humble grace of that sound shaped who I am and what I know music to be. Because that music was so haunting and so simple, so raw and so real, that everything else since falls into a kind of shadow. I remembered my dad and where I'd come from and where I was going to when I heard that sound and it cradled me in its arms as I lay there in my chains, doodling Elin's name over the desiccated wallpaper walls with her thick lead pencils.

There were holes in the floorboards on the landing outside our room and the sound of stuttering keyboards in the afternoons and early evenings because Jane was a piano teacher. She was gentle and understanding and looked at me with kindness. It was a confusing time. I tried so hard to be polite and conversational, but with the sober everyday paranoia on me it always felt like I was somehow being dishonest and that she could see straight through me.

I spent a few more years in Elin's bedroom, shivering and shaking; attempting to straighten out and then drinking again with Elin begrudgingly looking after me. We both smoked heavily and by nightfall the room was hanging with clouds and always stank of paints too. I developed an unsightly eczema over my face and would sit all day long covered in thick white cream to try and soothe the prickly irritation.

Elin got frustrated. I wouldn't get out of bed so she'd go out and leave me alone again with my crazy head. She'd started to rent an artist's studio on Jamaica Street and I'd have to lie at home on my own all day, starving hungry but too freaked out to go downstairs and make toast. I watched *Sesame Street* reruns and *Little House On The Prairie* and *Scooby Doo* on her portable TV. I watched *Rickie Lake*, *Donahue*, and *Family Fortunes*. The more mind numbingly boring it was, the better I liked it. But when the telly ended and it turned on to Ceefax, I sometimes burst into tears due to the overwhelming tension that refused to shift without drugs and alcohol.

****

Then, one unforgettable day out of the blue, she came back and was unusually kind, saying she'd been speaking to a friend of her mum's and that she wasn't going to have a go at me anymore. She told me that all the drinking wasn't even my fault and carried the portable TV away downstairs and began to stay at home in the daytime. She started to read to me from philosophy books. Nietzsche, Schopenhauer, Rousseau, even Plato and Aristotle. I'd never heard anything like it before and was soon mesmerised as a lost, forgotten part of me began to awaken and these books briefly but profoundly lifted me out of the prison I was slumbering in.

I believe those words went in so much deeper because of the atmosphere of love in which they were conveyed and the desperate situation (I didn't even realise) we were in. We needed those ideas for more than just some essay we were supposed to write for a college course, and I will always be grateful to Elin because she literally forced me to open my mind when I would never have been inclined to do so myself. Having been unable to pay attention at school, it was Elin who began to educate me. If it wasn't for her, I might still be watching Bert and Ernie arguing right now.

She showed me books with colour plates of Jackson Pollock and Rothko and weird Picassos. When I saw *The Three Dancers* for the first time it blew my mind. All those images and ideas mixed in with the endless records I'd been listening to for years and caught fire. Rock music has a side to it that is poetic and vulnerable and arty – and without knowing it, that was the bit

I'd always been drawn to anyway.

There was a dusty upright piano in our bedroom and I taught myself how to play it. Jane came in once, after she'd listened outside the door to a slow melancholy tune I was making up, and told me that I had a natural talent for music. I was secretly over the moon to hear that as it was the first encouragement I'd ever experienced from anyone who wasn't out of their head.

Elin also tried to influence me regarding politics and feminism. She was right. I needed to contemplate things other than my own pain. And one more time. She told me over and over again,

"You need to stop drinking, Patrick. You're an alcoholic. You're mentally ill."

No one I respected had ever said it quite like that.

One morning, the withdrawals got so intense that I started experiencing hallucinations. Rats running around in the shadows which sent me scuttling upstairs to be loudly sick in the bathroom. All of which traumatised Elin's schizophrenic brother who lived in the bedroom across the landing from us. This latest drama tested the patience of even gentle Jane. My eczema was furiously red again and I caved in and finally accepted Elin's ultimatum. That afternoon she booked me into an NHS treatment centre for drug and alcohol rehabilitation.

I was the youngest one there by well over 20 years. Day after day, hearing the tales of how the booze had completely ruined their lives was a mind-numbing, heart-stopping, sobering experience. Somewhere in the film-like qualities of all those horror stories, I made a more informed decision to quit, and with this new-found conviction burning in my ears I marched out after five weeks.

****

With treatment over and filled with a new lease of life, I began walking back to my mum and dad's house that same evening. They'd agreed to take me in again but without a penny to my name, it was a long trudge in the dark. The Robert Smith Unit was situated in Clifton and the beginning of that route back to their house carried me directly past Bristol Zoo. The traffic was crawling through the December drizzle when I heard the roar of a lion reaching out from his enclosure, over the grey stone wall of the zoo. I stopped and he started to roar again. Short guttural bursts one after the other. A trapped roar so loud you could actually feel it in your rib cage and at the same moment as I stood there listening, the idea for a song rose unbidden into my mind.

Arriving home, I sat at the dining room table, playing my dad's Spanish guitar. There was a picture of a mysterious woman with long black hair staring out through the sound hole. I'd been fascinated with her face since childhood. Having already written the disconsolate chords lying in bed at Elin's house, I put them together with the words I'd dreamed up by the zoo. Wow, it was that easy and I immediately sensed that the woman in the guitar was pleased and wanted me to finish the song.

I couldn't think of anything to go with the chorus chords so I just wrote, 'You Cruel Zoo You Cruel Zoo You', and sang that a few times, thinking maybe I'd change it later; I never did because it soon felt right. This was the first song I'd ever written down. Because although I'd invented loads of songs busking, they had always been on the spur of the moment and never got played again. This was different. I'd written a proper song and it was called *Zoo'd Out*.

CHAPTER 11

GET IN THE BACK OF THE CAR

A few evenings later I was once again walking the nearby streets. This time with my dad's guitar slung over my shoulder. Wandering around, getting out of the house, playing as I moseyed along, so long as no one else was close by. Not going anywhere in particular because I liked to make up eerie chords as I strolled past all the suburban houses. Suddenly, blinded by headlights, a car pulled over onto the pavement in front of me. It took a moment to work out but the driver was Dave Francolini, a guy who played drums and was part of the indie scene in Bristol. The door flung open and bounced back on its hinges and then flew open again.

"Patrick. What are you doing man?" he shouted over the growling engine

"Nothing," I said.

"Nothing. Come on man. Have you written any songs on that guitar?"

"Yeah, I have actually," I replied.

"Right. Get in the back of the car. You're going to be a pop star."

There wasn't anyone else quite like David Francolini and that's the truth. Whatever fire set this whole thing going, that started with a big bang and made the stars rage and the black holes ache was running through his blood veins with a horsepower the likes of which I've never witnessed before or since. As soon as he talked me in, I was thrown across the seat, bumping into the door and then back into him and then bumping my head on the passenger window with no time to master the sheer ferocity with which he screeched away from the curb, holding on for dear life to the neck of my dad's guitar.

Objects of all kinds were thrown in all directions. Cassette tapes and empty cigarette packets and patch leads and beatnik paperbacks and VHS videos, jumping up and down or cascading in clatters to the floor singing their little off-beat songs as they rattled around inside the car.

The roads were a racetrack and he took the blind bends on whichever side of the track suited his racing trajectory most favourably. Unlike any other driver I'd ever known, Dave didn't give a toss about the white lines they'd painted on to the tarmac and as a result you could have died at any moment. He had his driver's seat reclined to the maximum level of relaxation in mockery of the terror his driving invoked. I tried to shame him, in an attempt to slow him down, by saying that if I wasn't mistaken the Beetle's design had actually been conceived by Adolf Hitler. It was a cheap shot and on observation only made him go faster.

Before I knew it and high as a kite from still being alive, I was bundled up the stairs into an attic room at his mum and dad's house in Coombe Dingle. The guitar mic'd, a vocal microphone set up, and a brand-new cassette dropped into a Tascam Four Track recorder. I'd never seen a four track before. You could 'overdub yourself' on this machine, "Using normal cassettes," he said.

"Because normal cassettes have got four tracks on 'em, man."

"Bloody hell! Seriously?" It all seemed like some kind of wizardry to me.

Before beginning, Dave smoked a flat-out cigarette. He always smoked like it was his last one and afterwards ashen-faced 'straights' fell from his mouth exhausted into the ashtray. Every last bit of fire sucked out of them, their life force utterly extinguished.

Dressed in a black mohair jumper and pencil black jeans, he was rake-thin with unhealthy pockmarked skin, flashing green eyes, disorganised yellow teeth, and the rhythm of deep space flickering through his muscles. A contortion of fight, fight, fight, with absolutely no flight whatsoever to balance it up. Drumming on everything around him in a manner that relegated Stuart Copeland from The Police to something like a junkie gouching out on the pavement in Stokes Croft.

Dave would suddenly become so possessed by music that he would grab you and shake you and scream with enthusiasm about some B-side by The Fall. He'd turn the record player up to ear splitting levels and we'd dance around that attic room clutching each other doing Mark E Smith impressions, laughing our heads off.

At the same time, he also unnerved me. Because in our more sombre moments he was unapologetic and made no secret of the fact that he wanted to be successful. Not just successful, he wanted to be massive. Not just massive, he wanted the whole lot of those bastards to fall to their knees and weep and beg for forgiveness. It was unsettling to be around someone with so much ambition and I'd find myself secretly afraid because the way he'd rant with so much conviction about the failings of the current music scene sometimes made you believe we could actually do it.

He was generous and encouraging and almost angry in support of my talent. I'd never been friends with anyone like this before. I'd never met anyone like him. Someone with a burning earnestness who wanted to cause some real trouble in the real world. The people I knew before him were lazy and more into self-destruction. Dave was great for me and I totally loved him from the start. Despite the fact that his intense, controlling nature could come across as suffocating and incredibly bullish at times.

"Right then play this song then. What's it called?"

"*Zoo'd Out.*"

He wrote it down in scraggly writing on the top of the cassette box.

That was the beginning of Strangelove.

I had no idea my life was about to change forever.

When we got to overdubbing the middle eight section, I screamed down the microphone through loads of guitar pedals and it caused some kind of crazy feedback loop which we both thought sounded totally cool. This was the first time I'd ever considered how recording can take something you feel one moment and make it last forever.

I wrote more songs, quickly. *Snakes, Kite, All Because Of You, Nobody's There*; and Dave recorded them all with complicated drum machine overdubs.

He also reintroduced me to Alex Lee and Joe Allen and Jazzer, who all came along and played on top of the songs and brought their own musical ideas too.

A few years previously Dave had already attempted to get us together when we'd dropped acid at his flat above a post office in Filton. We'd played guitars all night long and you could actually see the electricity circulating between us like sparks from a Van de Graaff generator. We were into the same kind of bands and talked the same kind of crazy and that first jam was undoubtedly · an expression of some kind of star-crossed agreement. But at that time, I had no idea how rare this kind of chemistry actually is.

By the time Dave, Joe, Jazzer, and I had started making these new demos Alex had become a member of Bristol band The Blue Aeroplanes and was out supporting REM on a world tour. But between his schedule he'd come back and contribute guitar ideas at Dave's mum's house.

****

Now that I was sober, Elin found us a flat on Cheltenham Road in Stokes Croft. Right opposite the place where years later the Bristol Tesco riots would kick off. Jane had given us the deposit and the first few months of this new set up were full of promise. For the first time in my life, I had somewhere of my own to live and something to believe in. The band were demoing our early material and Elin and I were setting out together. Having been out of it virtually every day for years, this being-sober business was unusual enough to feel like taking a new kind of drug for a while. The eczema cleared up, I lost the boozing weight around my face and found myself writing new songs the whole time.

However, as the weeks continued to go by, for some unfathomable reason this novelty slowly began to wear off. I didn't have a clue about the true nature of alcoholism then and believed that by simply not drinking anymore I was now free of it. So, I couldn't understand why day-by-day the fear was back and ripening, waiting to pounce at the end of the bed as soon as I opened my eyes in the morning. That old familiar uneasiness in my stomach like rotten fruit, a poison reaching its way down into my fingers and toes and into my throat. In trying to cover it all up, I began to feel like I was acting in some shit B movie. That at any moment, I was about to be unmasked and humiliated.

I tried to talk back proud to the noise in my head or listen to music or walk around the streets or confide in Elin. But nothing I came up with worked to ease the chronic anxiety. The only thing that had ever been able to conquer this was drugs and alcohol. But I couldn't do them anymore.

In the end, Elin left the flat. Not when I was drunk or withdrawing but when I was six months clean, saying she couldn't handle the uneasiness anymore. However, I stayed on because she allowed the housing benefit to keep paying her half of the rent while she moved back in with her mum.

After she'd gone, I lay on the sofa disassociating and out of that came my creative contribution to the album *Time For The Rest Of Your Life*.

****

There was an Australian couple downstairs, both of whom had bloodshot eyes and permanent dozy grins. From the time we'd moved in, they'd insisted on telling us about strange occurrences in their place. Furniture being shifted around at night and how the next morning their living room was all different.

"Yeah mate. We got all sorts of weird shit going down in here. Don't you hear it. No? Spooks moving the sofa and chairs. Ha! Ha-ha! Ha-ha-ha! Total nightmare mate. Total nightmare. Ha! Ha-ha! Ha-ha-ha!"

"It's weird he thinks it's so funny," I'd said to Elin.

We hadn't heard anything ourselves and at first thought they were just making it up or that they were just stoners or that it was just something to do with them being Australian – as these were our first dealings with Aussies, apart from my Nick Cave obsession.

But that all changed one night.

****

Elin had taken her belongings and the flat looked dismally empty now. In the living room sat the landlord's three-piece suit and a dead laurel tree, which I'd resurrected from my dad's garden bonfire, standing six-feet high in a huge black bucket and smelling of petrol. There was an acoustic guitar, a wonky old 80s portable cassette player. Some cassettes I was recording song ideas onto, a mini-sized church organ given to me by my dad's best friend, Uncle Colin, and a Nick Drake compilation called *Heaven In A Wild Flower*. It was the only music I still owned, having sold or given away my entire record collection. In the bedroom there was only an old mattress on the floor.

Being clean and sober made it difficult to sleep and at night I'd lie on the collapsed brown sofa staring at the cream walls – further yellowed by the smoke of what I pictured were the fusty and uninhabitable lives of the previous tenants. Who were they to have left such a languid quality behind? Loneliness and insomnia were giving me the time to wonder.

It was four o'clock in the morning and just as I was finally dropping off, that guitar seemed to be calling again. When a chaotic place like Stokes Croft is quiet at night, it feels like the whole world is holding its breath and despite my troubled mind, the songs kept coming for a while, materialising whenever they wanted to and totally disregarding whether it was convenient or not. Back then they'd mostly arrive pretty much fully formed at night like new-born baby foxes. Wet and blinking. I never had to try. Just had to be awake to feel when they were coming. Like thunderstorms or something like that. This approaching song was called *The King Of Somewhere Else* and eventually ended up on a Strangelove B-side.

Everything goes dreamlike and time disappears when music is first coming through. The new song lured me away from my more usual heavy-hearted preoccupations and carried me through to the other world. Eventually, on returning, I always needed to record the bones of what had arrived straight onto a cassette because I can't write music and was liable to forget the precise melody and the particular way I sang it and the chords and the way they flowed. So, at about five o'clock, I pressed play and record and sang the song into the cassette player.

The next afternoon I listened back to the recording. All the way through you could clearly distinguish the voice of an old woman singing along in time, an octave higher, in a distant wavering voice. She sang in a vague almost unconscious way. Warbling the very same words that had only just come through to me. Not always in time but as loud as my own voice and clearly distinguishable. I listened again and again and it definitely wasn't an aberration of the tape. She even sang a few of the lines with her own inflections. But there was no one anywhere in the flat when I'd recorded the song and it was deadly quiet outside. It was five o'clock in the morning. After crossing off the possibilities there was only one remaining. Those Australians weren't mad after all and this was the actual voice of a ghost.

I played the cassette to Alex and Joe. To my sister Catherine, and to everyone else who would listen. We honestly didn't know what to make of it and on reflection it was strange how matter of fact I became about it.

In the chaos of the years that lay ahead I lost that tape. My good friend Domdee, who stole things (and admits to it because he says he 'couldn't help himself'), still swears blind he didn't take it.

Not long afterwards there were more unusual occurrences.

****

A couple in their mid-20s, who both had dark curly hair, lived upstairs. From Monday to Friday, they were dressed smartly because they worked nine-to-five office jobs. When you saw them on weekends going off downtown to drink coffee and read newspapers it didn't look right. Him in his Sunday jeans and a leather waistcoat and her in a black mini skirt. For some reason they came across as more themselves in their work clothes and on weekends appeared to emit an air of mild pretence. One Saturday morning, I heard Alice In Chains draining from their flat and suddenly felt terribly embarrassed for everyone concerned. It was always a relief to get them back to Monday.

I would often stay up all night occasionally sitting at the window and looking out onto Cheltenham Road. He usually kissed her as they went their separate ways in the morning and something about this ritual created an atmosphere of mournfulness around them. They were quiet people, you could imagine working towards something they considered better than this dilapidated house, and would one day have children and be kind to them. With Elin's recent departure fresh in my stomach, these reveries grew particularly poignant and even though I remained convinced that working for some insurance company was crazy, at the same time you could see that they really had something. Loved each other a bit like my grandma and grandad once had.

We'd exchanged a few words on the stairs and there was a nodding recognition growing between us. Eventually, they'd felt relaxed enough to ask themselves into my flat to see what it was like compared to theirs.

One evening I was lying on the mattress in the bedroom. I'd recently come up with words to a song Jazz had written the music for, called *The Return Of The Real Me*. I was practising singing the lyrics over his demo tape when I heard the thuds of someone throwing themselves down the flights of stairs above. I got up immediately because of the urgency of the steps and went to the bedroom door which opened straight out onto the landing. Just in time to see the face of the girl who lived upstairs coming towards me and the terror in her eyes. I could not get it out of her for a minute or so as she was hysterical and I assumed someone must have died.

"I was in the living room. Huh! A-huh! I was reading a book. Huh! Just reading. Huh! A-huh! Just reading a book. Huh! Huh! Huh! Then it went all cold. Huh! Then the picture on the wall came off the wall and flew across the room in front of my eyes. Straight across the room. Straight across the room and smashed on the other wall. On the other side of the room. Totally smashed. And the glass. Right in front of me. Huh! A-huh! A-huh!"

When I next paid the landlord at his greasy spoon cafe by the railway arches on Cheltenham Road, he told me what I'd already suspected. They'd moved out. In my mind, it was the ghost who had seen to that. I was sure of it. But why the old woman's spirit didn't want them around and why in contrast she'd sung on my tape remained a mystery.

****

A distant, apparently cold-hearted young woman moved in upstairs. Someone whom you could sense was up to no good and as a result the atmosphere in the building shifted once more. My sense of withdrawal from the world was growing and I was spending most of my time alone indoors. Dave was off touring with his other band Levitation, which he'd formed with Terry Bickers from The House of Love, and our demo recording was on hold.

Nothing musical had happened for a few weeks. I was sleeping through the daytime and waking up early in the evening. Seeing out the small hours without a drink to soothe the sadness of Elin's departure was growing increasingly challenging and I was hanging on to sobriety by my fingertips. With that struggle the songs stopped arriving. The desolation seemed to have its tides and there were periods when it gathered in intensity over a number of nights. Like it almost knew what it was doing. Like it was letting you know who was in charge. Like it was leading you somewhere that you could only imagine was even more unpleasant. Drowning out everything else because it needed to be the centre of your attention.

One night, I lay curled up on the living room floor in so much emotional pain that I seriously began to fear I might be going mad. All out of ideas and in desperation I found myself kneeling up and screaming out. Screaming into the walls and ceiling. A howl filled with so much trapped vitality that even after the reverberations died away it felt like the everyday objects in the room had been startled out of their deep inorganic sleep and were all awake now listening in anticipation as to what was coming next. The whole silent room, full of tiny little baby ears.

Inconceivably from the midst of that silence I began to discern a growing sense of peace. At the time it was the most unexpected experience I could have imagined. Back then, I didn't know anything about the kind of peace that is natural and doesn't come in a powder or a bottle. The air around me appeared suffused with a kind of lightness. Invisible to the eyes but at the same time fully felt. A lightness that gathered itself together and crowded around me and flowed into my body so that I lay down, flat on the sofa, smiling at the ceiling for the next few hours. In a rapture and utterly without questions.

That peace remained within me for a few days and I began to sleep and eat properly. With every object in the room alive I began to write songs again too. The isolation diminished and a renewed sense of being a part of something returned.

2002.
10 years later I was walking down Whatley Road in Clifton. Strangelove had split. I'd been sober for over six years and all memories of the events I've just described were pretty much forgotten. It was a sunny spring day, strolling back from the local supermarket. Feeling alive and well.

Suddenly, I was stopped in the street 50 yards past the health centre by an impelling inner awareness. An awareness so strong and somehow familiar that I was compelled to put down the plastic bags of shopping on the pavement and close my eyes, knowing 'something' was about to happen and comfortable enough by this point in my life to be able to completely give myself to the moment without caring about what it might look like to 'passers-by'. You could hear the birds singing and the breath of the spring breeze fizzing on your face.

In my mind's eye, I immediately saw myself curled up on the floor in

Stokes Croft 10 years previously. The atmosphere of that room reappeared in my inner senses almost as clearly as if I were there once again. Witnessing my younger self kneeling up and screaming; hearing that howl going through me with all its ferocity and despair and realising that this same scream for help was being cried out to me now where I stood 10 years later. Time had collapsed and both events appeared to be occurring simultaneously.

"It's alright. Everything's going to be alright, Patrick." I whispered back through the years "You're going to get sober. I'm here now and I'm alright. We're alive. We can live. You're going to make it."

My heart was alive with compassion for my younger self as he knelt on the floor in despair and I posted back through the experience of the moment that I now resided in. The sunshine, the breeze, the freedom.

"We're alright. We're alright. You're going to be alright. I'm with you. I'm here now. I'm alright."

I witnessed the peace and love of that moment filling the gloomy room with a 'lightness'. Filling it with the surety of knowledge that everything would work out.

Because when it finally landed, the truth was so strange.

All those years before, I'd cried out for help and help had arrived in the form of light and peace. And that 'help' had in reality come from my future self. And I'd now fully arrived into that future.

More strangely still, if I hadn't reached this place of inner peace within myself, I would not have been able to return it to my younger self and he would not have found the strength to carry on and so I would no longer exist.

I stood on Whatley Road in the springtime 50 yards past the health centre. Present to an act of the most mystifying healing. After only a few minutes the vision disappeared and I picked up the shopping again and continued to walk on towards my flat but I was never the same person again.

There are cracks in our everyday experience that lead into a deeper reality. I believe that reality is a deeper kind of truth. And I know without doubt that this truth has visited me on a few occasions and changed the course of my life. In many ways, that reality is what I want this book to be about as much as I want it to be about 'my story'.

CHAPTER 12

STRANGELOVE

In the final analysis, any rock 'n' roll band worth its salt remains a mystery. A synthesis of the individuals who make it up, and yet at the same time greater than the sum parts of those individuals. The music is the sound of that synthesis. The sound of people who together become something greater than themselves.

We lived within a few miles of each other and something about this particular constellation of individuals created a centrifugal force that dragged us all in its wake. That's a proper band. In plain sight, it places before the world a human potential to come together as one in music, offering the audience and listeners a chance to witness and partake in that connection and widen its circumference.

The drummers and bass players represent a kind of primal vitality, the guitars and keyboards the harmony and discord of our emotions, and the singer the tortured ego trying to find words and a meaning for it all.

In my estimation, when a band comes together in this way, the music they create represents a kind of idealised human form, which has harmonised these often conflicting energies into which we are all born – the drives of our primal urges, our conflicting emotions and intellect. That idealised form shows people who are watching and listening what they are capable of in themselves. How to blend and reconcile their own internal forces. If that connection within the band has formed itself successfully then it's easier for an audience to become a part of it. There is a kind of inevitability to a rock band that goes somewhere. A kind of destiny, a kind of hopelessness.

In 1991, Alex left the Blue Aeroplanes because of that inevitability. An established act, who were out touring the world supporting REM and recording in L.A. Despite all this, he walked because he had no choice. Something deeper than all that was happening. Something beyond any of our controls. Something that had a calling and a potential that none of us could resist.

Alex was only 21, but he'd already experienced a lot of rock 'n' roll and possessed an assured self-confidence that was almost unnerving at first and yet at the same time he was funny and self-effacing. He had cool blue eyes. He held your gaze and it was you who had to look away. Alex was the best guitar player I'd ever sat in a room with and could replicate any cool riff by any cool band you could think of.

He also wrote dazzling guitar music of his own and handed me a cassette with some tunes and asked me to come up with words and melodies. The music for *Hopeful* and *Time For The Rest Of Your Life* was on that tape.

He told us stories about Michael Stipe and the enormous audiences and what it was like to be in America. About meeting the Pixies in L.A, and how every night on the tour he and Rodney sang 'bury your love like Trevor' instead of 'treasure' when they did backing vocals on that Blue Aeroplanes song.

"No one ever notices," he grinned with a mixture of youthful mischief and scorn.

****

A few weeks after the scream. Joe, our bass player, came to live with me in the haunted flat in Stokes Croft. As well as running out of money, he'd also caused smoke damage to his own bedsit and needed to flee.

Joe was tall and gangly with good looks and so easy going it was initially like nothing had happened when he first moved in. He steadily revealed himself as forthright, philosophical, and contrary, with a sense of impending doom that ran like a golden thread through all his humour. He'd committed to the bass guitar in a way no other musician I've befriended before or since has ever come close to. Simply practising was for amateurs. Even if we were down the pub and a few attractive women wandered over to our table to get a light and then sat down to talk to us smiling, there was no coaxing him off course. I got used to watching the sparkle draining from their eyes as he slurred his latest eulogy to the four strings. Full of cheap cider and amphetamines and oblivious to the fact he was blowing our chances, or even that there were any chances to be blown.

Upbeat in his premeditated addiction to Benson and Hedges cigarettes he spent the dead time reading trashy science fiction novels and smoking. Leaping up from the sofa where he'd lain catatonic for hours and suddenly pacing around the room with his arms gesticulating, radiating with the spirit of some mad realisation he needed to jabber out in order to fully grasp. In the days of silence, when the courage was gone and we were hungry, he would write riffs on his Squire bass. Mostly in unusual time signatures.

On his playing them, I'd remark on these anomalies, but he'd insist they were all in 4/4 with just some extra bits added on. He'd count it out as proof and although he was blatantly wrong, would never concede so. However, the concentration he embodied in nailing these ideas was inspiring to be around and his talent sounded a dark light in the rooms of our flat. Watching his riffs grow, I sat by the bed, connecting with his spirit. The words for *Fire*, *I Will Burn* and *Sea* all started like that.

When they were teenyboppers, Alex, Joe, and Dave had formed a band together called the Coltranes and there was a strong sense of unfinished business between them. In fact, when they got together, they would often talk each other into a seething brotherhood of ambition.

****

Julian Poole, or Jazz as we christened him, was a country boy with curly hair who wore flowery 70s shirts and drove a gold VW beetle. He blinked out through round Lennon glasses and played in the Jazz Butcher, a band from Northampton built around the mighty Pat Fish. That's how Alex had first met him. Jazz made perplexing black-and-white art films on a hand-held camera and went to avant-garde student shows and galleries and at the same time was neck deep in mainstream culture. He'd turn up at Dave's with bumper-sized bags of popcorn or jelly babies and was constantly reading magazines.

"Hey, any of you tasted the new Marathons? Guess what right, they're called Snickers now. What do you reckon? "

Or

"I'm really, really disappointed with this sandwich…"

Or

"Yeah, my last band had quite a cool name Last Stop For Petrol."

Or

"Jesus man. I'd kill for a cold drink. Anyone know where the nearest slush puppy machine is?"

Maybe it was an Andy Warhol thing but we'd all look at him like,

"What the fuck, Jazz?"

Especially when we realised he wasn't joking or being ironic in any way.

Despite this unspeakable lack of rock 'n' roll credibility, Jazz played the guitar like a natural and already possessed a restless style of his own. When we were sitting around not doing much, he'd pick out weird sounding Grade Eight pieces that would send me into trances and he always made up his parts to songs the first time he listened. He'd studied classical guitar for years but when we caught up with him, all that music was coming back out the other way, rearranged by his eccentric talent. His contributions were infectious and often verging on virtuosic. He wrote his own music too. Quirky manic riffs on distorted electric guitars accompanied by minor inversions thrashed out on a 12-string. *Front* and *Walls* were his ideas. Crazy pieces of sound art that he cooked up on a four-track with Dave. Jazz also went on to source all our artwork.

Me and him as the relative outsiders of the bunch initially clicked over that too.

****

With Dave away so much with Levitation, Strangelove central moved to Alex's bedroom at his mum and dad's house in Cotham. His parents were liberal intellectuals; kind and supportive of our endeavours and his dad even came in and played violin on some of our demos. We'd stay up late with one dull, green lamp in the corner, writing into the night. The arrangements for most of Strangelove's first two albums saw the light of day in that bedroom.

At the same time, Alex had contacts in the music business and was on the phone to them on what appeared to be a daily basis. As a result of these calls a gig was booked for us in London. We still didn't have a name and were calling ourselves Words And Pictures while we desperately tried to conjure something else up. Many a summer's afternoon was wasted in Alex's garden making up joke names instead. Bizarre Bazaar! Although funnily enough, at one point we were seriously toying with the name Suede.

Alex had immediately fallen into the role of decision maker because he was the one most naturally suited to that position but also because the rest of us were still pretty childish when it came to any kind of responsibility.

However, it has to be said Alex had his quirky sides too – he hated to rehearse and although we continued to meet and record, we actually managed only one full band rehearsal before our first gig. There was a youthful arrogance to Al, Joe, and Dave, especially when they were together, and in their own minds they were already far superior to anything that might have been considered donkey work. Having no experience of being in a proper band myself and totally trusting their swagger it did not strike me as unusual whatsoever to be performing having done so little preparation.

****

We were the support act to a baggy band from Liverpool called Thirty Five Summers. On our arrival at the Camden Underworld, they stood on stage funk-jamming away their soundcheck. The rest of Strangelove flounced off to the nearest pub in a way too over-the-top musical protest and I walked by the canal, vomiting into the water with anxiety. The air was bitter cold and tiny snowflakes started to fall.

Would I be able to remember the words? Would anyone actually turn up? Would my hands and voice really stop shaking once we got on, like they'd all promised?

Too nervous to look up I stood, hands behind my back, and head down into the microphone. Too uncertain to adjust the stand. Not even knowing you were allowed to. The audience was sparse. Perhaps 25 people. You couldn't see them with your eyes closed but you could feel them listening. Their attention created a luminosity inside me and for long passages of the concert I swayed almost motionless, eyes closed, lips to the mic, singing inside a circle of light in my imagination.

That was the cacophony of the drums behind me; the guitars and the bass blaring out from the amps. That was my voice singing the words, coming back through the monitors in front of my feet. That was the sound of the same old chastising inner voice that haunted my every step and there was the room of light which the people had materialised with their listening. You had to keep your eyes shut and try to step forward in your imagination. Into the room of light. Still singing and still listening to the music, whilst at the same time fighting the chastising voice trying to drag you backwards, down into the void.

So 'that' was what doing a gig was like.

Echoing applause from the handful of people at the end of each song sounded anticlimactic in comparison to the colossal noise we were making and the brilliance of the room of light they were creating inside me. I had stood in audiences myself, of course, and immediately realised that they didn't even know what they were doing.

****

Afterwards the rest of the band were buzzing. According to Alex, we'd done well.

"What was it like for you, Pad?"

"Ahh. I wish I could have split myself in two, because I really wanted to be in the crowd and see what it was like from there, man. To know what we are. Or what we could be."

Al and the guy standing beside him laughed. A music journalist called Dave Cavanagh.

"That was great, man, really great," he mumbled in an Irish accent.

"Your drummer's in Levitation," he continued. "So, I was expecting some kind of hippy wig out but that was different. You've got proper songs."

Alex also introduced me to Cerne Canning and Simon Espiner, who at that time were managing the Blue Aeroplanes.

Soon after, Dave Cavanagh nodded me backstage into our crummy dressing room and without asking questions chopped out two lines of cocaine. I was too shy to say I'd given up drugs and alcohol. That I was a hopeless case. That I mustn't do this. Because I didn't want to appear uncool in front of him. Especially knowing he was a music journalist.

Immediately afterwards, I started drinking again too. My clean and sober time was gone. No one seemed to care. We were all young and happy. We'd just done our first gig and it had gone so well. How was I to know that this almost banal action, as far as the rock world is concerned, was going to be the biggest mistake of my life?

****

Back at the haunted flat things soon became chaotic and impermanent. Some nights there were ambulances and police at the door and, in between all the renewed debauchery, we played our second gig at Moles in Bath, having finally managed to come up with the name of our band: Strangelove.

Dave Cavanagh wrote a review in *Select*, a glossy music mag a bit like *Q*, and gave us a rave write up, focussing much of it on my performance and stage presence. In all honesty, this was the first positive feedback I'd ever received, in writing, in my entire life.

I walked a long way across town to show my mum and dad and read it back to myself over and over again with what felt like a pelt of wasps crawling over my body. My own name in print, in such positive rock 'n' roll terms was beyond words. That magazine was in every newsagent in the country and I felt almost distraught with gratitude towards Dave for writing it.

I began to get the distant notion that maybe I wasn't a waster after all and spent afternoons drinking cans and disappearing on the sofa, daydreaming myself into accepting all manner of music awards.

"Most of all I'd like to thank Dave Cavanagh. He gave us our first review and without that I don't think we'd be where we are today. I know he's here tonight and I'm still so grateful to you Dave that I'd actually like to hand this award over to you. Because it's yours Dave, as much as it's mine. Please come and accept it, man."

The assembled celebrities broke out into a subdued and uncertain sounding applause, as a dishevelled Dave Cavanagh approached the stage and I handed over some kind of a golden statue to him before he walked away blushing.

"Never forget who was there for you in the beginning." I yelled down the mic, stumbling offstage through the feedback.

Afterwards, David Bowie popped his head and smiling white teeth around my dressing room door and I met his eyes in the reflection of my star mirror.

"Lovely gesture, Patrick. Of course, my first reviews meant so much to me too, but I never thought of recognising the journalist like that. Nice one, fella. It kind of cheapens the rest of the awards for all those other wankers too. There's a small one at mine if you get a bit a 'Zoo'd Out' at the after show thing."

"Ahh cheers, David," I said. "Yeah I might do that. I'll definitely try and get away. You know what it's like, man."

"Ha, ha. Rather you than me, man. Catch you later. Just let yourself in round the back. My house is yours; your house is mine. Ha! Ha! You know that, Patrick."

Hours got swallowed on that sofa and it was nigh on confusing having to do all the in-between stuff. Seeing as you'd already made it in your head anyway.

CHAPTER 13

MONEY

Cerne and Simon were now managing the band and they'd procured an agent who was booking us prime support slots in London. We quickly put out *Visionary*, our first EP on a label they'd concocted called Sermon Records.

Cerne looked like he'd stepped straight out of the set of *Brideshead Revisited*, but rented gloomy offices by a strip club in Kings Cross, where he excelled in recounting various anecdotes about various stars. Lou Reed, Morrissey, Michael Stipe, and many more. He'd met them all at one time or another, yet traded in these stories without a trace of self-importance, genuinely fascinated by the eccentrics of rock 'n' roll and the trails of hearsay they left behind. At exactly the same time, he was party to every single scrap of gossip about every up-and-coming indie band in London.

I immediately warmed to him and his never-ending storytelling; also taking solace in the fact that he seemed to appreciate my role in the band in a different way to the others.

When the rest of us were together, we chatted away about guitar riffs and how the bass drum fitted in with the bass lines and what combination of pedals actually sounded the coolest. Different widths of guitar strings and the mysteries of compression. In all honesty, I was never a major contributor to these conversations because it was all slightly over my head at the time and didn't quite hold my attention anyway. In sharp contrast, we virtually never spoke about the lyrics. Maybe because they were so raw and personal but also because it was not what interested the others about music. That was fair enough to me and I'd never once worried or even thought about it much before. But when I was with Cerne he tried to get me to understand that, as the singer, how I came across as a person, how I dressed, what I said in the lyrics and to the press, would ultimately define the band as much as the music. He also took the time to ask me all sorts of thoughtful questions in order to work out where I was coming from.

Part of me recognised he was right and sensed that he was intrigued by some compelling quality he saw in me, and I tried to reflect it back. But in truth, secretly worried whether I was living up to whatever it was he could see. Cerne had a noted intelligence combined with an intuitive nature and an uncanny ability to be able to pinpoint the subtle aspects of a person's character. Those conversations uncovered strange fears I was otherwise unaware of and my self-defeating mind wouldn't allow me to settle on such things for long. As soon as we'd finished our chats, I'd walk away feeling inspired by him and then just as quickly launch myself back into the chaos and forget about what we'd said till the next time.

As a result, my early interviews with the music press were pretty disastrous. For some reason, it appeared to me that as well as being the singer, you also had to be a stand-up comedian. Through nerves I'd get so drunk I could hardly speak. Desperate to be in shape and appear cool and disinterested, I'd often peak about two days too early and once actually fell asleep in Camden in front of the *NME*. He was gone and so was his Dictaphone by the time Cerne came back to The Good Mixer to wake me up.

Somewhere along the line as a naive teenager, I'd sold myself this flimsy idea about rock 'n' roll singers. The myth that floats around in our collective unconscious. Back then I was so uptight that it seemed easier to embody that myth than to think more deeply and rise to the challenge of the kind of questions Cerne was encouraging.

****

Gig number six was at the Marquee and it was snowing again. The traffic was dreadful and we arrived late, missing our soundcheck as openers on a three-band bill. As usual, I played the whole set with my head down, eyes closed never looking at the audience. Dave Balfe, who'd played keyboards in the Teardrop Explodes, and Andy Ross from Food Records, were there to see another band but Balfey changed his mind and said he wanted to meet us instead.

A week later, Alex and I were summoned to London.

Alex already appeared to know quite a lot about Dave Balfe from reading Julian Cope's memoirs and he filled me in about him on our way up the M4; his uncompromising ways and all the acid he'd done. In the flesh, Dave was wide-eyed and uncommonly direct but with a gentle scouse accent. He immediately played Blur's proposed new single to us and with an intense stare asked what we thought. Andy, who'd previously been a music journalist for *Sounds* and *NME*, was more reflective, and then after a few pints he changed, told quirky rock 'n' roll stories and went out of his way to put you at ease.

****

After the office and then the pub, we went to Pizza Express in Camden where Cerne, Simon, and Alex were soon deep in conversation with them both. Tongue-tied and unable to face eating, I didn't order and was drifting a long way off as they munched margaritas and laughed amongst themselves.

Finally, Andy Ross broke through the joking rebuttals,

"OK, I'm going to be honest. Yes, we are thinking of signing the band but the one thing we're worried about is Patrick." Turning to me, "You don't look comfortable on stage."

For the first time that day, the full collective attention of the gathering fell upon me.

"I don't want to look comfortable on stage, man. It's not a comfortable place to be."

"Good answer! I like it!" spouted Dave Balfe, laughing. And then they all started laughing.

Unbeknownst to me at the time, that repost would be life changing. In the heat of the moment, something inside me had taken over and borrowed my mouth to deliver the right answer.

****

By the time our next engagement came around there was a problem. We were going into a studio to demo for Island Records but Dave Francolini was on a Levitation tour at the same time. By now we were decidedly unclear about Dave because he was rarely, if ever, around. Finally, as the day grew closer we got Cerne to tell him that we were getting a new drummer. Our growing momentum didn't have time to be waiting around for him anymore. There was no time to reflect and we didn't. We were young men and sometimes there is something quite cruel about young men.

Poor Dave had 30 years of crack addiction waiting for him and with all the other problems we were soon to uncover in Strangelove it was probably a blessing that he went then. He was already a bit of a liability anyway due to his fiery temper and need to control. A role which no one else was going to secure with Alex around.

Alex and Joe immediately chose John Langley, who'd recently quit the Blue Aeroplanes, as our new man. Ask anyone around at the time, he was truly gifted on the drums and already had loads of experience in music being about 10 years older than the rest of us.

****

As a result of our agent, we now began shooting up and down the country, thrown around in the back of a windowless rented van. John soon showed us how it was done. In the pitch metal blackness, sitting on amplifiers and wheel arches fighting the bumps along the motorways trying to light up cigarettes, swigging from various shapes and sizes of bottles, and snorting lines of speed off our own record covers by Zippo light. Many a line got wasted to the cold, shuddering darkness.

"Fucking hell, Steve!" someone would shout out as the van lurched over the latest pothole.

Steve Gray was our first driver and tour manager. Calm and pragmatic, he claimed he couldn't hear us because the rear part of that van was separated from the driving compartment by a thick piece of hardboard. Hence this permanent midnight. Out of sheer blind boredom, mixed with West Country cider and irrepressible high spirits, John would often be trying to snog us within a few hours of the longer journeys. With a certain amount of luckless charm and will power, he'd succeed and afterwards you could hear him cackling away to himself through the gloom as we lunged on to Glasgow or Hull. The shock of your first time was like breaking through to the other side of some weird initiation ritual into the dark arts of rock 'n' roll touring.

We called it being 'Langered', although that phrase also came to mean being intoxicated to the point of incomprehension. We once persuaded him, without too much effort, to throw some music journalist to the floor and do him at the end of the night. The *NME* described this experience as 'like a slug sliding through a scouring brush being scraped across your face.' That actually 'was' what it was like. So, they got that right at least.

What they didn't know was that John also had a brooding, contemplative side to his nature and would retreat deeply into himself for hours on end. He was fiercely sensitive. Constantly smoking. In the dressing room, staring into impossible novels with wounded blue eyes, tortoise shell national health glasses held together by Sellotape at the bridge of the nose, a reddish glow to his complexion and a greying Elvis quiff. Scruffy to the point of it being a natural gift. Before Strangelove, in his other bands, John had been known as the most drunk *and* the most sober one.

****

Our next London gig was supporting a band I'd never heard of. Two brothers from Manchester who were apparently loud mouths and always fighting.

As we arrived, they were sound checking. Motionless as waxworks, standing on the stage playing *I Am The Walrus* to an empty venue at ear-splitting volume and pulling it off. We'd witnessed a few bands by this time but here was something different. I was compelled to stand there and watch the whole thing.

After our soundcheck, I sloped around backstage at the Marquee and wandered off down some dusty hardboard corridor under the London streets waiting to go onstage. Bumping into their singer who immediately handed me the spliff he was smoking and mumbled,

"Nice one, man."

"Yeah, nice one, man. Cheers," I returned

We stood next to each other for a minute or so in the underground hum shifting about like truants whilst I took a few more pulls and then handed it back.

"No, keep it," he said grinning and looking slightly blown out. "It's yours brother"

Making the V peace sign as a means of saying goodbye, he strutted back down to the dressing rooms with all the druggy bluster he could muster. I stood there and finished the spliff.

"What's this band we're supporting called again?"

"Oasis."

"Their singer's cool, man. I just met him. Doesn't seem like a fighter though. He was so stoned he could hardly speak. Like one of those spaced-out northerners, you know. You can imagine him inviting us into his dressing room for mushroom tea more than you can imagine him head butting us."

****

We were talking to record companies and publishers – back and forth to London. Negotiations that I remained relatively unaware of happened right before my eyes. During these often tiring meetings in bright offices, I listened instead to the gospel that came crawling out of my head as I sat there in silence. Still living in the space-suit-self I'd climbed into as a stoned teenager, I'd decided that as 'lead singer' it would be tasteless and completely inappropriate for me to get involved in practical considerations in any way whatsoever and it soon became crystal clear, from inside that space suit, that my only job was to offer the occasional obscure comment that had nothing to do with proceedings in order to create a moment of confusion.

On reflection this conviction was probably as much to do with my Catholic upbringing as the sensationalised biographies about bands I'd flicked through as a 15-year-old. Because throughout this time, somewhere far in the back of my mind, the vestigial organ of my conscience kept broadcasting in the form of a distant feeling: 'No man can serve two masters'. And I was already owned by the bottle.

****

One morning, the whole band was in the van once again and I turned to Alex,

"What are we actually going up for *this* time then, man?"

"We've been signed, Pad. Food have signed us."

It took more than a few seconds to sink in. My head raced as the M4 blurred by in a series of grass verges. Finally, I turned back to him.

"Wow! Does that mean we're not on the dole anymore?"

Alex was often a source of strength to me, and without realising it, I relied on him to explain everything that was 'actually' happening

"Of course it does, you fucking idiot."

This was way before money had gotten its teeth into me. I turned to look out the window once more, still wondering if it really would make any difference. The trees that grew along the sides of the motorways always appeared weaker and somewhat sicker than their forest counterparts and when they waved their arms about it seemed to me like they were crying for help. I'd been on the dole ever since I'd left school and had assumed in some distant way that it would always be that way.

Maybe Alex was right. Maybe something really had changed and I was suddenly determined to actually listen at the meeting this time.

∗∗∗∗

We piled into some lawyers' offices and up a few flights of stairs. Our man was suited, booted, and sporting a scruffy 70s beard like one of Mike Oldfield's 1971 band when they played *Tubular Bells* live on TV.

The room was full of papers and old filing cabinets and we sat around a well-worn oak table. The contract was boring and repetitive and took forever to read out in that gobbledegook language. Eventually, it became so confusing that I had to actively concentrate on not listening, glancing round at the frowning faces instead; or following the flight paths of flies and making up theme tunes for them by humming at barely audible levels into my own eardrums; or digging my nails into the palms of my hands until the pain blocked out everything else. But you couldn't block it out. The gigantic seriousness of the place pushed down on your head like a giant foot. Suddenly you sensed it wasn't about gigs or reviews or songs or drugs or booze or records or even music. This is what rock 'n' roll took seriously. Every possible nuance of what might happen if you sold something, down to the most mind-boggling detail.

Finally, the moment arrived for us to sign and I was close to the edge. The last one to scribble my name.

The lawyer asked me the same question he'd asked the others,

"Do you understand what you're signing, Patrick?"

"No, I don't understand it!" I blurted, "Not any of it, but that doesn't bother me, man. I'm going to sign it anyway, 'cos I don't care about understanding stuff."

"Well, I can't let you sign then. I'm sorry, you have to understand what you're signing, it's a legal requirement."

The rest of the room suddenly de-focussed out of its own hypnotic trance and we all waited for me.

"Uh… OK, sorry… I *do* understand then," I eventually mustered.

He held my gaze for a few moments longer. I wondered whether some part of him was thinking, 'maybe I should teach this skinny little bastard a lesson'. But thankfully, for the sake of making it easy and claiming his fee no doubt, he re-slid the contract over and I scrawled my name in the scruffiest handwriting I dared, with all my cocksureness vanishing into thin air.

"Don't do that to me again, Pad," said Cerne out of the side of his mouth as we scuttled down the stairs. Off to the Columbia Hotel, for our post-signing celebration. A long afternoon's party that almost descended into a drunken brawl with the Buzzcocks. It got close, Steve Diggle was an angry man that day, but in his defence it has to be said that we were often extremely cheeky to strangers who tried to talk to us, whoever they were. Luckily, before it got really nasty, to calm things down Pete Shelley suddenly stood up and dropped his trousers and everyone ended up laughing instead.

CHAPTER 14

A CELEBRATION MEAL

A week after being signed, Joe and I *were* finally thrown out of our haunted flat and I moved with John and Dodge to an equally unsettling and ramshackle place in Cotham – 29 Hampton Road, which on the first day John re-christened Club 29. The party never stopped and when they flushed the lavatory upstairs, the effluence came up through the plug hole in our bath.

This was where we were living when the first money from our record deal came through. It was decided that we would be paid wages at the start of each month, but as I didn't have a bank account my money was transferred through John's. One sombre Wednesday morning, he came out of Lloyds clutching hundreds and hundreds of pounds. He'd withdrawn the entire month in cash for us both. John was always dismissive and cynical regarding the music business, having suffered a catalogue of fall-outs in his long stint with the Blue Aeroplanes, but never in my life had I held so much money in my hand. We went straight down to our local, the Highbury Vaults, and started buying drinks for everyone at the bar; immediately sky-high on playing the big shots.

"Yeah, we've been signed," I told the sceptical bar manager, who'd previously had to throw me out on a number of occasions.

By lunchtime, totally pasted and unable to locate amphetamines from the pub phone, John insisted we walk down to the main drag and find a restaurant. We hadn't eaten properly in months.

"Hey, are you hungry?"

"Aye, I'm hungry."

John was stooping down with his hand outstretched to two sleepy-looking tramps who sat begging on the road.

"Come with us, and we'll buy you some food."

We stepped into one of the poshest Chinese restaurants in Bristol, and it soon became clear that the two pie-eyed Scotsman stank to high heaven. It was relatively early and we were the only customers. It was eerily quiet in there, just the faintest Chinese classical music in the background. After scoffing ourselves stupid on extravagances, John began ordering rounds of Drambuie. The faultlessly obedient waiter carrying them through on a silver tray. Again and again, they came. Each drink, set alight, burning with a flickering blue flame and a coffee bean. We drank the flames and the alcohol in the silver shot glasses over and over. The two dour tramps continued to eat from the numerous plates that lay dishevelled over the table, in no way appearing grateful to either of us, remaining surly and especially suspicious of John, who insisted upon treating them like kings. Tottering under the guilt of all this record company money, he was attentive to their every need; encouraging them to order more lavishly, furnishing them with suggestions, handing them 10 pound notes, which they furtively pushed into their coats without taking their eyes off him, as we descended into incoherence. Tray after tray after tray of blue flaming drinks were brought to the table where they glowed in the surrounding hush of the restaurant like St Elmo's fire. The freaked-out Chinese waiter continuing to follow instructions to the letter.

"Another round of Drambuie, my friend," slurred John with his thumb waving in the air.

Till it all went black.

Waking a few hours later with the throbbing of a nearby bus on Whiteladies Road, the pavement was cool against my face. The yellow streetlamps were flickering on as the light of day drained from the sky. I sat up, next to me John lay unconscious on his back – commuters making their way home, stepping round and over our bodies. Too busy and too washed out to be anything other than slightly irritated by us. Shaking John awake, I suggested we get going before finding ourselves arrested. Sitting with our heads hanging on a nearby bench, my pockets were empty and John only had enough change left for a cheap bottle of cider from Sainsbury's. We drank it on the bench in silence and trudged back home to the flat knowing we were straight back to being skint again for a whole month. I collapsed on my bed under a pile of coats because we didn't have pillows or blankets.

****

Quite accustomed to begging by this point, and having already suffered years of homelessness, I still preferred to be pissed to withstand the hundreds of rejections and occasional contemptuous remarks or mini-lectures that had to be endured.

The next day, I sat down on Cheltenham Road because the underpasses in the Bearpit were already full of others with the same idea. When I first started, that was unheard of. Now, there were young beggars everywhere. The late morning was sunny, but the relentless grind of the traffic remained oppressive as the Drambuie hangover flamed on. People passed by in the rush of the day and I sat against the front of a deserted antique shop dreaming about cold milk and lemonade.

"Hey, are you Patrick out of Strangelove?"

He looked like a student in his Morrissey glasses. Pale and thoughtful.

"You're Patrick out of Strangelove."

He placed a one-pound coin on my jacket, a generous contribution at the time.

"It's you, isn't it? You're Patrick."

The silence hung between us for a few seconds as my head raced for an appropriate response.

"Ughhhh. No, I don't know what you mean, mate. Who's that? I don't know who you're on about. My name's not Patrick," I denied, doing my best Steve Diggle, faux-Mancunian impression.

He didn't look entirely convinced, but was too polite to continue his cross examination and paused for a moment longer before walking on his way with a self-conscious stride. Waiting till he was out of sight and with a racing heart, I picked up my jacket and scarpered, half running, half walking back to Club 29 with the shadow of our exchange in pursuit. Sweating in the clamour of the warm day and the blinding withdrawals, I couldn't think straight. Back home sitting on top of the pile of coats, swigging a can of cider with my back against the wall of the tiny bedroom, I couldn't quite grasp it. Something had just happened to my life.

We tried to record our second EP in Rockfield studios in South Wales, where Queen had done *Bohemian Rhapsody*. Donald Ross Skinner from Julian Cope's band produced the tracks, but Dave Balfe wasn't happy with the results. He sent us a letter saying that we should be sounding darker and that the others should start dressing like me, which went down like a lead balloon with the rest of the band.

Balfey then decided he wanted to produce us himself, but after his letter Alex and John simply weren't having it. So, one afternoon in Camden, in front of everyone, he suggested that I should leave Strangelove and be in a band with him and he tried to persuade me that I didn't need the others. Although I was already a long way out, I wasn't quite that far gone. I knew what my life had been like before I'd met Strangelove and was already bound to them by invisible strings.

However, it remained an unsettling time for us and we went through a fruitless phase where we tried out with a procession of big-name producers instead.

I can't forget overhearing a conversation between Alex and Mike Thorne in the live room at Trident, leaking through the mics and into the control room whilst I lay on the sofa bored witless.

"Can we just roll in a bit of low end onto that sound please, Alex?"

"No, I don't want any low end on it."

"Why not just give it a try, please?"

"OK then."

Various angular guitar played as the sound filled out a bit.

"There, what do you think?"

"Sounds shit," said Alex

Long pause.

"Maybe try another pedal?"

"I don't want to try another pedal."

Alex was 21 years old and Mike Thorne had been involved in making records since Deep Purple in the late 60s. But Alex wasn't rattled or overawed by anyone and would not be told anything when it came to guitar sounds. Especially in the morning. As a result, every single one of them we worked with pissed him off in some way or another.

Mum and dad on their wedding day, Oswestry, 1965.

Mum was born on August 9th 1939 at Porthmai near Tregynon in Mid Wales.

Patrick, 1968.

Grandparents Jim and Mary Duff at mum and dad's wedding, 1965.

Grandparents John and Florence Evans at mum and dad's wedding, 1965.

First day of school, St Ursula's. For the first four years of my schooling, I was taught by nuns.

Great uncle Ger was a Cistercian monk in a silent order.

With mum on the ferry back to Ireland to visit relatives.

Dad on honeymoon, 1965.

Patrick and Catherine, 1968.

Christmas pictures with my sisters Bridget, Jacqueline and Catherine from the early 1970s.

Patrick.

With The Beatles, 1980.

From left: Catherine, Patrick, Jacqueline, Bridget, Edward, Mum.

My brother Edward.

Strangelove. The first photo session. From left, Patrick, Jazz, Alex, Joe, John. (Pictures Beast)

GLASTONBURY

Astoundingly, a month or so later, with no other music successfully recorded apart from our EP, we landed a spot at the 1992 Glastonbury festival on the *NME* side of the pyramid stage. First band on Sunday morning. The Wednesday before, we were holed up in an indie club at the bottom of Park Street in Bristol, down the steps and under the road. We'd been up all the previous weekend and were still going strong when, by chance, Alex walked in. It emerged that to avoid the traffic jams he was driving to the festival that night so Gil, John and I jumped in the car with him. John – again with his entire month's wages – was paying for everything, as I still hadn't managed to organise my own account and Cerne was sorting me out with cash next time we hit London, having said to me in no uncertain terms that John wasn't the right person for me to have my money go to.

We hurtled over the Mendips in Alex's brown Talbot, drinking take-outs and singing over the top of the mixtape.

Al was staying with his girlfriend Bev's family in Pilton and we arrived at about six o'clock in the morning. He sensibly waved us off and disappeared indoors as we wandered around the village for an hour or so, trying to find somewhere to take speed where there wasn't a police presence. It had started as a joke but I was becoming increasingly convinced that we were being tracked by a new kind of robot dog and even went so far as to enquire of a policewoman whether such things existed – much to the annoyance of Gil, who was carrying our stuff.

We eventually snorted it off a flat grey rock in a lane somewhere in Pilton village; kneeling down by the nettles, imagining we had created a new kind of scene involving amphetamine ingestion in the open air, using primarily natural resources; harmonising the east coast/west coast split in the American music culture of the 60s.

Gushing this kind of hot air around the perimeter fence, we finally located an open gate and were ushered in by merit of our artist tickets. It was Thursday morning and the festival was already buzzing with punters – most of whom appeared to be drug dealers. As we stumbled around, John was unable to pass up even the slightest opportunity. His irrepressible enthusiasm for intoxicants of all kinds also spilled over into a sincere gratitude towards absolutely anyone peddling them. In this manner, he thanked each and every one with an open-hearted solicitude which would have seemed pathetic coming from anyone else but in his case was utterly genuine.

All of us doomed to self-destruction, in John's mind, belonged to one big happy family and it was his duty-bound responsibility to support the cause. In stark contrast to every other drug deal I ever witnessed, John expressed a sincere interest in the dealer; in his life, his hopes, and dreams. He'd engage in long rambling conversations, trying to discover something meaningful about their lives to repeat back and embellish, in order to make them feel better about themselves. They responded with curt, frowning replies in order to avoid drawing any more attention to the situation. Gil and I had to stand there listening, paranoid and scared shitless of most of them. Waiting and praying for that moment when the exchange would end, with John – finally satisfied – saying, "Thanks, Phil," (or Bonzo, or Mal, or whoever), "Great to meet you, my friend. Send my l-l-love to your sister. I really mean that. I hope she gets better. My name's John. My name's J-J-John."

Whence he would shake the hand of his new mate with warmth and raise his thumb in the air; for a brief moment confused about which direction he was now supposed to be going in; checking for his tobacco and money by patting his shirt and trouser pockets, resulting in a nervous back and forth dance followed by a final stumble onwards, as if some guiding hand was giving him a firm but gentle shove further down the road to oblivion.

By two o'clock in the afternoon, we had ingested a staggering cocktail wandering through crooked miles of the festival crowd. Pills and powders, hash cakes and a variety of hallucinogens, both natural and otherwise.

We'd already been awake for days and as the festival started to fill out we marched on into the faces, following John who I eventually recognised was slightly veering off to the left at all times and thereby leading us around in ever decreasing circles as the veer became more exaggerated. Lost and rudderless, completely disoriented, he was unlike himself, agitated and turning back to repeat.

"I've spent hundreds of pounds and I'm not even out of it!"

"Hundreds of fucking pounds and I'm straight! I'm fucking straight! I'm not even fucking out of it! I don't believe this!"

Tears fell from his eyes as we staggered on through the sunshine. Eventually, I could no longer keep up and fell to the brown grass in the heat with unintelligible physical symptoms, having found myself unable to speak for hours with a critically dry mouth. I watched him disappearing into the crowds with his hand still outstretched to shake the hand of every passer-by.

"My name's J-John. My name's John. My name's J-John, pleased to meet you."

****

Gil was nowhere to be seen when I woke up a few hours later raw with sunburn. Begging a nearby stall owner for a cup of water. I'd no tent, no money, and no stomach.

"How the fuck am I ever going to be able to get up on stage?"

This was Thursday evening and we were due to play Sunday morning. I vomited bile behind an ice cream van to the hum of a thousand generators and wandered off through the ever-thickening punters. The air was cooler now and the crowd was changing as numbers filled out. More and more happy-go-lucky people arrived, enjoying themselves in the evening gloam. Their healthy shine made me even sicker. I walked, lost in dreary reflections, until what I assumed must have been the hallucination of a pale, frowning face emerged out of the endless smiling and bantering.

"Elin? Elin?"

I woke up in the front compartment of a red tent looking into her eyes. It took some time to remember where I was. She was smiling and stroking my hair. It had been a long time since she'd shown me this kind of tenderness. Through force of habit, I went into profuse apologising but for once she didn't appear irritated by my forlorn state. Rather, she smiled and continued to stroke my hair. For a brief second, I wondered whether I was dead.

"I had no idea you were going to be here, Elin. What the fuck are you doing? Are you on E or something? Why are you being so nice?"

Our relationship was so clumsy on my part by this point that I didn't even know she was involved in an art collective who were erecting some kind of Glastonbury festival gallery. We were at that very moment in the front section of the organisers tent. Apparently, when I'd come across her, I'd passed out with the shock of seeing her face and collapsed to the ground.

"We had to carry you back here," she laughed, "You look so ill, Pad. I can't help feeling sorry for you."

When her arty friends arrived back at the communal circle, I pretended to be asleep until they went out for the evening. Curled foetus like in the front part of a tent which was too small for my body, passing revellers sending yelps into the night, as I slipped in and out of a sleep that mixed itself into the sounds around me and on, into a series of festival appearance nightmares.

The next morning Elin woke me.

"I'm taking you home," she said.

It was dawn and the ground was slimy as we tiptoed our way through the miles of canvas trying to work out how to get out. Groups of teenagers who'd been awake all night scurried about and there were food stalls still blasting house music. The odd 30-something dildo dancing like a broken robot with his top off, gurning at passers-by. There were students and lost souls, hippies and crusty punks, pagans and middle-aged men who'd done acid in the 60s and never got over it, and even weirder people dressed in the kind of attire that says, 'I am spiritual'. We trudged around searching for the exit when Elin found a bank bag with a few tabs of acid inside it. She was always finding things on the floor.

Hours later we arrived at the bus stop to Bristol and by the late afternoon were back home in bed eating sweets and watching TV. I slept for hours and woke up at midnight.

"What did you do with the acid?" I said.

"Don't be an idiot, Pad," she scoffed.

When Elin woke on Saturday afternoon it was already time for me to go back to Glastonbury.

"Why, oh why, oh why, did I bother to take those trips?"

My skin was crawling, hands shaking, intricate globes of spinning yellow light floating around the bedroom before my eyes.

"Please let me stay in bed? Don't make me do it?"

But there was no way I could get out of this one.

Elin organised a taxi to drive me back down and I fell asleep in the front seat with my head on the dashboard. Coming round in the baking sunshine the dashboard was covered in a circle of yellow sweat. The Indian driver, eyes firmly fixed on the road, took the money and shot away, leaving me at the gate with my artist's wristband. I stumbled back through the festival confusion and within five minutes by pure chance bumped into Alex, who was going back to his girlfriend's parent's house in Pilton.

There were a few tents in the garden, mostly belonging to Alex's friends and I spent the evening slightly detached, still slightly tripping, listening to them until they climbed in through their zips. I didn't have a tent, so I sat on the grass alone on top of a shrink-wrapped tray of about 20 cans of Fosters. I must have drunk every one because when morning came they were gone and I was sitting on the cardboard covered in dew and surrounded by empty cans.

It was Sunday morning. Steve, our tour manager, gave me his worried look. He'd loaded the van and was ready to drive down to the stage with Al and Bev in the front. In order to avoid the humiliation of having to walk through the crowds in the state I was in, I jumped in the back with the equipment. It was another rough ride in the dark. This time over a muddy field, coming down off a load of acid with 20 cans of weak lager swishing around in my stomach.

They unceremoniously flung open the doors. A stagehand who looked like Lemmy with dreadlocks appeared silhouetted in the sunlight. He fronted a posse of about half a dozen sunburned middle-aged men dressed in black with wrap around shades and studded belts with keys and mini tools attached to them, eager to unload our van.

Perched on top of a vox amplifier, I peered squinting into the light, and when they saw me for a brief second, they all stopped, and stared back in silence.

"Fucking hell!" one of them eventually muttered, and I knew he meant me.

Because it wasn't until that precise moment that it finally dawned on me that this time I was in trouble. Because I already knew that when one of 'those' guys say you're in trouble, you really are in trouble.

****

An hour before we went on, I lay on the floor of a prefabricated dressing room hut with stomach cramps. John, seeing me, confided in solidarity that he knew how I felt but that in his case, because he hadn't gone back to Bristol for a bit, it was worse for him. The rest of the band sat around on the chairs in silence. Each one nursing his own private hangover, apart from Jazz.

"Hey, does anyone want one of these satsumas? They're great. They're really juicy. I mean it."

No one answered that one or even looked up. The dressing room was a deadly anxious place in Strangelove. A sense of impending doom hung over us before and after every gig we ever played, regardless of any amount of adulation we received, and the intensity of our collective doldrums had already been noted by the record company and managers, journalists, groupies, and anyone one else deluded or unfortunate enough to have ended up there.

****

With minutes to go, standing backstage on the dusty grass, we waited to climb the staircase to the stage and it came to light that John Peel was introducing us. We'd no idea and it was suddenly extra terrifying to hear his bearded highness read out our name in those famous laconic tones.

"And... they've the slightly unenviable task of opening proceedings on this somewhat cloudy Sunday morning.

Ladies and gentlemen; Patrick Duff, Alex Lee, Joe Allen, Julian Poole, and John Langley. Strangelove."

About halfway through, everything started going blurry, as If I'd been turning like a mad, whirling dervish all night long and had suddenly come to an abrupt stop. Glastonbury festival was spinning round me like a broken roundabout trying to reboot itself and I finally realised that I wasn't going to be able to stand for much longer. There was no more faking it. I was going down by my own hand. Kneeling into a semi crouch and then down onto my heels. I was going to have to lie down. Surrender to a 10 count. The wounded animal in me was taking over. No doubt about it. I lay on my back looking up into the festival sky singing the gig into the white heavens. There was no-one now, apart from me and the clouds and the sound of young Strangelove being blown around on the breeze in a valley of mud and dust and generators.

At the end, John Peel emerged and I heard him say over the applause.

"Well, I think you'll agree that was rather good. Ladies and gentlemen, Strangelove."

Still lying on my back, a shadowy, bearded face with twinkly eyes popped into my eye view.

"Well done, very good young man. Let me give you a hand."

He didn't say it down the mic or try to make it into some kind of joke. He just offered me his wrist and lifted me up and escorted me back to the side of the stage with his hand on my shoulder.

"How was that for you then, Patrick?"

"I don't really know, man. But thanks."

"Look after yourself."

Bloody hell. John Peel just said my name.

"He said my name. He knew who I was," I bleated.

I put my arm around Joe as we walked away, ecstatic.

"He said my name, Joe. Did you hear that? He called me Patrick. Did you hear?"

****

Just one week later, we walked through the art deco arches at Maida Vale Studios in London to record a Peel Session and it was my birthday.

I'd learned by now that it took ages to set up the drums and get the amp tones happy, so I wandered off. Maida Vale was a labyrinth of scruffy corridors. Full of hangover adrenaline, you could sprint along them, bounding up little staircases and running down other long, submarine-like passageways. Past vast wooden studios with cavernous ceilings and recording suites and radio broadcasting rooms and huge rehearsal complexes, lobbies, janitors' cupboards, and the smell of soldering irons. The corridor décor was shabby 70s with creamy, crumbling paintwork and worn carpets.

Through the endless twists and turns of the place there didn't appear to be another soul around until I peered through a window in one of the countless doors. An entire orchestra, sat in a horseshoe of chairs, were engaged in a muffled discussion with their conductor. All of a sudden, they played one short phrase. The first time I'd ever heard an entire orchestra play. Even through the door, the sheer volume and depth sent an electric current through my body. The next outburst seemed to alter the chemical nature of my DNA. I awaited an encore but they went back into the chin-wagging for so long that I had to find my way back to our session. However, I couldn't stop that deep musical phrase playing through my bodily organs for the rest of the day and I heard its melody superimposed and morphing over all our Strangelove music.

A few weeks later in a studio in North Wales, we heard our session coming out of a radio in the pool room. John Peel complementing the band and reminiscing about how much he'd enjoyed our Glastonbury performance. We'd properly gotten away with it, man. As a youngster, I'd lain in bed at night listening to his show crackling on till I'd fallen asleep. That voice had unlocked all sorts of musical directions for me and his endorsement of our band was like a direct communication of the most extraordinary kind from the closest thing to God Almighty we knew at the time.

****

Before we'd even started, Alex had a snobby attitude towards music videos. He'd long ago suspected that most video directors were pretentious wankers and that any cool band was supposed to detest the process and was backed up in this suspicion in every respect by John. The two of them had already recorded a number of records, videos, TV appearances, and interviews and because of that greater experience, what 'they' said had an unspoken gravitas in our band. Their combined insistence that this was a shit thing to be doing immediately became band policy.

Behind the scenes though, Jazz was coming from a different angle. I could tell he wasn't convinced because I already knew he loved music videos, having witnessed him in studios spending entire days watching MTV. Splayed out on a sofa eating a giant bag of gummy bears mouthing, "Brilliant", as Van Halen pranced around on the other side of the screen in an orange suit drinking Coca-Cola. So, when Jazz heard we were making a video, unlike the others, he perked up.

Despite the churlish atmosphere, he couldn't hold it in anymore and blurted out a series of inspired, massive budget video ideas, completely off the top of his head, channelling mad idea after mad idea; looking slightly crestfallen when we all burst out laughing at the grandstand randomness of his mind.

"Fucking hell, Jazz. What are you on, man?" we said.

And he was the only one of us not on drugs.

In fact, the video we ended up making couldn't have been any further from Jazzer's technicolour imagination if we'd tried. Just one day before shooting, Cerne and I met with the directors in a grotty Camden pub.

"Yeah, basically we love the song, Patrick. Really love it. We want to use a combination of bright strobe lights to capture a stark, bleached-out, psychedelic live performance of the band. To go along with the lyrical ideas of the song *Visionary*."

Having already done an exhausting day of interviews with journos who seemed to ask sly questions, I suddenly found myself possessed with a second-wind contrariness.

"When I was living in our flat on Stokes Croft, man, and trying to stay 'off' drugs, I wrote the words about that.

"How when I was clean the ordinary objects around me started taking on a kind of illusory feeling. Like they were in some kind of a conspiracy. Do you know what I mean, man? This song's got more to do with a kind of tyranny of the physical world and longing to be freed from it. An oppression, you can't be freed from, man.

"It's not about going into some kind of heavenly, bleached-out, psychedelic, trippy landscape. It's about being trapped in the mundane, man, and at the same time sensing it isn't even fucking real."

To their credit, without any complaints or arguing, they graciously agreed to go and think it through again for the following day.

****

Next morning, we rolled up to some video shoot black box in London at an unfeasibly early hour. The directors had brought along a load of tat from junk shops. Standing lamps, beds, wardrobes, cupboards, chest of drawers, tea chests, wooden tables and chairs, even an old tin bath. Initially pushed to one side of the room.

"OK boys, so this is what we're going to do. Having spoken to Patrick yesterday, we've changed the spec."

The rest of the band were staring at me now, but I kept my tired eyes fixed firmly on the director.

"We're going to set you all up here and you're going to perform the song. As the performance progresses, we're going to cut in different versions of you playing surrounded by more and more of this junk. Just in the same way that we acquire all these objects as we go through life, but why do we really do it? What does it all mean? Why do we need all these things anyway?" The director nodded at me with his trendy London arty vibe.

He hadn't understood anything of what I'd been trying to convey the previous day. Pissed out of my head explaining it, the whole thing had been lost in translation. It was six in the morning and we were in tatters and I was far too polite that early on to cause any more trouble.

"Yeah man, yeah cool," I mumbled.

We were ushered away to an upstairs room while they screwed about with their lights and cameras and slightly predictably, we launched into the booze and drugs.

"Fucking hell, man. What the fuck are they doing down there? We've been waiting around for almost two hours now. Why couldn't we have just got here now. It doesn't make sense getting up at fucking five o'clock for fuck all like this. This is so badly organised. I fucking hate doing music videos," said Joe.

"Yeah," growled the rest of Strangelove. This time including Jazz.

In fact, this moaning continued for a further five years, every time we ended up on a shoot – and sometimes even when we weren't. John and Al remained the most adamant but Joe overtook them on volume and sheer outrage on a number of occasions. We did loads and loads of waiting around in vans as we travelled between cities, but there was something about waiting around when you're standing still.

Despite band policy however, staring down from our dressing room window and witnessing so many people running around with camera equipment and lights was becoming rather intoxicating to me. Especially once the speed kicked in. They were down there doing all this work because of us. Because of our music and our ideas. There was no doubt about it, I was secretly beginning to enjoy all this and starting to feel somehow 'important'.

Firstly, 'I' was summoned downstairs on my own. The director said for starters to get into the bath and sing the song from there. I really didn't want to do that especially when I saw the others looking down from the window laughing but was again too polite to say so.

'Why, oh why, did I ever say anything about what this song was about in the first place?' I thought, 'If I'd only just kept my mouth shut I'd never have to do this.'

"Yeah, sure thing, man," I muttered, climbing in.

"All right Patrick, you ready? Camera one position. We're rolling."

Out of your head at nine o'clock in the morning in a pitch-black studio, lying fully-clothed in a tin bath surrounded by cameramen and lighting men and miming to a song you'd written about alienation, I discovered, can make the world appear mighty strange?

****

The next video we commissioned was for our second single, *Hysteria Unknown*. This time we *all* met the director a week beforehand. A different guy from London in the same grotty pub.

"Yeah, boys. Saw you at New Cross, loved the gig so much and I've got this idea. Basically, it's an intense live performance with strobes. Kind of bleached-out."

"Yeah, that sounds great," I butted in, "That's just the kind of thing we want."

CHAPTER 16

TIME FOR THE
REST OF YOUR LIFE

Alex, Joe, and I were often listening to Julian Cope's latest album at this time. Paul Corkett had produced that record and Alex suggested we approach him. To kick off, he remixed our next single successfully.

In Paul, we had finally found a producer who Alex could stomach and who the record company would agree to. So, at his suggestion we met at Jacobs Studio in Farnham, Surrey, where Copey had done *Jehovakill*. Here, we began work on our first album, *Time For The Rest Of Your Life*.

On arrival, it came to light that the Smiths had recently recorded there, along with Status Quo, because this place had two main and entirely separate studios. The engineer/tea boy was an affable northern lad in his early 20s. He told me that Morrisey had spent the whole time in his room writing lyrics and refusing to engage much with anyone else. The very thought of that kind of single-mindedness sent a shiver through me.

Status Quo on the other hand had broken windows and put cars in ditches. Each night, after recording finished, into the early hours Francis and Rik would stay up playing 12-bar blues songs with mountains of cocaine. They'd also set up a waist-high microphone in the corner of the studio attached to a DAT tape and every time someone belched or farted they would launch themselves over and press record. Then, on their last night, they got especially wasted and in the wee hours listened to the whole fart tape at ear splitting volume, rolling around in hysterics. That kind of single-mindedness, on the other hand, made me feel slightly queasy. Deep down I knew of course, out of the two bands, which was the cooler way for the singer to behave and that comparison spooked me from the moment I put those two stories together.

****

Over the next few weeks, it became clear we'd fallen on our feet. Paul had total commitment towards everything he did. A careful, meticulous sense of sound, a dedication to the band, a penchant for late, late nights and like most of us, just the one outfit. A tangled black mohair jumper, black canvas drainpipes ,and a pair of scuffed, sloppy biker boots worn soft and curvy with age, also black. He shuffled around in the daytime blinking. Shifty and nervous until the sun went down. Despite this, he spoke softly and always put you at your ease. He was gentle, a practical man, who was focused on the work. A slight frown that never left his face as he fiddled with microphones and then sat twiddling at the desk.

"The bass drum again please, John. Thank you.

"The bass drum again, please.

"And again. Thanks, John.

"Again, please. Thank you.

"Please.

"And again, John.

"Keep going, John.

"Thanks, and again, please".

A Benson and Hedges never left his fingers and the control room remained clouded in heavy, cumulus veils of smoke that slowly shifted around at all times. That first day, I lay on the sofa sipping my new favourite drink, vodka and lime, hypnotised by the drum sound and Paul's polite, quiet voice. Joe had turned up with a bag of mushrooms and in the excitement of being in a new place miles from home we were unable to resist – apart from Jazz of course, who was up to no good in his own way.

"Wow. We can use the phones here. I just called L.A. on the one in the dining room."

"Really, Jazz?"

"We'll probably end up paying for that," said Al, rolling his eyes while rolling another joint.

The first night was spent jamming. Making up songs about an imaginary uncle who could supply our every desire. Each spontaneous number, alive with a different aspect of him. I was making up the words and pictures like there was no tomorrow and as the night gave way and the sun rose the relentless jamming intensified and everything became clear. Hitting me like a revelation from the scriptures. The imaginary uncle was me. He was a hidden part of my psyche, man.

"This is what we should be doing. Fuck the other stuff. We should make the album using these jams, man. Let's just do *these* songs."

Did Paul realise we were tripping? He recorded it all diligently. Next afternoon, Al said to him in a voice like a slowed-down dalek.

"No, I don't think we want to listen to last night. Let's just get on with the plan."

****

Paul came along with his wife Rachael and their dog, a black Labrador called Harry, who'd breathed in more smoke than any dog ever in the whole studio dog world. Having Rachael's female presence around was akin to drinking clear spring water after a heavy night. She was friendly and prone to an endearing gale of the giggles and now that we had switched back to the original plan of actually recording our tracks instead of the 'A Man Called Uncle' album, the others were getting their sounds right, which took bloody hours. Rachael and I began a series of skittish conversations that continued throughout our stay and helped me through the endless waiting.

Harry contributed another layer of calm to proceedings too. Even in the live room with the guitars barking like hellhounds, he would only very occasionally prick up his ears and peer quizzically, seemingly if they went out of tune or he considered a particular chord was ill chosen. At that point, he would slowly, very slowly, make a decision to get up and go into another room.

Paul wrote the names of all our tunes out on a big blackboard. Alongside each one he wrote down the parts which made up that song and the name of the player. John: Drums; Joe: Bass; Al: Electric Guitar; Pad: Singing; Jazz: Electric Guitar; Jazz: Acoustic Guitar; Al: Keyboard; Pad and Al: Backing Vocals.

Most tracks were recorded completely live followed by guitar overdubs and keyboards. Then the vocals to see if we could do better than the live pass. It was with a sense of enormous satisfaction that I watched those chalk words on the blackboard being rubbed out one by one and turning into music you could listen to through massive speakers.

****

Alex was a hardened night owl by this time and incapable of anything other than a slightly irritated grunt till the late afternoon. We worked from about 4 p.m. to 6 a.m. Joe, John, and I were all dedicated to amphetamines, so time had no particular meaning for us that wasn't connected to the terror of our own mortality. On the other hand, and without anyone quite noticing, after completing his parts and watching a bit of MTV, Jazz would often sneak off to bed early, with a cup of milky hot chocolate and some mini marshmallows sprinkled on the top, which his mum had packed for him.

He kept them in the fridge in a plastic container. His mum had written 'Julian' on a piece of paper in her ink pen handwriting and firmly sellotaped it to the lid. Much to his chagrin that box got knocked about quite a bit by the constant relocation it went through having to accommodate the unimaginable numbers of Stella bottles that were night and day whizzing in and out of the refrigerator whilst the studio bill soared. After a couple of weeks Cerne got wind of the Stella bill and one day there were no more everlasting bottles in the magic fridge. We were suddenly being strictly rationed and it was nowhere near enough. If we wanted more, we'd have to cadge money, lifts, or taxis to an off licence a few miles away as none of us had a car there apart from Paul. That's when we made friends with the people who owned the studio who would occasionally drive us across. Nevertheless, a serious problem with running out of booze haunted the album sessions from that day on.

One afternoon I'd only just begun the day's session, having mistakenly smoked grass with Alex and John beforehand to get in the zone. How on earth those two could handle the quantities they blazed away was a mystery to me. I was pretty much incapacitated now, but it wasn't till stepping outside with Paul that I realised how out of it I actually was. Jacobs Studio was a scruffy rambling house with large bay windows sitting in the midst of substantial grounds and the green, green, green of the lawn was burning my eyes, baby.

Almost immediately, a black jeep turned into the long and winding driveway. Followed by another and another, another. In fact, five identical black jeeps driving in a convoy coming towards us like a funeral procession. Inside those jeeps were The Cure. We'd been told they were coming, but now it was actually happening. My heart in my mouth, the stoned paranoia racing around my blood track. They appeared to be driving in slow motion. An eternity passed for them to reach us as we stood nailed to our spots, mouths hanging open.

"I wonder which one Robert's in?"

'Probably the first one,' I thought, 'Gotta be'. I'd seen them on *Top Of The Pops* when I was about 15. White make-up, bright smudged red lips, scruffy back-combed hair, Ray Ban sunglasses. As they purred by, an animal terror twisted my stomach.

To us, people like The Cure were more like characters from the pantheon of Greek Gods than real people. They lived on the other side of the screen. It was unimaginable that they were suddenly on this side. Our side of the screen. The blacked-out jeep windows flashed by inches from my face. I could hardly believe that the real Robert Smith was actually in one of them.

****

The fact that they were now in the adjoining studio was a bit like living next door to a nuclear bomb factory. You could just kind of feel it somehow. That first night Paul and I, who were fans, couldn't stop talking about it and at about 11 p.m. I turned to him.

"Shall we go and have a look?"

Paul was quietly stoned by this point.

"Yeah alright, Pad. Why not?" he slowly deliberated.

We sneaked outside into the dark, tiptoeing through the sorry-looking rose garden. A low, muffled rumble emanated from their studio but nothing you could differentiate. We stood in the darkness trying to catch a phrase, looking at each other quizzically. I'd really only just met Paul.

"Let's get a bit closer," I whispered. "The window's a bit too fucking high to see through. I can't pull myself up."

"Hang on a sec." Paul followed, trudging through soil to the wall. "I'll give you a leg up."

The glass was steamed but I caught a glimpse through into a room with orangey light. Paul didn't seem too strong and I was holding on to the window ledge at the same time. They sat in a cramped circle on the floor. Crimped hair. That's all I could see – crimped hair and orange light – before Paul gave way and we both fell back into the rose bushes. The pain from the thorns shot through my body and I heard Paul stifling a giggle. We sat there holding our noses terrified they might come out and discover us, whilst at the same time desperately trying not to laugh. I couldn't even look at Paul. Like when you're at school and you know you're in shit and you're desperately trying to stop laughing. We sat in the throbbing muddy stillness. The rumbling noise stopped. Oh no. I prayed they wouldn't come. Please. We didn't move or make a sound for a good two minutes.

Eventually, I plucked up the courage to look at Paul, who rolled his eyes as if to say I think we've got away with it, let's split. We limped back across the gravel, closing our studio door super-quiet. There was mud and blood on my hands and thorns in my legs and sides. Breathing hard, my jacket and trousers were filthy but this was still a success. I'd seen Robert. It must have been. We smoked ourselves into a deeper and sillier satisfaction and listened to our own music loud, till dawn.

Almost inconceivably, a few years later Paul would go on to produce The Cure and eventually become their full-time live soundman. In fact, he did the sound at their iconic gig in Glastonbury in 2019.

****

In a typically supportive gesture, on our arrival at Jacobs Studio, the band had encouraged me into taking the main bedroom with the giant double bed and the large bay window looking out over the rolling countryside. They said it might inspire me to write. However, whenever we smoked grass together, I still heard those whispers in my head; that they all hated me and that I needed to go upstairs and drink wine on my own. Almost every time I smoked that shit, I went into acute paranoia. It had been going on like this for years. Despite that, I couldn't seem to stop myself when it got passed round and there was always one going round in Strangelove. So, most evenings at some point during those sessions I ended up in my bedroom drinking off the neurosis. That's when the owls started talking to me.

One night with the lights off and the window open, listening to the leaves, I could sense another presence in the nearby oak tree. Was there something there or not? I reached out further with my senses and eventually it started calling out into the cool night air. That sound, so gloomy and intoxicating.

"Twoo, twit twit twoo …"

I was about 13 when I first recognised an almost unnatural talent for cupping my hands together and playing a warbling tune. The obvious one was the Ennio Morricone ditty from the Clint Eastwood westerns. But I could do a pretty fair 'Bohemian Rhapsody', as well as *Yesterday* or in fact anything by the Beatles. I could also muster a pitch-perfect owl. Finally, here was my chance. The first time I sent it back, an almost identical response, the owl paused for a good long while. I thought maybe I'd scared her off, but eventually the gaping silence broke again.

"Twoo, twit twit twoo…"

"Twoo, twit twoo twoo…" I was back at her before she had time to think.

This time the pause was considerably shorter.

"Twoo, twoo, twoo," she mournfully enquired.

"Twoo, twoo, twoo," I replied.

"Twit, twoo, twit twit whoo."

"Twit, twoo, whoo whoo whoo."

Our conversation continued, in roughly this way, for perhaps 20 minutes. True, it was a very different exchange from the one going on downstairs at that moment in the control room regarding bass levels. Nevertheless, something about 'this' particular communication lifted me clear out of my stoned terror in a way I'd never experienced before. All the paranoia was vanishing, and in my imagination I could see myself outside the window hanging in mid-air. The house and its shadowy gardens and fields spinning below. The round earth playing slow round notes. Something was here with me. Something that was telling me it would all work out. That one day in the future we would know peace. Just like when the barn owl had flown onto the window ledge in Wellfield Avenue all those years ago at the height of the war.

The great thing about Strangelove was that the next afternoon, sitting around the dinner table just before the session began, it all came tumbling out.

"Hey, guess what. An owl was talking to me last night. Sitting by my window. Telling me all sorts of weird stuff."

"Yeah, yeah cool, Pad," Joe absentmindedly nodded.

Alex, looking up from fiddling around with his rizlas, yawning,

"Ahh, right. What, upstairs?"

"Yeah."

Jazz didn't even bother taking his eyes off MTV and just let out a kind of mildly interested, high-pitched grunt of recognition.

"I've had that kind of shit happen, I know what you mean, man," said Joe.

That was the end of the conversation. As if talking to owls was nothing more than that. On reflection, a lot of other bands might have seriously considered kicking me out at that moment but to Strangelove my particular version of the world remained nothing whatsoever out of the ordinary.

****

A few days later, I stumbled bleary-eyed down to breakfast at about three in the afternoon. The Cure were in our kitchen playing bar billiards. I poured out a bowl of muesli and didn't say a word. I couldn't even lift my head, but did manage a super-furtive glance over at Robert. He was grinning to himself. You could immediately sense no one gave a shit about winning the game. It was more about the jokes and piss-taking. Leaving quickly, I'd swallowed it all even quicker. He seemed smaller than I'd imagined him. Smaller and slightly happier and much more vulnerable. Gentle and a bit lost. But not as lost as me, I thought.

"Fucking hell, Jazz. Pad's allergic. I told you, man, get that fucking moggy out of the dining room," said Joe in his slow trippy voice as I walked back into our lounge.

I'm highly allergic to cats and it was often an uncomfortable situation for me at Jacobs, as there were a few of them wandering about and Jazz would encourage them to come in cos *he* loved cats.

The other continuing problem was booze. Especially since Cerne had stopped the unlimited studio supply. We were drinking day and night and kept running out. Early in the morning, desperate I'd started to search madly around the house and went into the breakfast room. In a small defunct fridge by the bar billiards table there was a bottle of red wine. Oh my God! Alleluia! So I had that. Drank it all. I'd never tasted anything quite like it. "Bloody hell! Hope it's not too expensive or something." I collapsed in my room and got some sleep for the first time in days.

****

Most of Strangelove had lived in cities all our lives and it was something of a culture shock to be out in the middle of nowhere. As well as the stars, bright as you'd ever seen them, there were also the countryside sunrises. One morning, summoned by the early morning birds, I stumbled outside in an advanced state of comedown desperation. Perhaps this time I really had gone too far. 'Strangelove Singer Dead In Studio'. I couldn't breathe properly. LSD and speed and Valium and alcohol had shrunk my whole world down to two sacks inside my chest that I had to keep sucking air into if I were to survive, whilst at the same time terrified I might be distracted from this responsibility by the white noise in my head. Wandering away from the house. Breathe, breathe. Black wolf, white wolf, fighting it out in the bag. Head down looking for my feet, my face about to fall out into my hands.

Boom! I was shocked out of one panic attack and into another by a great pounding on the earth. Muddy vibrations trampling up through the soles of my feet. What had I done? The ground was giving way as I scrambled for some explanation until my eyes caught the flash of a great brown hare running to the hills. I'd somehow disturbed it and there was nothing to do but watch it flee. In the disarray, it had stolen all the good that was left in me. Stuck to the spot without strength or power to follow, I watched it running to the horizon with my soul, its heavy feet sending dull drums back through the ground. With all its potent brown grace vanishing through a distant hedge. Leaving me dumb.

The relentless birds yacked their malevolent chorus about a new day as I walked back into the studio bereft, robbed. Went to my room, locked the door, looked to the hills and put my head to the window. Bastard. It wasn't till years later that I realised. That hare hadn't stolen anything at all, and was just looking after it until I was ready to have it back.

****

Next day, The Cure left. I'd wanted to watch the jeeps going down the drive but had crashed out till the afternoon. We'd all missed it, even Jazz.

Andy, the studio manager, having had us around for a few weeks, appeared both amused and sceptical of Strangelove.

"Robert wasn't too impressed about his bottle going missing," he said in a clipped voice.

"That was me, I didn't know it was his," I spouted back immediately with an extra shot of Catholic guilt.

"Well, that's the end of that little mystery," he sarcastically continued. "And Robert also said to me that he didn't understand why Strangelove didn't speak to him."

We were all splayed out around the dining room. Why Strangelove didn't speak to him? No one had an answer for that. True, conversations were pretty much night-time affairs now because of Alex, but as the quiet smoking continued, I noticed a deeper silence fall between us. Andy walked away and it slowly began to dawn on me.

Fuck! All I had to do was go up to him and say: "Hi Robert, cool to meet you. Always loved your band man. Love all your stuff actually. What are you up to over here?"

Maybe he might have invited us over for a drink. Maybe we could have hung out. Maybe we could have made friends. Maybe even gotten invited to do a gig or even go on tour with them. I didn't know. I didn't know you could talk to popstars. I didn't know that you were allowed. That he would ever have had the time of day for someone like me. That, fucking hell, he was just another person. That same guy who'd played those amazing harmonics on *Play For Today* was a person. A fucking person and I could have told him how cool that guitar part was. How much he'd inspired me. Or I could have just said hello. I could have, fuck. I could have said: "How are you doing, man?"

CHAPTER 17

IS THERE A PLACE FOR ME?

With The Cure gone, I'd discovered a substantial stash of wine in the locked oak cupboard of a dining room set aside for the other band's studio. A small key was just left there, in the lock. Now that they were gone, it was relatively easy to steal in there whenever we ran out. I'd have a bottle away. Just one, maybe two. Over the next few days, no one said anything about it and anyway, I was going to replace them at some point, man. Yeah, replace them, definitely.

It was around 1 a.m. The booze had run out again. However much we bought, it was always the same. John especially didn't give a shit about alcohol protocol when he was out of it.

It was an uncomfortable process, opening a door you weren't really supposed to open; walking across a carpeted room you weren't really supposed to walk across; unlocking a cupboard you weren't really supposed to unlock; taking a bottle that wasn't yours and drinking it. The guilt drained away in exact proportion to the amount you drained from the bottle, but it came back the next day to join all the other guilt from all the other times. A great, big ball of guilt that was waiting for you when you woke up. So big that you'd never have been able to swallow it in one go and too large now to be able to spit out.

I opened the door and stepped inside the room again. Even in my whizzing, drunken state I sensed that something had changed and that instinct stayed my hand from clicking the light switch. There were people. Sleeping people. I immediately shut the door behind myself and stepped inside to prevent the yellow light entering from the hallway and plunged us all back into darkness. One of the figures appeared to lift its head and look towards the door but I couldn't be sure. As my eyes adjusted to the room, I started to make out five shadowy lumps scattered across the floor. I stood in deadly silence as the humps shifted around, occasionally letting go of sighs. Bouts of snoring, rising up and falling away. The unmistakable smell of men who were in a band. Tobacco, body odour, booze, applause. Napalm Death.

We'd been told that they were coming at some point over the next few days; that they were playing some gigs and driving down afterwards. They must have arrived early. A quiet moan arose, a short indecipherable mumbling, and then a return to the communal breathing and restless shifting around. I would never have been capable of mustering the courage if not for the fact I needed that fucking wine.

Slowly, ever so slowly, I began to edge forward, holding back with each step. Searching with the soles of my feet for creaks in the floorboards by allowing my weight to slowly come into each step before being sure I could place my whole poundage into that next one. Across the carpet between the lumps. 'Napalm Death, Napalm Death', the words kept sounding in my head. In truth I'd never heard any of their music, but the name 'Napalm Death' had registered an impression within me on flyers in the music papers.

Here in the dark, with these shadowy forms, that name had taken on shapes. 'Napalm Death, Napalm Death'. It was as if each time I edged forward, a land mine might explode. Holding my breath, tiny tears came into my eyes. Having to semi-step over one particular lump with a little leap. Landing the other side as ungracefully as a six-year-old ballerina, I prevented any more stumbling forward motion by an immense exertion of will over my frame. Standing in the middle of the room throbbing with a fear so vibrant it was almost thrilling. Stepping on. The key clicking in the cupboard. Opening the oak door quickly in one precise intense movement and stopping it with the same exactitude to avoid its creaking.

I reached in, clutching the first one I fingered. The unmistakable cool smooth swan-like neck of a bottle of wine. The foil top, on running your thumb upwards. One clink as the bottle was lifted out. The cupboard was too low to be able to lift this bottle higher than its sisters in the rack so it had to be lifted and tilted. Lifted and tilted. Another clink. The awkward pain in my spine as I bent it into an unnatural curve in order to stoop for the cupboard. The sense of freefall once the bottle got free and could be pulled unhindered through the air of the room. The realisation that there was another route out, not so convoluted, where the skip over the body could be avoided. Turning back at the door. The last moments. The door creaked, slightly. Closed and creaking again. Back into the hallway. Another bright world which had no connection whatsoever to the room you'd just escaped. Like being teleported. A daddy-long-legs flew around the light bulb. Impossible to explain its agitation. How could anything so strange and otherworldly exist? It crashed into the light and crashed into the light again.

Upstairs I drank the bottle in my room, straight out of the neck in the dark. The red heat guzzled down my throat. The amphetamines kept on pounding.

What was I turning into?

What kind of a person does something like that, man?

Who the fuck am I?

What have I become?

****

We heard nothing from Napalm Death until three days later. At about 10 p.m., a head came bobbing round the door of the control room where we sat working on a track. Long black hair with a centre parting, a round, smiling face, a sprightly American voice.

"Strangelove, right? Howdy! Anyone wanna smoke a bong? Napalm Death here, reporting for duty, sir?"

The rest of his body stepped in wearing a dazzling white shirt, all the buttons undone over a white t-shirt and black boot cut jeans. Shaking everyone's hands whilst still clutching his bong.

"Hi, hi, hi, hi people."

He immediately precipitated a little buzz amongst us and work stopped with the surprise of his arrival. He started to load before we'd even answered.

"This bong is going to blow your fucking minds, Strangelove," he chirped.

"I found this little baby in Mexico and she's dangerous. Get ready to check this motherfucker."

"You can forget all that," he laughed to Jazz, who was tuning up his guitar and waiting for the tape to roll.

Within seconds, we were nervously laughing with the sheer audacity he had shown in entering a room of strangers without any social anxiety whatsoever. The antithesis of Strangelove, we loved him straight off and he soon rattled on, talking about Napalm Death in the most jovial and disparaging terms.

"Arghhh-hh, we're so fucking dark, man. Aaarghh, arghhh arghRRR, GRR, GRRR, GRRRRR," he did an impression of the throat singing – whilst playing air guitar with his head down, shaking his hair about – that actually had us laughing out loud.

Exuding charm, chatting 19 to the dozen, his long-fingered hands busily prepared the resin and within a few minutes, the bong was alight and each member of the band was called over in turn whilst he administered to us. He showed an irrepressible enthusiasm and nothing delighted him more than to see a man reduced to a fit of coughing that was fit only for the dying.

"See I told you baby, she's a python. Ha! Ha-ha! Aha baabyyy! Keep it in! Keep it in!"

Jazz never got swayed by peer pressure but that American was the closest I ever saw to him descending into the dead end of drugs.

"Well," he said to us, when he finally realised he'd met someone who could not be persuaded by his high spirits.

"Good luck to you, baby. I respect a man who knows his own mind," whilst wiggling the end of the bong tube with a lazy smile in a parody of temptation.

"Never forget, she's waiting for you if you ever change your mind and you want to get your skeleton out and see your bones dancing."

Soon after this, already exhausted by our own relentless schedule, we were sitting back in our chairs silenced. Little red lights flickered over the desk and up into the compressors and the cool oppression of the air conditioning suddenly came sharply into focus.

"Play me some of your stuff then, man. Roll me a song," he said eventually.

So Paul played him *Time For The Rest Of Your Life*, which was already mixed and mastered and ready to go.

"Fucking hell, boys! That's a monster! Totally! I love it! I totally fucking love it!"

With that he became Strangelove's new best mate and turned up every night at about 10. Most of the others went to bed around sunrise, but me and him stayed up longer playing acoustic guitars long into the mornings. Hypnotic jams, staying on the same strange open chords for hours. Doolally till he disappeared off with his high spirits finally flagging. Then I'd continue on, playing the piano. The grand at Jacobs was haunted by a sad ghost that seemed to be trapped somewhere inside the wooden casing. Strange classical sounding pieces of music came through to me and I sat for hours sometimes till late afternoon, on no sleep, patiently trying to get my hands to do what the ghost was trying to tell me.

The sessions were drawing to a close and our friend from Napalm Death left the same way he came, without explanations. We'd completely run out of money now and John and I would get a lift from Andy into Farnham and busk Syd Barrett songs to get funds for our drink. On a few occasions, there was torrential rain and one time it got so bad we tried to find shelter in a nearby church.

"Let's get in there, Pad. Come on, quick before you get washed away."

It was lashing down, the drains in the street couldn't take it. The sound of the rain pelting down on the soaked concrete like horses clip-clopping over my coffin. There was no chance of busking and we were getting drenched.

John shook the door of the church. A-shaking and a-rattling. We'd both been brought up Catholics but neither of us had set foot inside a church for years. He almost pulled the door off its hinges but could not under any circumstances get it to open. We stood there in the rain like two drunks who hadn't bothered listening to Noah. He looked across at me with a limp roll-up hanging out of his mouth and blind rage in his eyes. He spat the useless tobacco to the floor and had one more go. Grabbed the handles and shook them like the apple tree at the end of the world but to no avail. He hung his head back into the pouring rain and hollered up at the skies,

"The House of God is locked!"

I was immediately convinced we should call the album by that name, but on arrival back at the studio the others – equally convinced in the opposite direction – said no. They didn't like it, especially John. So we called it *Time For The Rest of Your Life* instead.

All the chalk words that Paul had written on the blackboard weeks ago had now turned into music. There was just one more guitar overdub Alex wanted to try on the intro to *Is There A Place?*

"I don't know what it is, but we need something," he insisted.

Towards the end of our time we'd been working non-stop to finish the record, which had ended up becoming a double album because we'd recorded so many songs. There were a million finishing touches and Paul had not left the control room for three days except to piss. He hadn't slept a wink in all that time and had existed on only coffee, weed, and Bensons. Eventually, he went distant. Superimposing his dreams over the desk, lunging around the control room like some Captain Ahab searching for the wild, white whale at the end of the album.

The sun was coming up over the wobbly fields of Surrey, but the moon still hung on in the sky – defiant, like a bald, white scream. After weeks and weeks of concentrated music-making and debauchery, a strange chaotic spirit had risen up in our collective. That morning it materialised and launched itself at Alex and he took it by the tail and thrashed it into his guitar playing. He stood in the middle of the control room with the big speakers as loud as we could possibly stomach them to make it feel like something was actually happening. We rolled the tape one more time and he started playing with an abandon we'd never witnessed in him before. The slow build of the ominous intro, the rumble bass and drums, off-setting it all by channelling the cold, dumb rage of our band. Suddenly, as he was playing, we all spontaneously rose up out of our seats standing on our hind legs howling. Shouting and screaming as he played.

"Go on man, plaaaaayyyy!"

"Woo-hoooo!"

"Come on Al, fucking kill me!"

"Come on! Come on! Come fucking on! Kill me! Kill me! Kill meee!"

The true renegade spirit of Strangelove was baring its teeth. Beyond the rock 'n' roll and the prancing around out of your head and the tensions and the laughing and the hurt feelings and the boredom, beyond even the music itself. The hairs on the back of my neck stood up like the ghosts of drowned sailors. The noise of it all, the chaos and the years we'd all spent sunk on the dole, the songs we'd written that were to bind us together for a lifetime whether we liked it or not and whatever anybody fucking thought about it, all fused together in that moment.

There is only one life we know about and that moment changed mine forever. In my imagination, silver sparks were cascading across the skies and falling into the sea. Even though the ship was going down – and deep down I think we all knew we were a doomed vessel loaded up with tar and whizz and vodka and smoke – we'd all decided to stay on board and go down together. It all flashed up in a terrifying vision on a 60-foot silver screen in my mind. I saw it. We were all going down together!

Is There A Place?

Out, out of my hands
These prisoner's hands
That carved me through with stone
And that's the stone of my heart
A prisoner's heart
That can't feel love I'm told
Told of another time
Another way
Another
Is there a place for me somewhere?
Is there a place for me somewhere?
Is there a place for me somewhere?
Is there a place for me somewhere?

I've got to find somewhere
I've got to find somewhere

CHAPTER 18

RADIOHEAD

We received positive and encouraging press from all the magazines and newspapers for our first album and around this time Radiohead invited us to go on a UK tour. Cerne showed me an interview Thom Yorke had given in *Q* praising Strangelove and John played me the first version of *Creep*. A memorable song that on first listening sounded slightly American to my ears, but John immediately corrected me by saying they were from Oxford. Radiohead were not a particularly well-known band at that time and the venues were small. Joe called it the 'Toilet Tour'.

Strangelove arrived that first day poisoned with hangovers. The gruelling traffic jam to Wolverhampton in our pitch-black van had been made even more unbearable when Steve, our long-suffering driver and tour manager, got stressed out about our collective lateness and refused to stop at the off-license as punishment. We were well into the withdrawal phase when late afternoon a string of skinny corpses trailed into the venue.

I'd turned up wearing a full-length 70s leather coat, recently purchased from a second-hand shop, and in my humble estimation looking decidedly like rock 'n' roll royalty. That coat had first started whispering to me from a dusty row of leathers in Uncle Sam's on Park Street.

"I've been waiting for you, my man," it seemed to say.

The guy who ran the shop was grinning from ear to ear as I stood swaying before the mirror. Looking so cool it was laughable. Something about the wide lapels, the skinny arms, the shiny black buttons, the way it swished when you walked and the feline odour of some distant perfume of the previous owner immediately filled me with an intoxicating sense of arrogance. Pop in a piece of chewing gum and walk down the street with that leather on and you were far, far more worldly than was ever remotely the truth. Floating above everyone else in the town because me and that coat knew something they didn't. I should have sussed and walked away the moment I'd put it on, but it looked so cool and I was weak.

One day, far away in the future, I'd come to realise that this particular leather coat was cursed.

Thom was polite and friendly and despite the fact you could see it wasn't easy for him he held out his hand and said,

"Welcome on tour, great to have you with us. My name's Thom."

Alex, Joe, and I stood before him – the living dead. Wearing the coat, and only just becoming accustomed to its aloofness, it persuaded me to make only a cool, distant response to his good-naturedness and I watched the enthusiasm drain from his face.

****

After the Sheffield gig, it was a long solemn drive to Glasgow and the daytime band seemed even more withdrawn than usual. Something was up, the paranoia was unbearable, and it wasn't much of a surprise when on arrival Steve said he wanted a word.

He took me off to a bar round the side of the venue.

"Do you know what happened last night?"

"What do you mean, man?"

"Onstage, do you know what happened?"

"Just say what you mean Steve?"

"Do you remember telling the audience to fuck off. To fuck off and go home. And then walking off stage?"

I pulled the coat closer round me,

"Did I?"

"Yeah, Pad, you did. Look man, people have come out to see you. They've paid money. You can't do that. Why don't you wait to have a drink until after you come off?"

****

John and I met a dead-eyed Glaswegian in a pub round the corner from
King Tut's who gave us a handful of barbiturates because John had already
insisted on putting him on the guest list. John immediately shared them out
equally and we swallowed them straight down. Back in the venue, Alex had
scored ecstasy and all of us, apart from Jazz, dropped a few of those. When
the curtain call came, I tiptoed down the stairs from the dressing room to
the stage, feeling incredibly fragile.

'SWISH' – John lightly tapped one of the cymbals. It was the most
incredible sound I'd ever heard.

"Do that again, man, it sounds amazing."

'SWIIIISH'

"Wow, cool, man. Do it again."

'SWIIIIIIIISH'

Every time he touched that cymbal, the fear was diminishing like he
was some kind of mad doctor.

"Let's just do that for the whole gig, it sounds so fucking cool."

Alex went into the riff for *Dancing Queen* by Abba, which we used to
play as a joke in our rehearsals, and so we did that as our opening number.
It sounded breath-taking. Then, he went into the opening chord for *Glue*,
a forlorn little song I'd written about glue sniffing and nothing to do with
our setlist. *Glue* sounded enormous. Slow and profound. I sang with a wide
Cheshire Cat grin plastered across my face.

'I'm glue-ing out of my mind
Glue makes me feel like I'm wanted
Glue makes me feel like I'm real
Glue makes me feel like I'm the kind of person that you'd really like to get
to know,

Glue I love you
Glue I love you
Cause you're cheap
And you make me feel
Like I'm not cheap'.

Those lines resonated around the derelict room like a proclamation from the land of the dead and were delivered with pure and restrained depth. My voice coming back through the monitor was the best I'd ever heard it. In fact, this was the first time I'd *ever* properly heard it. Suddenly, a joke song about glue sniffing metamorphosed to sum up everything pregnant in that moment. The audience appeared to be captivated and the gig progressed in this haphazard way, flitting between lost Strangelove songs and bizarre cover versions pulled out of thin air. All the strange things we'd done in rehearsals in moments of boredom came flooding to the surface and the set drifted by on this laughing gas.

The ghosts of rock 'n' roll were rising from their graves and transmogrifying into a massive finger made out of smoke that was breaking through the clouds and down through the roof and pointing from heaven right at us, just so that everyone in the world would know. I was a thousand feet tall and didn't have to move to make no point. My presence filled the grotty, old King Tut's Wah Wah Hut and for miles beyond with pure, unbridled love.

Because I was the one who had to love everyone. The same love that was making the electricity work in the amplifiers and in the sound man's fingers and in the eyes of the shining girls at the front. My love, that was making the cars go by on the road outside, making the motorways turn blue, making the sun go round the earth. I strolled the stage now with the utmost confidence. Coat swishing, the head down days were over.

The drunken guy who'd given us the barbiturates was getting carried away, jumping about so much that he began to crash into the people around him. Foaming at the mouth and starting a fight and collapsing to the floor and being thrown out by the bouncers. Nothing could wipe the smile from my face as we continued to shower the audience with the giant waves of love. This was the reason I was born. The only truth I'd ever known. From having told them all to fuck off in a black-out in Sheffield the previous night, this audience were subjected to a very different side of Strangelove.

****

"Hey, man, we ran out. You don't mind, do you?"

So full of love and generosity 'myself' that night, I was sure it would be OK to take some of their lagers, as it was clear they didn't drink, but when

Thom came offstage and found me in their dressing room, plundering the rider, he didn't appear impressed. Another sleepless night, through the early hours of some bed and breakfast in Glasgow, it began to bug me that I'd done the wrong thing. We'd watched Radiohead every night, and to me even though they only seemed to have one great song then, it was such a great one. Thom had totally nailed something a lot of us felt at the time and Jonny's part when he attacked the guitar was priceless. They'd always been friendly and welcoming and had generously praised our band. Why would I want to fuck that up? The remorse was intense and probably over the top due to the now rapidly disappearing love chemicals.

Next afternoon, searching for the soundcheck, we came across each other on a thin thoroughfare at the end of a bank of seats, on a wooden balcony overlooking another wooden room, somewhere up north. He strode towards me.

"Hey, Thom. Wait a second, man," my voice was thin and croaky. "I'm sorry about yesterday, I shouldn't have taken those drinks from your dressing room. That was uncool. Forgive me?"

"I'm busy," he said, sailing straight past, brushing up against 'the coat' and almost knocking me to one side. I turned to watch him walk away, purposefully disappearing through a door at the far end of the hall.

Still coming down, but still wide open, I was suddenly struck with an unsettling and powerful intuition.

'That guy is really going somewhere, Patrick. One day he is going to be a huge star and, unlike him, you have a lot more darkness coming your way.'

Strangely, that night on stage we came up with another fistful of gold. Everyone said so. In fact, John had played such a blinding set that their drummer Phil was reduced to tears before they went on because he felt he simply couldn't follow him. But I'd already sensed it wasn't going to be the taste of things to come, however much I tried to push it from my mind. They would increase and we would decrease. I would have to stand by and watch my band and my life go down the drain. Why wouldn't that idea leave me alone?

****

However, the next day it was Thom who got drunk when we played in

Manchester. He'd been cruelly taunted and dismissed in the latest issue of the *NME* and had holed himself up in a bar all afternoon. Unhinged at the soundcheck, and on stage that night he was the most unsettled we'd ever seen him. At one point, he stopped the gig to shout abuse about journalists. I stood there swaying in my new coat, feeling safe, loving the way the whole room went quiet and no one knew what to say. Loving the chaos. Strangelove all agreed it was the best gig they'd done so far because of that.

"Sorry, that was not good," Colin and Ed said to us afterwards in bewildered tones.

"Are you mental? That was the one," we insisted. "That was amazing. It was proper. You were fucking brilliant."

But they weren't having it, however much we promised.

Apparently Thom was forlorn, and so I barged into their dressing room again.

"Look, man, for what it's worth, you were fucking brilliant tonight. That was the best one of the whole tour."

"Whatever," he slurred.

Drunkenness didn't suit him.

"I mean it, man. We all thought that. Look you've got nothing to worry about. Fuck the *NME*. Your band's great."

"Fuck, yeah!" he dismissed.

"I mean it Thom. Honestly."

"Get the fuck outta here, man," he slurred, whilst chucking me a can. I caught it.

"Thanks, man," we both said at exactly the same moment.

If it hadn't been him and they hadn't made it so big I probably would have forgotten all about that incident, but in the intervening years I've remembered it many times.

****

Thankfully, after that night in Manchester, the weird vibes between Thom and I disappeared and in the dead time between soundchecks and gigs we even began to console each other about the music press and how cruel some of the reviews could be. How powerless you felt knowing a scathing personal attack was now in every newsagent in the country. How angry, how much it hurt. Talking to another singer who actually knew what that was like allowed me to recognise it was OK to admit how much it did get to you.

Because absolutely everyone else said you had to rise above it.

In truth, we did receive loads of great press and so did they. In fact, for both bands at the time it was probably more good than bad, but we agreed that for some reason it was the nasty ones that went in deeper and the ones you ended up musing over. Why was it that the singers were always the ones who always seemed to cop the real venom? The same strange reason why they got the most adulation too.

The journalists who didn't get Strangelove accused me of not being 'for real', of being overly dramatic. Faking being highly strung and paranoid. Pretending to be fucked up. Considering what I'd already been through in my life, it was pretty confusing trying to work out what that meant. I totally relate to why Richey Manic carved '4 REAL' into his arm with a razor blade in frustration. Many of those so-called clever men, itching to be recognised themselves, with their pens and their Dictaphones and their cocaine-nose jobs and their detailed maps of the music world and its history, didn't seem to quite trust in anyone who was still lucky enough to be alive. In fact, if you were still alive you must be some kind of a fake.

On the other hand, Radiohead were accused of 'not' being rock 'n' roll enough. Dismissed and ridiculed because they drank tea after their gigs and didn't take drugs and weren't fucked up. And how dare they not be fucked up.

You couldn't win either way.

★★★★

In Newcastle, towards the end of the tour, we were sharing a dressing room. By this point, we were sitting around together before the gigs, exhausted. Usually in silence, staring into the white noise graffiti of the walls.

Many backstage rooms on these 'toilet tours' are like this one – covered in mad scrawlings. Band names and curses, girls' names and dirty jokes, fantasy breasts and crass philosophical musings, chains of banter and derision and multifarious erect and often ejaculating penises drawn in marker pens galore. Years-and-years' worth of bands you'd never heard of with impossibly doomed names like Emperor Ming, Backdoor Boyz, Jelly Attack, or Last Stop For Petrol.

Nursing your wounds, waiting for the next gig to dawn, you found yourself drawn into deciphering these decades of scribblings, whilst wondering to yourself: Exactly who were these ghosts from the past, whom you'd never heard of and whom you were about to share the same stage with? Where were they now? What was it you were actually getting involved with here? Were you somehow connected to them all now? What the fuck was all this? All these smartass idiots trying to outdo each other with wicked wits or just pure offensiveness.

Suddenly, after weeks of these silent and undisclosed reveries, Thom jumped up with a massive red marker pen, standing on the backs of the sofas whilst careering around the room, giving marks out of 10 for the graffiti. Like he was some kind of English teacher. '3/10 Very Poor. 4/10 Could do better. 1/10 Cheap.' He kept up the exasperated energy for a good five minutes whilst the rest of us sat in an exhausted silence. The scraping of the marker pen on the wall squeaking with livid Oxford. Until Terry stepped in.

Terry was our American roadie whom I'd made fast friends with. He was tall and handsome, skinny with a black bob, and looked far more like a popstar than a roadie. We'd shared all manner of intoxicants and had by this point become roommates. Our room, the naughty one, where everyone hung out at night. As usual we'd been drinking together in the van. It was the end of the tour and Newcastle was a long way. Terry wasn't used to it and this time he'd overshot himself. Beyond drunk, a Californian drawl infected the room.

"I've been on this tour for weeks now and I want to say something."

The whole room was already collapsed with tiredness anyway.

"This is supposed to be a fucking rock 'n' roll tour, man. Fucking rock 'n' roll. Who the fuck are you people? The only fucking person whose got any rock 'n' roll in their fucking bloodstream that I can see is Patrick. Fucking Patrick, man. The only fucking one"

I genuinely prayed for the ground to swallow me up. We'd finally got a good vibe going on this tour for fuck's sake.

"Don't, Terry," I said. "Please don't."

Terry remained adamant as he stood there swaying. He'd always liked it and had commented on it many times throughout the tour and so for the first time that afternoon I'd let him try it on. He was wearing my coat. He'd only had it on for a couple of hours and it was already spinning its black magic around him. I didn't realise then. How could I? It didn't strike me till years later. But the coat had got Terry by the puppet strings too and it wasn't going to let me off the hook that easily.

"Patrick's the only fucking one, man."

"Terry, please?"

****

The last gig was in Belfast. There were tanks and armed troops on the streets and the whole city was sinking in thick, cold fog. Not so many people showed up and at the end both bands danced around together in the venue to The Doors. Radiohead were about to go to America and unbeknownst to any of us, everything was going to change for them. They were about to become one of the biggest bands in the world. Just before we all left, Thom went up to Alex and said,

"If I ever lose one of my guitarists, I'll give you a call."

Next morning, we woke up having stolen hundreds of pounds worth of wine from the kitchen of our bed and breakfast, which Steve now had to pay for out of gig earnings.

"Why didn't you just wake me up when you got back in? I could have opened the bar for you instead of you drinking the expensive stuff," said the offended, red-faced bed and breakfast man.

Steve wouldn't let us have any more money for drinks and we had to stay sober on the ferry back.

Withdrawing once again along the M5 near Birmingham in our big blue van, which Steve had rented off some travellers, we suddenly overtook Radiohead in their white van. Waving out the window and making faces.

"Come on, Steve, floor it, fucking go!" we shouted.

But Radiohead had a posher van. A modern thing that crept up beside us. They looked smiling and waved back at us through the windows and then took off. Leaving us for dust.

****

Not that long afterwards, Alex and I were hanging out in the studio in London where they were recording *The Bends*, trying to nail *My Iron Lung*. It wasn't going particularly well and there was a definite tension in the air.

"Sounds a bit like *Dear Prudence* in a spin dryer," I chirped, when they came back into the control room.

"You're still drinking then, you fucking wino," said Thom, grinning with a steel light dancing in his eyes.

We hung out for a few hours, whilst they tried various takes of the song and played us some of the other ones they'd done. We were witnessing musical history in the making but didn't know it. I couldn't help reflecting on how different it was to the atmosphere in the studio when Strangelove were recording and became convinced that's why they were having problems. I encouraged them to get pissed and loosen up a bit. But only Colin succumbed to a glass and he sipped it like we were at a South Kensington art gallery. They listened back to their music like kindergarten school kids watching TV. A single-mindedness that was endearing to behold. Total concentration. Thom, combining a little frown and a little grin on his face, eyes closed as his head nodded up and down. There was no shouting or drug taking whatsoever.

"Fucking hell, it's really like serious when they're recording, isn't it?" I said to Al as we left the studio.

"Yeah," he replied absentmindedly.

Because it had been inspiring to have been there for those few hours. To have shared that time together. Music that soared and went straight into a melancholy heart and moved it somewhere more thoughtful.

****

On the way out, Jimmy Somerville from Bronsky Beat and the Communards was sitting in the communal lounge, staring at EastEnders. When I was a kid, I'd seen him shy and smiling on *Top Of The Pops* at Number One. As always with these pop stars you couldn't help but feel some strange fascination in actually seeing him on a sofa. They always looked so much more vulnerable than on a TV screen and despite all the success he'd once had, here in the flesh I never saw a man who appeared so terribly alone. The sadness hit you like a tube train. I'm sure it was just a moment, like we all have, but it left me with a chill. Music was so generous and so cruel. It used whoever it wanted to for as long as it wanted to.

****

Food Records now merged into Parlophone and we were subsequently signed alongside Radiohead and Blur, just as their stars began to ascend. Both those bands were being treated like royalty around the EMI offices and Colin told me that Radiohead had insisted to the people at Parlophone,

"You've got to sign Strangelove. You've got to. They're amazing."

Altogether the times were a-changing. Pete Paphides, a renowned journalist who'd once slagged us off, wrote a heartwarming apology in the Melody Maker, expressing a newfound admiration for our latest gig; and Radiohead – now hitting the big, big time – pronounced Strangelove as their favourite band of the moment. In a later interview with Caitlin Moran, Ed O'Brien was quoted as saying,

"Radiohead are definitely post-Strangelove. We toured with them for *Pop Is Dead* and we changed quite a lot after that. They were inspirational."

There was more love coming our way in the press from Richey Manic too, who eventually invited us to support The Manic Street Preachers, and we played the penultimate gig before his disappearance, at the London Astoria.

CHAPTER 19

SUEDE

Suede also invited us on a European tour. *Dog Man Star* had recently come out, Bernard had walked, and they'd just recruited young guitarist Richard.

We bumped into the band on the evening ferry from Dover. Both on our way to the first gig in Strasbourg where this book began. Suede appeared relaxed, cracking in-jokes with their crew.

Introductions made me nervous, so I slipped away up to the deck. Hanging onto the cold steel rails with the ferry chugging into the night. Peering at the lights from the port and the lights from other boats. This was one of the first times I'd been abroad and, in the excitement, the dark blue horizon leaned in and whispered,

"Is this what you want?

You can have all this for real if you want it."

Suddenly, my heart was racing and great waves of hope came crashing through my chest. Being around all these bands who were going somewhere was beginning to have an effect on me. Throughout Strangelove, my intuitions about our future would sway back and forth between opposing poles.

Maybe it was all going to work out?

I was filled with an intense urge to phone my mum and dad and say thank you.

"Thank you for giving me life."

Music was taking us to faraway countries. I watched the white cliffs vanishing into the rumble of the engines and the lapping black waves and the salt spray. Out at sea, surrounded in darkness with the blustery air blowing over my face, my blood beating in my ears. There, in that moment, for the first time I really began to feel that maybe, just maybe, I could be someone – and not just in my imagination.

****

We went out and watched Suede playing most evenings. Whereas Radiohead were just about to hit the big time, Suede already had and these were larger indoor gigs than we'd experienced before. Sold out gigs. Hundreds of people with a tangible sense of excitement in the venue every night. Fans hanging around afterwards and waiting for their moment with the band, asking for autographs and clutching albums to be signed.

As the tour progressed, we started to get to know each other and it soon became apparent that Suede were also considerably more together than we were. They had setlists with bold song titles printed out on A4 paper by a computer. On those setlists they had hits. They had a proper light show. They had extensive merchandise. On their tour schedule, under every venue, they had the names and addresses of nearby gymnasiums. Brett had a special tea that he drank before concerts to help soothe his throat. He let me have a swig of that tea sometimes and it worked. They also had proper stage clothes which they changed into before the gig. They sent those clothes off to the laundry on arrival at the next venue. Those clothes came back clean and you could see them hanging on rails backstage. Nudging Alex and pointing out to him from the corner of some huge communal dining room in Germany,

"Look, man, they're ironing their fucking trousers."

As we stood there dumbfounded, who could ever have foreseen that Alex was going to be playing with Suede a few years later?

Despite these surface differences, Brett and I clicked immediately. In our conversations, we discovered we had both sniffed glue and lighter gas as kids, both liked *Starsky and Hutch*, both knew all the words to all the Crass songs, and both had long lists of dark-humoured, drug-taking anecdotes. Unlike his worldly, slightly aloof persona in the press, Brett was sensitive and thoughtful and self-deprecatingly funny. So dealing with the nightly adulation he received from his fans was a complicated business for him.

As the tour rumbled on, and we all started going insane, Brett would be coked up and shouting out to the Italian audiences between songs, "You fucking love it, you scrubbers! You love it! You fucking scrubbers! Scrubbersss!" And the cheers just grew louder. Something about all this theatre of the absurd strongly appealed to the drugged up me - and instead of simply daydreaming I continued to consider in a more practical way what it might mean to be famous.

It became clear that Suede had created a kind of umbrella for a certain type of outsider to stand under and feel part of something. When you get a few hundred people, who often consider themselves to be pretty isolated, going through something of a transformation of that kind, becoming one with each other and the music, in the same place at the same moment, it's a powerful experience and leaves a profound impression when you witness it night after night.

We shared something in common with Suede, though our music was darker and less considered, their European fans opened up to our vibe and the tour was bringing our band closer together. It was a happy time for us.

"All right. Good evening. We're Strangelove. White trash from the South West!"

****

On the sleeper bus, you came round from your coffin in a new town or capital city every morning. Stumbling out into Stockholm, we were playing the Cirkus, a plush venue holding a couple of thousand people. I began to revel in the sweet simplicity of each day, having foreign adventures and doing a gig every night with nothing else to worry about.

Outside our bus, in the cool sunshine of early morning, a funny old man dressed like a tramp sat on a stool, recounting a story to 30 or so young children who stood around, faces transfixed. His click-clackety Swedish voice rang out with a variety of larger-than-life characters. It was a radiant spring morning and for no particular reason I stepped onto a small ferry boat that had pulled up 20 yards from our parking place.

The sea was clear and sparkling and the pale sun low in the sky. The only other people on deck were an old couple, with their backs to me, dressed in fine clothes, standing in the bow. Those two strangers in their dark winter coats, silhouetted against the sun with the expanse of water before them and Old Stockholm coming into view on the horizon, evoked an almost worshipful response from within my heart. My mind went completely still and I had a strong premonition that one day I would be free to know a love like this myself, but it would not come till late in life and despite the wait I'd be happy one day.

Wandering from bar to bar, I was approached and then accompanied by a growing posse of what eventually became about 20 Suede fans who recognised me from the music papers. All full of myself, I invited them back to the venue and let them in the stage door to the soundchecks. I'd never felt so important in all my days and the coat swished from side to side as I danced into our dressing room. The gigs at the Cirkus – two sold out nights in a row, performing to wildly enthusiastic Scandinavians – lifted the tour to another level.

****

In southern Spain, we were due to play a huge stone amphitheatre carved into a hillside in the middle of a desert somewhere outside Granada. We watched the sun going down on the Moorish landscape with the reds and browns of the distant mountains. There was just one tiny dirt road up to the amphitheatre and we couldn't work out how all the people would get there. But as sunset deepened, the fans – mostly dressed in black – started walking across the desert from the horizons, arriving in all directions as we stood by the dressing rooms on the top of the hill. Like some ancient rite unfolding.

This was the first time we'd played outside at night. It was still warm. Under the stars, I sang the whole gig looking up into a huge, demented orange moon as it rose over the desert; wrapped in the almighty enthusiasm of a Spanish audience of thousands. The noise of their caterwauling was like being hit by a 50-foot fist. When Strangelove shone (which wasn't all the time) there was nothing like it, and for some reason that night we blazed, sending the showers of silver back across the sky again. The distant hills erupted with the noise and in my estimation, something happened to us as a band of individuals. That night something fused together in the tumult of the excitement and the witness of the audience that can never be undone.

****

On reflection, I consider this is why a lot of bands, who shine and then later crash and burn, attempt these reunion tours over and over again. As an awkward, skinny, insignificant young person you suddenly become the focus for some kind of mass transcendence and it's completely mind-blowing. Your life can never be the same again. It's too easy to roll your eyes at acts who go out kicking their hits back into life. Anyone who has ever actually known the experience of that specific kind of voodoo would be left with some part of them wanting to recapture it. A wishing well that never runs dry. That's the price you have to pay for the experience of Granada.

****

Afterwards, the fans queued to get our autographs. The women strolled up laughing, chattering in Spanish and lifting up their tops. Unable to reflect on whether this was the right thing to be doing and having already witnessed Brett oblige without a flicker of interest in his eyes, like he was signing on at a dole office, I went ahead. The first time I'd ever signed breasts. The marker got stuck on the skin and all my early attempts looked like the scrawlings of some poor soul in a lunatic asylum trying to scrape their name in the flowerbeds with a special stick. It was also mind boggling having to deal with all the different shapes and sizes, but you got used to it quicker than you'd think. Especially once you got your knack. The scrawls became more legible. I even started looking them in the eyes. I got blasé. Overconfident. I used the right-hand nipple as the dot over the 'i' in Patrick.

We had a compound of dressing rooms around a small plaza. It was a gruelling after show party, as Matt had given out loads of backstage passes to whomever he considered were the most interesting looking fans, although Brett complained bitterly that he'd only invited goths. In all the laughter, our friendliness with Suede developed to such an extent that we ended up covering each other's songs. We played *Killing Of A Flashboy* and Suede played *She's Everywhere*, a song I'd recently written with Alex.

Brett announced it from the stage in Zaragoza.

"This next one is a cover song by the soon-to-be-enormous Strangelove."

Happily, and it has to be said to the enrichment of my life, enough of a connection remained for me to count on Brett as a good friend to this day. Even now we hang out at the Bishop's Palace in Wells drinking green tea, laughing and going to obscure, sacred music concerts at the cathedral.

****

The next day, travelling back from Spain, staring dead-eyed at the outskirts of Zaragoza, was the first time I'd flown in an aeroplane. Gaping out the window and witnessing the clouds down below; realising how they circulated the earth, loitering above us. Fluffy white parasites who sucked out all the water they could. So that was it. No wonder I was so dehydrated. Simon sat next to me in his rectangular sunglasses.

"I have to give up cocaine," he said.

"Me too, man," I agreed. "And drinking?"

Lovely, sensitive Simon. He was right. We remained pensive in the prolonged silence that followed our simple exchange and sipped medicinal Pernod till Heathrow.

Cocaine, the handmaiden of the ego, was always a shit drug, but in the years to come it got even shitter when rugby players with dyed mohicans started taking it. On that plane, in a moment of clarity, I recognised that there was nothing cool about it whatsoever. I'd never felt particularly connected to the headline hedonism of the 90s and in stark contrast wanted to get my act together instead. I didn't want to blow our chance. I'd had a taste of something sweeter on this tour and wanted to concentrate on music and not on talking hot air 19 to the dozen. However, at that very moment and without me realising, my black leather coat was above our heads shoved into the locker, listening to Simon and I and looking down on us with its own agenda.

****

We returned to England and played more sold-out shows in Blackpool and a final one at the Albert Hall.

One of the anomalies about being in a band on the road is that you arrive at a virtually empty venue every afternoon. You wait for hours while stage-hands fuck around with wires and occasionally shout indecipherable phrases across to one another, but they disappear off at times too and then you're left there alone; the other musicians back at the hotel, complaining about cricked necks or lost inside their headphones.

On a tour with venues that were so much larger and grander I'd find myself drawn to the stages at these quiet times. You are free to jump up. Free to stand there and look back at the empty seats, the balconies, and the high-vaulted ceilings. There you begin to learn about the qualities of silence that hang around in the emptiness. If you stop listening to yourself for a moment, shut your eyes or stare and wait, the atmosphere of that silence starts whispering. You can hear its silent language in your bloodstream. More and more, finding yourself pulled in as the noisy days and nights roll by, your listening grows on beyond your ears and it soon becomes apparent that the silence in the Luna theatre in Brussels is different to the silence in the Auditorium Flog in Florence, is different to the silence in the Arena Auditorium in Valencia, is different to the silence in the Empress Ballroom in Blackpool.

In each place you start to experience that silence talking back to you like a saint who holds the keys to all the gigs that were ever played there in the past. The nameless saint of each particular venue, who watches over the remnant spirits of all the people who have left a small part of their listening in the walls and ceilings and in the air molecules. Their unwitting gift to the theatre. In the silence you can still hear that listening, as still as the dead, and you sense all the music that was ever once played there. Forever playing on in the silence. A silence that's now waiting to be filled by you. A silence that roars back and fills you with reverence and eventually makes you realise that you're just a small, small part of something much bigger, called music.

Day by day, you are humbled to a greater and greater degree and then finally most of all, by the silence in the Albert Hall. It was giant. A giant, bigger than the Albert Hall itself. In fact, the silence in the Albert Hall could have filled 10 Albert Halls standing on top of each other like German acrobats. Three o'clock in the hungover afternoon and utterly alone, you are partaking in something so mysterious and so profound and so insistent that it weakens you.

Standing alone in the Albert Hall, that silence began to replace me to the point where I became overwhelmed by a growing annihilation so intense that I had to turn my back on it. Terrified that something so giant and so strange could ever even allow me the time of day. I went back to our dressing room, sat down on a chair, and cried.

****

After the gig, I was alone in our dressing room again, this time vomiting blood into the white sink. My mum and dad had come to the concert. This was the first occasion they'd ever seen Strangelove in all the years of me being in the band because when we were away Cerne had invited all the parents.

They didn't have to tell me, but I kept receiving the messages regardless. Piped through an ancient looking intercom. You couldn't turn the decrepit speaker off.

"Message for Patrick Duff," the woman's voice crackled once more.

"Patrick, your family are waiting for you in the green room."

"Message for Patrick Duff, your family are waiting."

"Message for Patrick from Strangelove."

In the end, our roadie Mark came through the door.

"Get your arse up there. Your mum and dad are waiting. That's your mum and dad, I don't care if you're fucked. Get up there you fucking…" he insisted in growling cockney.

Dad was a bit pissed, but for the first time ever I sensed him almost nervous around me. Slightly uncertain of how to approach. He smiled a watery, almost humble smile that I'd never seen on him before. Yet he wasn't diminished in any way.

"Look, Pad. I was really proud of you tonight. I mean it. Really proud," he said.

"Really proud."

I stood there speechless. Without truly knowing it before, I'd been waiting for this moment all my life. But when it finally came, so easy and natural there in the green room, I was too sick to receive it with even a flash of the necessary grace. The Snow Globe Albert Hall was all shook up and I couldn't see straight and the words landed soft and hollow and dead in my ears. Alcohol and drugs had killed the love inside me.

"Thanks, Dad."

"Let me get you a drink."

"No, Dad, there's loads of it free in our dressing room. Actually, I have to go back down there because there's stuff we have to do at the end. I'd better go. Thanks for being here."

My voice sounded like it was being beamed in from a thousand miles away. Some voice in a shit B-movie coming out of a cinema screen. My mind raced uncontrollably as I walked slow motion back round the circle of the hall and down the stairs. I'd messed up. I'd fucked up something important. I hadn't even waited for mum either. As I heard the hustle and bustle of the party fading, a cold rain started to fall inside me and it didn't stop. Without knowing it, this was the moment I started to open my eyes. Slowly but surely, as the blizzard got worse, a light shone out in the distance and over the coming weeks and months that realisation grew. I found myself beginning to hate alcohol and drugs and the so-called rock 'n' roll lifestyle. At last that tired, old romance started drying up, and I started to realise who I actually was despite it all. Something sweet and tender, dying on the branch.

When I shut my eyes, I could see. All those stories I'd picked up in music papers and sensationalised rock biographies as an impressionable kid. I'd sucked it all in because I was lost and lonely and needed something and I'd connected all that white noise with the actual power of music that already reigned supreme in my body. Those words had taken me over and given me an identity that was now destroying all the good things in life.

I never had another drink that didn't deep down feel like a cup of poison. I never snorted another line that didn't stink of ashes. And sure, Keith had snorted 'his' dad and it was funny and all that, but from that day on the joke was on me.

****

However, there were all sorts of other people involved in the running of the tour with Suede, who agreed it had been a great success, and after that final gig at the Albert Hall, I headed to the countryside in Wales. We'd planned to write new material on the road but had barely accomplished a note due to a combination of partying and exhaustion. So, I still needed to write words and some songs for our imminent album sessions. After watching Suede and seeing with my own eyes what it was possible to achieve, everything looked different.

CHAPTER 20

GOING UP COUNTRY

I'd enquired from Cerne whether he could get me away from Bristol where all my cronies lived, knowing that by hooking up with them, even once, the possibility of doing any work would most probably evaporate. So, he'd rented a cottage about half a mile outside a village called Talybont-On-Usk in South Wales.

I asked Elin to come along for support and the first week was wasted shivering in bed from the withdrawals and trying to get her to look after me so I could straighten myself out to be able to write.

"When we were in Strasbourg, something happened."

It all came tumbling out, confused and stumbling. I hadn't meant to tell her.

"I went into a church. I was running away from these beggars and there was this little boy and I cried out in front of a stained-glass window. Something happened to me, Elin. It was like God or something. I know you probably think I'm insane, but honestly. Something actually happened. I'm not lying. It was like this kind of weird light. This whole chapel disappeared into it."

She sat cross-legged at the foot of the bed where I was lying in a tracksuit soaked with sweat. Elin prided herself on being a radical feminist, Marxist, atheist at that time, but after a short reflection she turned her gaze away from the window and caught me straight in the eye.

"I always knew you needed something like that to happen to you, Pad."

I was totally taken aback by that response. She'd always known me better than I knew myself and to experience a moment of that intimacy between us once more was crushing.

"Please help me Elin, I love you, I'm so sorry. Please help me."

But Elin was not up for the role of nurse anymore, and remained more interested in being an artist. She disappeared on walks and sketched quietly in her notebooks and pretty much left me to face myself; eventually returning to Bristol. Disinterested in my shaking, neurosis, and lack of appreciation or understanding for the beautiful surroundings we found ourselves in. Watching her scruffy black hair and fine face frowning at me through the window of the one bus out of Talybont. I didn't know it then, but it was over between us, and I'd never really see her again.

****

It was a creepy old cottage in the middle of nowhere and at night you were completely enveloped in agricultural darkness. With only a fire in the grate lighting the room. I played acoustic and listened to the demos with a relentless wind rattling the doors and windows. Those restless sounds reminded me of Emily's house. The house of horrors, where at the end of our benders, my friends and I would sit coming down in her unfurnished front room. The cold through the floorboards. The windows rat-a-tat-tatting out their messages. Somewhere within those memories and the restlessness of that cottage, my creativity started to flow again. In a few days, I'd written the lyrics and melodies for *Casualties*, *Twentieth Century Cold*, and *Living With The Human Machines*.

Alex came to visit, as did our producer Paul and his wife Rachael. They drove me up to the top of the Brecon Beacons and we wandered around in the mist, smoking ciggies with the lost sheep. Alex and Paul appeared pleased with what I'd achieved and it was comforting to be somewhat clean and connected back into making music again. So pleasing in fact that after they'd left, I decided to reward myself with a night out at the Star Inn. Just down the hill in Talybont. Just one night off before getting back to writing.

This marked the end of any more lyrics in that particular cottage, and much of what unfolded over the next few weeks went in and out of black out. Getting lost for hours in the pine forests near the reservoir. Coming round to find myself busking Syd Barrett songs in Abergavenny town centre. Back at the Star Inn with a vague recollection of some kind of argument. Giant

DT spiders the size of cannonballs crawling out through the walls in the bedroom and sending me scuttling terrified down the stairs in the early morning glow. The red public phone box by the Talybont Stores where I'd rang a few of my friends who'd driven across to stay for a while, further straining relations with the villagers. I eventually ran out of money and on the last morning, whilst waiting for the interminable bus to arrive, was informed by a scruffy old hippy in wellington boots, whom I'd never seen before, that I was banned from the Star Inn.

However, there had been some initial writing success and so a few weeks later we tried again. I pleaded with Cerne to find me somewhere more remote. Somewhere with no inns, or telephone boxes, or village shops of any kind within walking distance.

My red-haired sister Jacqueline dropped me off with a big bag of groceries from my mum. This place was deeper into the Brecon Beacons. In fact, I have it on good authority that Salman Rushdie was hidden away in this same cottage for a while after the Fatwa was put out against him. Cerne had surpassed himself. We motored over the old Welsh bridge and on through a cloudy afternoon. Up into the bald hills until I was asleep, and on arrival collapsed face down onto the bed, unreachable. After agonising for a while, there was nothing else Jackie could do but leave me there.

****

Early Morning Birds Early Morning Birds Early Morning Birds Early Morning Birds Early Morning Birds Early Morning Birds Early Morning Birds Early Morning Birds. That first morning I awoke to a cacophony of birdsongs, all competing for survival in my ears as they greeted the sunrise. The relentless world was still turning around unstoppable and there were no curtains and nowhere to hide from the light, apart from under the piles of dishevelled woollen blankets. The earth was a monstrous juggernaut that kept on rolling, regardless of how bad you felt. Grinding on to God knows where. You could shout STOP! at the top of your voice but it simply did not make any difference. I wanted to get off so bad but I didn't know how to, and anyway the truth was I didn't want to die.

One of the worst things was waking up. Alcoholism and addiction and the ensuing battle against my own body had put me in the ring against nature and all its mystifying rules. And now those birds were starting to defeat me. You could hear it in the malevolent joy of their singing. Those birds were mocking me, man. Or warning me. Or they didn't even care. That was more like it. They were just doing their thing. Creation didn't care about me or my weird feelings. I was all alone. Peeking out from under the covers, the sunshine silhouetted a branch across the whitewash walls like the diagram of a poisonous headache. It was clear this second cottage was a more rustic affair and I immediately suspected, after the last fiasco, a lot cheaper to rent. More like a glamorised bird-watching hide.

Wandering through the open air, I stared across at the bare hillsides and heard no answers. Coughing blindly into the distance. Further away, scattered against the green of the cultivated ground, black-and-white cows moved around nonchalantly. Possibly by remote control. It wasn't easy to work out who was moving them or what they were actually doing over there, apart from the indifference of eating grass.

What the hell was this place?

I strayed onto animal paths that ran in straight lines and seemed to know what they were talking about and I'd start following them and get weirdly hopeful and then forget why. Eventually, most of my walks developed into crooked ellipses around the hideout because I kept having to remind myself that I had more than it takes to lose that cottage.

I discovered a few derelict stone abodes on the hills nearby. Burnt-out carcasses of buildings with loops of plastic hose inside, old blue rope and fertiliser bags scattered under layers of dust and mouse droppings. People had been here, but they weren't here now.

Back home at night, insects flew pestering around the light bulbs. Outside over the rolling hillsides, I sensed that the vast dark skies with sharp, bright pinhole stars were supposed to be inspiring but I wanted someone with arms to hold me.

Occasionally in the daytime, small aircraft flew over and momentarily interrupted the isolation. They made such an annoying, thin racket that you could hear them coming from miles away and easily avoid surveillance. Didn't they realise those birds woke me early and I was more than ready by dawn? Mind you, they may have powerful cameras on board those planes and perhaps they were just allowing me to think I'd fooled them.

You could almost hear them crackling away on their walkie-talkie things.

"He's hiding in the old barn again. What a loser. Over."

"Just fly past, but *don't* circle around and make him think we haven't seen him. Over."

Yeah, they were on to me, man. I needed to get back to somewhere where I could lose myself in a crowd.

One morning, I simply couldn't take another blackbird, and decided to follow the faint tyre tracks along the grass road my sister had brought me in on. They led to a dirt track that led to another dirt track that led to a small road that led to a bigger road. Now, occasional cars were passing by with diffident countryside faces at the windscreens. However, I successfully hitched a half hour lift in the back of a white van to the market town of Brecon, installing myself in the darkest corner of a god-awful pub by midday. They were playing a Beautiful South album and it wasn't long till I was on the phone to a friendly dealer who came from Bristol and taxied me home that afternoon with no lyrics. Apart from the words 'Died of Exposure' written on the front of my empty notebook.

****

A few weeks later and short on songs, we holed up in Chiswick's Eden studios, to record *Sway*. A song I'd started writing late one night in Jacob's. Alex had recently come up with some chords for a middle eight section, which I then wrote lyrics and a melody for when arriving in London. On his suggestion, we also collaborated with a string quartet, playing a score written by a young arranger and violinist called Audrey Riley.

We listened in the control room as they sat in the studio playing through the dots. This was the first time we'd ever made music with people outside the band. The arrangement sounded graceful and melancholic and the skill of their musicianship and the mellow tone of the instruments sent a shiver through you. Something which had started its life as a distant yearning inside me was now beginning to sound distinctly sophisticated.

The rest of the band and I slouched on the sofas in front of the mixing desk, stoned out of our heads, listening to the classical musicians' conversation coming through to us from their mics. They were unaware we could hear them.

"Is that cheese sandwiches again?"

"Well, I like cheese – better than your salmon spread, it smells awful."

"Well, at least I don't eat Wotsits, Felicity, they actually do stink."

We were speechlessly high and could hear every inflection and nuance in their voices coming through on those big speakers. That giggling, so natural. Those voices, reserved and wholesome as we sat poisoned.

"Get lost, I like Wotsits," said Felicity, with faux petulance.

"Hah! Hah-ha-ha!" The whole control room was filled with bright, echoey laughter.

It was hard to believe that people like this actually existed and didn't get crushed alive. Voices floating in from a completely different world. Their apparent goodness was like a knife being slowly plunged into my heart.

****

Following the *Sway* session, I returned to Bristol to hang out with Gil. Listening to the song around at his flat, through completely different speakers, it continued to resonate. Gil was earning his living as a music journalist now and assured me that the track sounded brilliant for all kinds of other sociological reasons too. The thrill hung in the air afterwards. We listened and listened again. Even compared to the music we were into, it still sounded cool.

There were times when I connected with the reality of what was happening. When I suddenly realised how blessed I was to be making music with people who were so talented. To have created something so subtle as a song that reflected in part my own feelings, but was also the synthesis of all our talents which I could hear so clearly across the recording. Machinery had captured something mysterious about Strangelove that would last forever and just for a while that night a profound sense of gratitude descended upon me.

But after Gil crashed out on a passing whim, I decided to end my life by taking a load of Paracetamol. Waking up early the next morning miles away, having collapsed halfway along my mum and dad's road. Having tried to make it back to them without remembering. Still half alive I had enough sense to turn around and walk back to town and ended up in Horfield where I wrote the words to the *The Sea Of Black* round at my sister Bridget's house. Lying in her bed while she was out at work.

I could barely lift my hand as I watched the whole song in my mind's eye like a strange film superimposed over her wardrobe doors. All the walls in her tiny, dark room were churning up into a great sea that seemed to be swallowing me and I was sure I could hear ghosts on the stairs outside. Breathing hard and shallow, the veils were thin. My heart suddenly beat so fast that I'd fall into intense sweats which seemed to be dragging me through to the next world, before scribbling down the next line.

Remember where you're going won't be long.

CHAPTER 21

LOVE AND OTHER DEMONS

A few weeks later, it was time to start the recording of our second album, *Love And Other Demons*. I didn't want to go up to London with the rest of the band because the paranoia was getting worse and normal social interaction was becoming too complicated. I'd hoped to have straightened myself out for these sessions, but hadn't been able to accomplish that, and I couldn't let them see me like this on the first day of a new record. Catching a taxi from Bristol to the studio in Fulham, I would just have to detox up there. But the naughty taxi driver and I got pissed up on cans driving along the M4 motorway.

I arrived in a mess. Luckily, on the first night there was nothing for me to do. So, when Brett phoned the studio and invited me to an impromptu party at his house in Ladbroke Grove, it was an easy decision. By five in the morning, everyone else had gone home and Brett was downstairs with his girlfriend Sam. You could hear them laughing as I walked around in circles in his front room waiting for the off licences to open. I locked myself out of his flat and didn't want to ring the doorbell just in case they were having sex. So instead, pushed the cork in and found an early morning black cab back to the studio in Fulham.

That day was the beginning of *Love And Other Demons*. 6th May 1995.

On arriving back at the studio, I was greeted by the sight of John wolfing down a fry-up veggie breakfast in the bar area and we broke into a pointless argument. Falling out with John on the first day was the worst possible start, so I shuffled into the empty recording room. Sat down at the piano and began to write *Elin's Photograph*. When the inspiration struck, tears

began to pour down my face. Alex came in, early afternoon, and I showed
him the new song, although in all honesty I could barely play it.

After he left, the shame washed over me and I realised I'd have to clean
up, there and then, if there were any chance of me being able to participate
in the rest of the session. It was a real blow to have to face the fact that I
couldn't hide how bad it had gotten from them anymore.

****

No one I knew had any idea about detox programmes back then. So when
the time came you just had to ride through the withdrawals on your own.
Take to your bed and lie there dying till you didn't die anymore. This process
was always a rough ride and I already knew what was coming. I'd been
allocated a small, suitably alienating bedroom at the studio in Fulham from
where I phoned through to reception and pleaded for a portable television.

My personal withdrawal programme, which I'd developed over the past
four or five years involved watching shit TV and eating sweets for three
days to try and numb out till the nightmare passed through you. But the
TV set didn't arrive till early evening by which time the shakes were already
on. There were only four channels back then, flicking through the black
and white portable trying to find something stupid enough to zone out to.

No more Elin and no more sweets. I lay on the bed staring into the
flickering black and white screen. A grey old man was walking through
a grey desert with a grey sky. Despite the fact that there was something
unappealing about the 80s video quality of the film I settled on it. That
movie, airing on Channel 4, turned out to be *The Last Temptation Of Christ*
by Martin Scorsese and it was at a point near the beginning of the story.
Despite all the shaking and shivering, I was soon transfixed. The narrative,
with its proverbial sorrows, plus a few more twists and turns, held my
attention in a way that other entertainments were not capable of. Because
many of those scenes were so familiar, rising up from my childhood to meet
the screenplay. Alongside the faces of my mum and dad, my sisters, my
brother, reading a junior bible in kindergarten with the nuns, my first holy
communion and the recent episode in the church in Strasbourg. All these
memories began to flood into my awareness at the same time, creating a
terrible sense of dismay.

The three-hour film built towards the intensity of the crucifixion when Jesus, recognising his true purpose and having transcended a host of temptations, cries from the cross, "It is accomplished." The desperation was now too overpowering to refuse and, falling to my knees, I tried to pray. Fumbling to recall the Our Father or the Hail Mary. Prayers I had recited on countless occasions as a boy, whose words I could no longer recall. Forgetting those prayers in that particular moment seemed such an appalling betrayal of myself and my family and the fabric of my younger life. I'd utterly lost myself and the roots of my past and I began to cry out. As in Strasbourg, calling out into the emptiness. Crying out to a God I didn't believe in anymore. Crying out to a past that I'd cut myself off from. Crying out on my knees in an empty room in the dark in front of a portable television set that I'd now turned off.

Unlike the church in France, no sense of peace or transcendence arrived in Fulham. The emptiness towered over me like a great hammer, about to crash down upon my head. I waited in vain and wept. Certain that I had pulled all this dead air around myself with my own hands. That a great cloud of ashes was falling from the sky upon me. That I was disappearing. That I'd betrayed my own grandparents. That I'd placed myself beyond help.

****

However, the next morning I awoke with a sudden leap of the heart. Like nothing you could have imagined, a clear 'voice' sounding from within me.

"Put your clothes on."

"Put your shoes on."

"Go on, take the door. Take the lift. Walk through the studio reception."

"Outside. Turn right. Keep going. Turn left. Turn right."

No, it wasn't an actual voice, more a sense of knowing, but there wasn't any resistance in me to these assurances. In fact, this 'knowing' was unquestionable and for perhaps half an hour, I was ushered along London streets that I'd never seen before. The sun was shining, it was springtime, and the symptoms of the withdrawals, which usually took days to leave, had vanished. The world danced before my eyes and the whole of life appeared infused with a shining benevolence. My body tingled with a kind of quickening and every person who passed me by appeared so innocent that their presence filled me with sweetness. We were all here together. Vulnerable. Alive. At the same time in the same place.

A yellow and green washing-up sponge discarded in the middle of a small side road radiated with quiet beauty and yet at the same time, beneath the shadows of the buildings, it seemed to be suffering, and inspired great waves of tenderness to rise from within me. I felt drawn to pick it up and stroke the grubby scouring pad and it was only the knowledge, some place in my mind, this was such a socially unacceptable action, that continued to stay my hand. I stood in the road, pulled in two directions, looking down and unable to abandon it, until a van driver tooted me out of the way and the road was suddenly filled with cars.

I continued to walk on and after a further 10 minutes or so arrived outside an octagonal building of red brick and glass. Possibly a small library for people 'in the community'. A completely impersonal building. I would never have been drawn towards it otherwise. However, there was no doubt about it, this was where the 'knowing' had led me. The front door was locked, the lights were off and wandering around the building I couldn't work out its significance. But the inclination to continue, that had taken hold of me in the studio, had fully disappeared.

I finally noticed a piece of white paper on the front window of the entrance folded and blue tacked to the glass, recognising at once that this paper was the reason I'd been led through the streets. I prized it from the door and unfolded it. Written with blue ink in small, elegant handwriting were the words:

'The Holy Eucharist is available here Sunday morning 10.30 a.m.'

It was suddenly as if I stood before some ancient gate. Scenes and images from the previous night's film flashed across my imagination like sheet lightning as I continued to walk around the building in circles like a lost animal, carrying on till once again I became nervous of drawing attention to myself. Sticking the paper back on the door and walking away. Slowly but surely retracing my steps back to the studio. In my mind, a candle was burning without a flicker in the midst of a derelict house. The image, bold before my eyes. And at the very same time, I had fallen in love with London and with every street I walked along and with every person who passed by without even noticing me.

That day myself and Jazz wrote *#1432* together and recorded it in his room on a four track. His wife Jackie, sitting on the bed next to us. Him on guitar and me doing the words and singing. That's the version you hear on the album live from that room in Fulham. There was no one else like Jazz. So genuinely off the wall and free of cares that I don't believe he even noticed what a mess I was in. Through those round glasses he was still able to look straight through to the way it had always been between us. The place where we'd always been friends. Right from the start. The music flowed and the words flowed and the singing flowed and that natural, easy-going outlook of his helped sustain me through the dry days ahead.

****

Because there was an intense, ghostly atmosphere around the recording of *Love And Other Demons* and the veils between the worlds remained paper thin. I stayed clean for 10 days and a new album slowly began to materialise. However, the sense of connection with the 'knowing' and its radiance began to fade and be replaced with a more familiar paranoia. With the straight-edge intensity of each day growing, it became clear that I simply could not handle the rest of the band being around when doing my parts. The thought of them in the control room listening to me sing brought about such a state of mental gooseflesh that I could no longer perform with authenticity, in trying to hide it.

So from then on, I achieved each pass with only Paul and myself in the studio. The mood darkened as a result. We'd never worked this way before, and everybody having to vacate each time I did a take did not create a harmonious or collective atmosphere. Eventually I snapped, and began to drink again.

Brett came in and sang on *She's Everywhere*. Also, Brett and Richard did backing vocals on *Living With The Human Machines*. But without drugs to undermine the alcohol intake, it got messy. The next afternoon I began insulting other bands who were using the studios, shouting, screaming at the bar piano and smashing glasses. Paul decided we should all go home and leave him there alone to work on the mixing for a while.

Worst of all, on that last evening I started an argument with Alex. The first and only one we ever engaged in. Taking his ever more frustrated attempts for us to get on with things as some kind of personal accusation, I'd finally gone on the attack. Because on reflection, for want of a better candidate, I'd allowed 'him' to take the place of my own conscience. That same conscience I was doing my best to ignore, that told me I needed to change. That kept whispering to me that I was losing it. The same conscience that I was running away from had ended up staring out of his eyes at me. I didn't understand that I was actually staring into a mirror and that all the pent-up rage that came flooding out that night belonged somewhere else far closer to home.

Without knowing it however, the damage was done and from that day onwards the foundation stone of our band slowly began to crumble.

****

Sensibly, Paul decided we'd better try another studio, as I'd created such a weird atmosphere around us in Fulham, and we decamped to a secluded place in Somerset called The Wool Hall.

****

Music for *Beautiful Alone* had now arrived from Joe and I was finishing up the melodies and lyrics as we worked on some chords for a verse. Alex had come up with the music for *Spiders And Flies* and after hearing it for the first time I went drinking with my sister's fiancé Dave, and woke up two days later underneath some electricity pylons in Gloucestershire. It was the sound of the electricity going down those interlacing cables that gifted me the lyrics and a melody for that song. A moment that was a catalyst in fusing together some of my recent forebodings.

Weeks previously, in London, Jazz had suggested we should check out an Internet café – something I'd never heard of before. On arriving it was full to capacity, and so we stood outside waiting our turn. Glancing in at the people who sat at tables with headphones on, staring into screens so close to their eyes you feared for their retinas. It was the weird computer light across their faces that first haunted me. I couldn't get that picture out of my mind afterwards. Because in their eyes they were here and they weren't here either.

They were somewhere called the 'Internet', I was cheerfully informed by Jazz and at that moment I sensed many others would soon be leaving with them and their departure unsettled me. Even though I didn't have a clue about where it was, for some reason I immediately had a strong intuition that I didn't want to go there. Perhaps because these weren't the dumbed down eyes of people who watched TV shows? These eyes were hungrier. More restless. More vigilant. Colder. Or was it simply the eerie silence coming out from what they'd called a cafe that was full of young people? Or just the fact I'd never seen anything like it before and the unfamiliarity spooked me?

As we stood waiting, Jazz continued to insist that this new Internet thing was 'awesome', but he couldn't explain what it actually was clearly enough to my satisfaction. So, when a space finally became available, I remained outside none the wiser. Despite Jazzer's enthusiasm I refused to go in there with him. Something about that cafe was turning my stomach.

Where was it they were all staring into with such fascination?

Who said it was even really there?

Whatever the answer, that questioning of technology became one of the lyrical themes of *Love And Other Demons*. That and Elin's departure. And my addiction and the sense of death being close and the sense of some distant light that was trying to break through into my life.

Jazz waved me off smiling through the window as I walked away. Funnily enough, he went on to make a good living out of the 'Internet' after we split up.

****

We sat around in the new studio in Somerset with Paul in attendance. Still needing one more song, but it wasn't happening. Jamming, there was an edgy vibe in the band with awkward silences and uncomfortable absences, as different people took leave of the restlessness in the room.

"What about the one you played me in Fulham?" Alex wanted to know.

"What song's that then?" I asked.

"You made it up on piano."

"No, man, I don't know what you mean."

"Yeah, you do. You played it to me."

"No way, you dreamed it, Al. I haven't written anything lately."

"Yeah, you did."

Alex moved across to an upright piano in the corner of the room and played the verse and chorus chords to *Elin's Photograph*.

"Fucking hell, man!"

The truth came flooding back. I'd totally forgotten the song and the morning I'd written it, but grumpy Alex, half asleep, on witnessing one shaky play through weeks before, was able to march across that rehearsal room and play it perfectly. As soon as he picked out the chords, the broken-hearted words came bubbling up from my psyche.

Paul nodded and said,

"Yeah, it's got something."

Immediately, the band fell into its neuroses. A familiar musical noodling filled the room as people twiddled on their instruments, making up parts with the amps turned low. John, eyes closed, nodding his head and drumming on his jeans. Joe too, as if he were listening to something far inside himself. His playing and the lines he came up with on *Love And Other Demons* remain some of my favourite bass playing of all time on any record. *Elin's Photograph*, one of my favourite Strangelove songs, wouldn't even exist if not for Alex's singular musical memory.

Within minutes, Jazz had written a perfectly poised intro on the 12-string and Alex conjured a middle eight using diminished chords, which was just the extra viewpoint it needed. In my mind's eye, I could see all these bugs crawling up the wall as I listened to him play. Actually having to force back tears as the arrangement started to take shape. Because despite all the difficulties, there was something in the room holding us. Despite the argument and the cracked foundation stone and all the erratic behaviour and the effect it was having on my contribution, they were still somehow able to stand with me. Music has the power to bring people together and sustain them through the most troubling of times, and the dark heart of Strangelove was beating strong again when *Love And Other Demons* was ready to go into the final sessions.

****

We'd spent a week or so working up these songs at the Wool Hall before recording them. Unsurprisingly, the studio was a total mess within a few days. Overflowing ashtrays and dead green Stella bottles everywhere. One evening, the rest of the band were sitting around watching TV in the main house and I'd gone back over to get my cigarettes because there was a taxi arriving to take me to a nearby pub. On stepping into the studio's rehearsal room, a cleaner was crouched down over by the microphone stand, in the exact epicentre of my particular messiness. He was moving the scores of empties and trying to open a cupboard.

"Hey, man," I offered, "Don't worry about those bottles. I'll clean that shit up myself."

Having someone to tidy up after us always made me feel like some kind of spoiled brat. Especially as we always turned everywhere into such a state. Preferring to imagine that I was going to do it myself, I would often tell them not to bother. Encouraging them to have a drink and even take some drugs if they were up for it, which usually got rid of them *and* immediately alleviated the 'cleaner guilt'.

"Hey mate, don't bother with those bottles," I repeated with more gusto, "I'll do it. I'll do all that, honestly. Seriously, don't worry about it, man."

This particular cleaner, whom I hadn't met as yet, was squatting down and swivelled around on his haunches to stare right back up at me. Unusually unkempt, even though he was wearing reasonably smart slacks and a brown shirt, his hair was wild and thinning. His eyes wide and black and smouldering with rage.

We waited, staring at each other across the unhinged atmosphere he was putting out. Cleaner guilt distorting in my brain sacs. What the fuck was this guy's problem?

For some reason, perhaps the strange intensity of the moment and my already unhinged psyche, I suddenly reasoned that *he* was the taxi driver I'd ordered. He was in here trying to nick something and I'd caught him. That must be it. Cool by me. I wasn't going to grass him up.

"Hey man, no worries. Are you the taxi driver?"

He was standing now and sizing me up. Like two cowboys at a shoot-out waiting to see who'd draw first, but I didn't want a fight with anyone.

"Hey. Are you alright, man?"

He didn't say a single word in reply. Standing there with a vein like a hosepipe throbbing in his temple. So, I quickly picked up my fags and backed out of the room without taking my eyes off him.

"See ya."

Still, he never spoke, but his eyes carried on, burning holes through the back of my head as I lit the next cigarette and walked across the grounds and waited for the taxi at the top of the driveway. Having to concentrate to stop myself from tripping over. Woah! What the hell was all that about? Looking back nervously at the rehearsal room where the lights shone and a shadowy figure loomed at the window and then disappeared.

****

Shortly afterwards, one of the technicians from the main studio strolled across the courtyard just as the sky began changing into its darker blues.

"Hey man, what's the problem with your cleaner?"

"Cleaner?" He replied.

"Yeah, man. I just met the cleaner. In our rehearsal room. The guy's a proper loon. He just totally stared me out for no reason."

The technician looked perplexed until his whole face lit up.

"That's Van!"

The cleaner/taxi driver was Van Morrison.

The Wool Hall was his studio.

No one had told *me* that. Mind you, they never did tell me much. To be honest, I hadn't really heard of him back then anyway. I knew the name of course, but wasn't aware of his music and certainly didn't have any idea of his status.

But the technician was laughing his head off. Especially when I related how I'd addressed him as the cleaner.

Over the next few days, I was encouraged to retell this tale to everyone who worked there. They responded, eyes sparkling, with their own bitchy stories about his world-famous temper. Greeted with smiles wherever I went now, I'd unwittingly become the hero of the Wool Hall. The rest of the band remarked on how I was brought coffees, furnished with larger portions at mealtimes and more than tolerated when helping myself to booze from the kitchen. Welcomed with open arms into the dysfunctional family. All whispering about 'dad' behind his back. How could you hate someone that much who you didn't actually love? I became intrigued. And it wasn't long until I caught the bug myself, growing to like something about him, to laugh at the never-ending stories and take an interest in his music as a result.

When I got to hear how good some of it was, the nagging question wouldn't leave me alone, but they all continued to assure me.

"The only reason he didn't go completely mental with *you*, Patrick, was because he wouldn't have been able to believe what was happening."

****

On the last night of recording at the Wool Hall, Paul knocked at my bedroom door and brought me outside to witness the full moon. It hung in the sky like a great round door. He'd set up the mic so that I could record singing *The Sea Of Black* outside on the balcony. The sky was full of stars and out here in the countryside with no light pollution you could witness the unfettered blazing glory of the night. Alex had come up for the music to this song and with the sadness of his guitar coming through the cans, the scene inspired me to capture the mood of the words on the first few takes.

"Remember where you're going won't be long…"

Life was soon to change forever for me, but I had no idea of that as I sang out into the night.

"Yeah, Pad. That was great. I think we've got it. Have another go if you want though," said Paul.

"No, man. If you're happy, I'm happy."

"OK great, come in and have a listen."

"No just run it, so I can listen out here in the cans if that's OK, man."

Love And Other Demons. Against all the odds. We'd done it.

CHAPTER 22

SATURDAY, JANUARY 20TH, 1996

B ack in Bristol, I was now renting a room in another house in Cotham. Club 29 had imploded after John's new girlfriend (my old girlfriend) Marnie had moved him out because of the chaos. Dodge and I had been forced to relocate quickly and our new place was in a large shared house with Joe, my sister Catherine, and various other drifters.

My new room was called the Murder Room, because the person who'd rented it before me was a junkie who'd been stabbed to death in there a few months previously. Unsurprisingly, it had a bit of a weird vibe. So I slept mostly in with Dodge, top to bottom, or with my sister Catherine, and Joe, who were now expecting their first child, beautiful baby James.

We had a housewarming party and sat in Dodge's bedroom watching Strangelove playing on a late night ITV show called *The Beat*. This was our first TV appearance and my drug buddies and I crowded around his little portable. All at once the noisy bantering stopped when we came on and my face appeared. There on the other side of the screen. Secretly I'd been excited about being on the telly, but in reality it was strangely unsettling because I suddenly sensed that my wasted friends didn't trust me anymore and the band who were behind that screen with me didn't trust me either. For very different reasons.

After they all trailed off at about six a.m., we'd run out of booze. Still wired, Dodge and I drank a bottle of methylated spirit that he found underneath the kitchen sink. He diluted it down with tap water but the taste still burnt. But even that was better than being left wide awake and having to deal with the guilt and confusion. Next morning, as the light crept in on my headache, the empty spirit bottle became evidence of a new low. Dodge said we shouldn't ever tell anyone about it ever.

Days after this incident, Strangelove played the main stage at Glastonbury for the second time and it went out on channel four. My face, swollen with boozing. Then it was on to the Maker Shaker tour.

****

Four bands chosen by the *Melody Maker* travelling together on a coach and playing venues up and down the UK.

Strangelove, Powder (Pearl Lowe's band), Pusherman (some drug dealers from Camden), and Elka (the bastard sons of London taxi drivers all). A week in, I'd made firm friends with all three other bands and the 24-hour rancid carnival. One morning, wandering around Manchester in a stupor by the time I found my way back to the coach, they'd been waiting an hour.

The drivers and tour managers were sorely unimpressed, but as I climbed up on board the rest of the coach erupted into laughter, applause, and cheering; the party still going strong from the night before. At the front, by the big windows with my wine bottle aloft in the air. Cheering. Yeah! Come on. Yeah! 20 sets of feet stamping on the floor and rumbling the coach. Yeah! Woah! Yeah!

"Let's hear it for Sammy Davies Fucking Junior!" I wailed for no apparent reason.

The returning ovation was like scoring the winner at the FA Cup Final.

Looking up to see all the smiling, laughing faces at the back, I passed by Strangelove, who were sitting at the front of the coach. They weren't cheering. They weren't laughing. They weren't impressed. They had their sunglasses on, staring out the windows looking bored. I won't ever forget that moment. It still haunts me to this day. My life was completely the wrong way round.

****

On the last night of that tour, I stayed in London and went round Soho with Justine. Alex from Blur's girlfriend. We'd first made friends when Justine had handed me a load of pills after the Q awards. She liked drinking too and she was skinny, pretty, sarcastic, and funny. This time, having already consumed a staggering cocktail of intoxicants, I handed her my wages and asked her to score me whatever drugs she could because I didn't know the London people or places. In and out of the bars and clubs we sailed.

Late night early morning back at their flat in Soho, Alex was lying on the bed completely unconscious.

"He's just been on *Top Of The Pops*. Yawn! Yawn!" she giggled. "Probably pissed out of his head."

I poured glugs from a bottle of red wine over his pretty face trying to wake him up and say hello but he was dead to the world and so we went back out again. Justine needling me and saying she didn't believe that I used to be a tramp.

"You're just trying to be ever so doomed and romantic. Ha! Ha! Ha!"

So I decided to show her how good I was at aggressive begging.

The city was just waking up and businessmen, with bowlers and pinstripe suits, were up and about on their way into work as we walked across Trafalgar Square and down Whitehall.

"Stop a second, man! I said stop, man! Just stop for two seconds."

"Come on. Look, I haven't got any money and you look like you've got loads. Yes, you have it's obvious. Why don't you give me some of yours? That's only fair. Surely you can get that. Come on, man. Don't walk off. We're all here together on this rock. That's the sun up there. Up there shining. The sun. It shines down the same on us all. Zippy *and* Bungle, mate? Come on? Me *and* you. You *and* me. I'd help you if it was the other way round. I would. I really would. Come on. Come on, man. Share. Remember. Share!"

We rolled around on the pavement laughing and singing the *Rainbow* theme tune.

'Paint the whole world with a rainbow…'

Trying to get that drum fill exactly on the money until the police turned up.

Although I got my name right the first time, a date of birth was proving more difficult. Hallucinogenic drugs and numbers have never gone well together in my mind. So they arrested me.

"Fuck off and leave him alone, you wankers! Fuck off! Don't touch him! Don't fucking touch me either!" she railed. And a wide-eyed Justine got arrested too.

****

At the police station they asked me to turn out my pockets. There were hundreds of pounds that Cerne had given me at the end of the tour screwed up into a kind of ball in my trousers. Possibly the largest amount of cash ever discovered on an aggressive beggar. Confiscated into a plastic bag along with the stub of a cheap looking eyeliner.

"What the fuck are you wearing, you prick?"

One of the policemen booted me hard in the backside and I slid 30 feet face down the corridor along its polished floor like I'd fallen over on ice. In my 70s suit, trouser bottoms cut with a pair of scissors to three quarter lengths and black tights underneath. He picked me up by the scruff of the neck and shoved me into the cell where once again I fell to the floor. You could hear Justine shouting in the distance. Doors slamming, sat on the bunk now with whatever drugs racing round my racetrack. Head in hands. Heart going. Shit. Shit. Shit. Shit. Shit.

"What are you on, you fucking prick?" An hour or so later the same small, snarly face appeared at the little grill.

I was in a prison cell out of my head on more drugs than I'd ever taken in my life and I didn't even know what half of them were. My poor, tired brain completely gave way under the pressure and it became an entirely sensory experience from that moment on. A kind of groping marathon run behind closed eyes. 15,000 deafening heartbeats later, a kinder voice greeted me through the same grill and asked if I'd like them to phone anyone on my behalf.

"Can you phone Andy Ross at Food records for me please," I mouthed all humble.

30 minutes later I was out, and they handed me my money back.

Justine was released an hour later and we got pissed in Charing Cross zoo.

"I'm going home," she said in front of the monkeys. "Can't handle you anymore, love."

For the next couple of weeks, I crashed with Rob from Powder and his friend Sarah in Tooting Beck. Going round and round, lost on the tubes all day. Stumbling up to London transport officials.

"I can't get to King's Cross, mate. I've been down here for hours. Please, please help me… No mate. Listen to me. *You've* got to help me. I can't understand that fucking map. *You've* got to take me to King's Cross."

I couldn't make my way down there anymore.

Occasionally, I actually managed to turn up at Cerne's office and plead for money.

Sick again, I was walking down Oxford Street with the early-morning terrors looking for somewhere open, selling the cure. From the corner of my eye, I suddenly caught a glimpse of a shadowy figure who seemed to have lost all direction. Some kind of a vagrant. A shudder went through me on turning to recognise it was my own reflection coming off a large shop window in the sunlight. But it was too late. In that glimpse I'd caught myself. Clothes dishevelled, torn and filthy. Standing in the road, the sound of car horns blaring in my ears. Shouting and stumbling up the road till I found a place open. Ironically, Strangelove had a big article in the *Big Issue* that week.

A few days later, drunk again early in the morning, I was back at Cerne's office and trying to talk money out of him. This time he wasn't having it. Apparently, I'd phoned a few days earlier in a black out shouting, "Help me! Help me!"

Cerne repeated once more that he'd been speaking to someone I needed to talk to. He was straight on the phone organising and as luck would have it this person could see me immediately. Cerne insisted that I should travel to some offices further into west London. He wrote down the address and directions on a yellow post-it note.

"Don't disappear this time, Pad. It's important. I mean it. Rayner's my friend."

****

I was travelling to meet Rayner Jesson. Nick Cave's manager. A few tube stops along, I couldn't stand the tension anymore and had to get off early at Hammersmith. They hadn't opened yet but I begged a cleaner in the nearest pub to sell me a bottle of Holsten Pils. This time it wasn't Van Morrison. I handed him the note and waved the change because he said he couldn't open the till. Descending back down into the underground for the remaining stops I opened the bottle on a ticket machine and drank it on the tube train in three or four swallows.

Putting it down by my feet, the tube suddenly jerked away from the station and the empty bottle escaped me and began rolling up and down the carriageway. The almighty racket it caused as it rattled around and crashed into the ends of the carriages close to smashing was indescribably intense. I was trying to distance myself from the responsibility of that noise by hanging my head and avoiding the eyes of grumpy-looking working men, who stood upright in the alienation, holding on to the bands that swing from the roofs.

Under my arm was a book called *The Drinker* by Hans Fallada. Knowing I was about to talk to Rayner about alcoholism, it suddenly seemed ridiculous to be turning up with that particular title. So I abandoned it on the tube. Left it on the seat along with the empty bottle of Holsten still rolling around on the floor. A bottle which inconceivably, turned out to be the last drink I'd ever take in my life, to this day.

****

Although we'd never met before, Rayner greeted me at the door of his office with a knowing grin.

"Well, finally," he piped, looking at me as I leaned against the door frame.

"Right, in you come then."

We sat in his office and he looked me up and down for a minute or so, still half hanging my head with exhaustion.

"Right, you're a fucking mess and you're going into treatment."

Without waiting for a reply, he was on the phone to the head of EMI, Mark Collen, who agreed without a moment's hesitation to help. A decision which undoubtedly saved my life. Over the years, I've heard a lot of negative stories about record companies. I'm sure many of them are true. Not this time. I was there. Mark Collen didn't even have to think about it. And this was way before people knew about addictions, the way they do now.

Rayner was old-school rock 'n' roll management. He was in his early 40s, chain smoked, wore a Crombie and had a full head of hair cut into a scruffy salt and pepper quiff. He was good looking and his whole face beamed in craggy lines when he smiled. My hands were sweating, my heart was fluttering and my mouth was dry but something about Rayner's presence settled me. Something in his demeanour immediately allowed me to recognise I could trust him and deeper than that, there was a curious sense of the familiar too. Like I'd known him before. Like I was truly welcome. Like we'd met a thousand times already.

"What do you smoke, then?"

"Well, Benson's usually," I said.

He went over to his cabinet and pulled out a duty-free bundle of two hundred Marlboro and threw them at me.

"Well, you're smoking these now," he laughed.

"Where's your stuff?"

"It's over in Tooting Beck"

"Right then, we'll go and pick that up."

"Can I use the loo first, man?"

****

In the toilet there was a battered wooden plaque hanging from a nail. Glued to that wood was a torn-up scrap of paper with a poem.

FOOTPRINTS
One night a man had a dream. He
dreamed he was walking along the
beach with the LORD. Across the sky
flashed scenes from his life. For each
scene, he noticed two sets of footprints
in the sand one belonged to him, and
the other to the LORD

When the last scene of his life flashed
before him, he looked back at the
footprints in the sand. He noticed that

many times along the path of his life
there was only one set of footprints. He
also noticed that it happened at the very
lowest and saddest times in his life.

This really bothered him and he
questioned the LORD about it. "LORD
you said that once I decided to follow
you, you'd walk with me all the way. But I
have noticed that during the most
troublesome times in my life, there is
only one set of footprints. I don't
understand why, when I needed you
most you would leave me."

The LORD replied, "My precious,
precious child, I love you and I would
never leave you. During your times of
trial and suffering, when you see only
one set of footprints, it was then that I
carried you"

On that particular morning, I assumed Nick Cave had written those words. Because every single other poster hanging on the walls in that office had something to do with him. It was a natural conclusion. I decided that this was a poem by him that people had not heard of, something more private. Something Rayner had been privy to as his manager and that he'd kept as a memento. Something gentler and more vulnerable. But words that also seemed to chime so peculiarly with the visions and voices I'd been experiencing. I could see that beach clearly in my mind's eye, and I could feel its distances and the darkening blues of its sky and I could see the footprints.

Returning to the office, Rayner ended his phone call.

"Yeah, Nick was in a treatment centre," he said, putting down the receiver. "I remember him down there just like you, not so long ago. And I was in there myself seven years ago."

In his smoky BMW we crawled through the London traffic, listening to *The Dirty Three*. Another Australian band who he was managing. The growing melancholy of the violin against the ramshackle guitars and drums in the standstill was making my heart race. On leaving his office, Rayner had insisted I should crash out in the back. Compliant and exhausted, I lay curled up on the seat like some kid being driven home sick from school. It was almost unbelievable that at that moment I was being accompanied into a treatment centre by Nick Cave's manager. Nick Cave, my teenage hero. The last thing I would ever have imagined when I'd woken up that morning.

Rayner sat there with the wheel in his hands turning round to grin at me every now and then. He'd been clean from all drugs and drink for seven years. Seven years. It was almost impossible to imagine. And he was smiling and relaxed and cool as fuck and I felt at ease in his presence, despite his music credentials. What was this world that I'd suddenly stumbled into? What kind of rock 'n' roll was this? What kind of voodoo?

Rayner had something else that day I'll never forget. Time. Time for me, and time to abandon his day and drive me. We left London behind heading south, faster down the A roads.

"Yeah, Nick was in a treatment centre not so long ago," the words kept turning in my head.

****

We drove towards Brighton and eventually pulled into Farm Place, a 17th century manor house huddled in the sleepy village of Ockley, Surrey. Britain's answer to the Betty Ford Clinic. Back in 1996, it cost you £200 a day to stay.

"What, I have to share a room?" I blurted out horrified to the grey-haired woman at the desk who came across all firm like a hospital matron.

"You're not a pop star in here," Rayner chortled. "You're just a patient like the rest of them."

"Quite right, Rayner," she testified.

The tiny bedroom had four single beds. A beamed ceiling so low that you had to duck all the way to the corner and a floor so uneven that it made you feel like you were already pissed up again, on some cross-channel ferry. There were also three sets of luggage around each of the beds that left me in no doubt that they were occupied.

Rayner, already known to the staff and obviously well liked, gave me a hug on departure.

"Here's my telephone number," he said. "Call me any time and stay put, you crazy bastard."

****

My first engagement was with a doctor. It was Friday afternoon and, by chance, the day he arrived on his weekly visit.

The examination went on longer than I considered necessary. His hands were cold and so was the room but mercifully I was just about convivial from what I'd got down myself that morning.

Finally, I jumped off the table.

"Everything OK there then, doc?"

"No it's not OK," he said in an unfriendly manner.

"What do you mean?"

"You're in a serious condition, is what I mean."

"What do you mean serious?"

He grabbed my hand and placed it on the lower part of my abdomen

"That, young man, is your liver, and it's severely enlarged," raising his voice. "I've rarely seen anything like it in a man of your age before. It's a disgrace."

The weird protuberance, I'd never even noticed, was tender to touch.

"Am I going to die?" I asked.

"Yes, you are," he said.

Stunned, I swayed in the middle of the room for several moments unable to assimilate his words. All at once breaking down and weeping as he watched dispassionately offering no consolation, before adding…

"We're all going to die.

And it's going to be a lot sooner for you than you realise if you don't do something quickly."

Slowly dawning that he hadn't given me a death sentence, it was with great relief I watched him leaving Farm Place later that afternoon. And though I never knew whether he was just trying to frighten me, either way it was a sore lesson. The protuberance lasted a further few months but eventually disappeared.

Heminevrin and Valium helped with the withdrawals and I stared into the flames in the fireplace of the empty lounge. The matron said it wasn't time to meet the other patients and I was led upstairs to pass out on the bed. Waking at about midnight, the room was alive with snoring and the night nurse found me wandering around in the corridors.

"The sounds from those others are totally doing my head in."

So she sat up with me till dawn. Eventually, after much persuasion I returned to the bedroom and managed to get about an hour's broken sleep.

****

Saturday, January 20th, 1996. I woke up on my first sober day. A school bell began ringing from downstairs and under the covers of my sweaty bed I kept my eyes closed and listened to the others getting up until the room fell silent. Almost immediately a buxom, middle-aged nurse waddled in tutting and opened the curtains.

"Up you get, up you get. I know it's your first morning, so I'll let you off this time. But we don't lie about in bed here. Up you get. Up you get."

Something about her no-nonsense northern accent had me scrambling for my clothes and downstairs at the double. The plain truth was, without a drink I was nervous around authority figures. Despite the fact that I was fully aware of what an uncool situation that was, for someone who was supposed to be a rebellious rock 'n' roll star.

You had to get up at six every morning and do chores before breakfast at seven. Which I carried out, from that day on, without so much as a whimper. Each day was structured like a school, with lessons concentrating on various aspects of addiction and recovery. Some more factually based, others arising from the experience of our lives. The councillors, quiet and yet insistent, forced you to consider the certain doom you faced in continuing on without change, heaping the evidence over everyone in spades.

Most of the 26 patients in Farm Place came from the upper classes. The youngest a public schoolboy, 19 years of age and addicted to weed and coke. The oldest a sherry-guzzling alcoholic in her 80s and a friend of the Queen no less. We sat together in a circle of chairs in a large oak-panelled room with a deep stone fireplace. It was wintertime and the fire blazed and crackled away all day long. The councillors left me alone at first. All I had to do was listen and stare out the windows whilst the other patients 'shared' examples of powerlessness and damage.

Many members of the group seemed happy to spill their guts and talk through any number of harrowing incidents. Often overcome with guilt they'd burst into tears. Gently shaking their heads and accepting tissues from nearby care bears. Turning their faces to one side and mumbling apologies into the air with their eyes half closed.

On the other hand, some of the older men, especially, appeared reluctant to admit their drinking had caused much trouble at all and came across as belligerent. They'd often been forced into the place by loved ones or work and did not accept that they needed to be there. As the days went by, the councillors would sometimes confront these types with a letter from a family member. A letter that was 'shared' with the group. Often a raw, highly emotional account. You sat there as some posh businessman heard the words of his own daughter, and what she thought about his drinking and the effect it was having on her life. All eyes in the room fixed upon his face, watching his head beginning to hang as the truth crashed in. Delivered by his own flesh and blood but coming out of the mouth of an impassive councillor. All his pomp and ceremony crushed. You could hear a pin drop every time and afterwards they'd let the silence hang like an execution.

Then, as if that wasn't enough, they would encourage other group members to chip in with how they too had seen through his arrogance and lack of empathy. How he was a control freak. How he was quite frankly rude. How he was in 'denial'. Secretly, for some reason, it was satisfying to watch these guys being cut down to size and witness their brain wires grinding to a halt. But it was also unsettling to consider when exactly the tables might turn upon me. Everything happened slowly, inch by inch and they'd always leave them there to soak it up in the burning silence.

After a few days of this kind of listening, without any effort, the doors of my own memory began to shake open and many unsettling incidents arrived in my consciousness. And, unlike the drinking life, I actually had the space to consider these memories in the breaks between groups. The faces of a lifetime who appeared before my eyes in sober reflection. All of whom had at some point or other turned away from me, hurt or angry. Finally, it was my turn. An unusual experience to speak in public without the manic rush of alcohol and drugs to back you up, and one I had not been accustomed to for years. It became apparent, once I opened my mouth, that the amount I drank and the depths to which I'd sunk were extreme, even for a place like this. And the councillors soon insisted that before speaking I had to begin with a preamble.

"My name is Patrick, I'm an alcoholic and an addict. I'm a sick person trying to get well. Not a bad person trying to get good."

Speaking of the troubles that addiction had pulled down upon everyone around me, and trying to stick to the facts rather than dramatise, suddenly gave them an added gravitas. Some of these tales I'd already recounted in pubs, but then as a joke with dark humour and twisted exaggeration. It wasn't like that here. The room seemed to go into a kind of trance the first time I revealed some of my trials of homelessness as a teenager. The kickings I'd taken and the heartache my poor mother had gone through when she saw the state of me. The shit I'd put Elin through. Two women in the group started crying. I'd never been listened to like this before apart from Uncle Ger the Cistercian monk. The group listening was like some vast circumference that made you feel small and yet at the same time held you suspended in a circle of light. Every time you spoke the circumference grew bigger and it got brighter and you felt smaller and smaller. Telling truths to a room full of patients who were simultaneously opening to the truth for themselves, and that collective attention falling upon you, was an intense, unsettling, and yet at times almost exhilarating experience. Not completely unlike Strangelove gigs to be honest, once you started to get used to it.

These hours of reflection grew into weeks and I witnessed the chaos and heartbreak replaying itself in my mind over and over and there was nothing I could do to stop it now. My conscience had come home to roost. This was what I'd tried to avoid facing. Something inside me had recorded it all and seemed to be insisting I look now. On and on it went like a never-ending revolving door of faces. I'd remembered far more than I'd ever realised.

****

After a patient had stuck with treatment for about six or seven weeks, they were required to write a 'life story' and read it to the group, who sat around in the circle evaluating. These 'Peer Evaluations' came with a special form and boxes to tick. Arrogant, Selfish, Dishonest, Immature, Inconsiderate, and many more. Whilst listening to the story, if you caught the whiff of any of these defects of character it was beholden upon you to tick the box. There were also sections where you were encouraged to offer thoughts of your own regarding the failings of said person. What you believed they needed to do in order to stay clean and sober. What you'd noticed about them over the weeks. Strengths and more especially weaknesses. In this way, each reader was encouraged to face their shadow and assimilate the insights of the group whilst reappraising their life as they trawled through the forms at a later date with the support of their councillor.

****

I stood at the top of the grand wooden staircase that led down into the main reception hall of Farm Place. It was a Saturday afternoon, when most other people were receiving visits from their families. Reluctant to descend into the restrained social hum percolating from the lounge, I paused at the top of the stairs and was suddenly filled with a now almost familiar sense of light. My experiences in Strasbourg and Fulham returned and I recalled the night Aunty Ethne had died in our house and how as a child I'd heard the voices of angels singing. Some invisible presence was alongside me again and for a moment it whispered loud and clear about the possibility of a new life.

****

A guy called Richard turned up. About 10 years further down the line than me. His face was red, almost purple, with ruptured blood vessels. On arrival, he was terribly shaky, inching slowly into the dining room with a councillor in attendance. Everybody stopped and looked up from their life stories. He walked as if across enemy territory. Every step, a bed of nails. His trembling left hand raised before him as if he was checking the validity of the air, or reaching for imaginary support, or defending himself against imaginary attackers. His eyes and skin were severely swollen with alcohol abuse but worst of all it was clear that somewhere underneath his frightful appearance there lived a terrified person.

A few days later, I watched him fall to the floor of the smoking room and go into a withdrawal fit. Writhing and smashing his head into the legs of a chair, biting his tongue, blood and foam oozing from his mouth. The nurses were all over him as we patients sat frozen with our cigarettes, stunned into inaction whilst they rolled him out into the recovery position. On returning from the hospital and heavily sedated, he eventually began to share in the groups too. Richard had come to treatment five years previously.

"But I didn't listen," he warned us.

Chris was a cocaine and gambling addict, who had blown hundreds of thousands of pounds in west London and spoke like Prince Charles. In the Saturday morning family sessions, his father described the last few years as 'a living bereavement'. My new friend shifted about in his chair while his mother and the rest of his siblings were encouraged to 'get honest' around the anger and fear they'd experienced as a direct result of his behaviour. I thanked my lucky stars that my mum and dad didn't even know I was there and wouldn't have to be put through this kind of public ritual. Even though Chris insisted it had been a healing experience for all. I wasn't sure my family would have understood the need for it.

Despite all the intensity, I'd become strangely comfortable at Farm Place. With all other responsibilities lifted from my shoulders, it was actually a relief to finally be breathing clean air without having to face up to anything else apart from the bloody truth about drinking. However, having completed three months, I was also positive I needed to get back to work. Even though the councillors insisted I needed to stay longer. We still had an album ready to go with no release date and I felt I owed it to Cerne and the band to be available again.

Saying goodbye to all my new friends at the treatment centre was a surprisingly moving experience. We'd been through so much together and in many ways, they already knew me better than anyone I'd ever met. Going back 'Out There' as people called it, felt decidedly nerve wracking.

****

In my last few minutes, I spoke to Richard as I stood on the porch outside waiting to leave. From the trembling wreck who'd arrived, a sensitive and thoughtful man had emerged from inside him.

"I'm never going to drink again," he told me. "And make sure you don't either. People like us have to do the right things. We actually have to surrender. White flags and all that, Patrick."

His eyes were sparkling as he stood before me, buzzing with newfound optimism. I tried to assure him I'd do my best.

"Thanks, man. Look, I mean this," I said. "You've been an inspiration, Richard. You were a mess when you came in here, and you've changed right before my eyes. It's a miracle. You're a walking fucking miracle, honestly."

He glowed, smiling with a slight tremble under his eye.

"Thanks, Patrick. Don't worry. I'm never going back."

A year or so later I returned to Farm Place for a reunion and it was the first thing I asked about. Richard had drunk within weeks of leaving and was dead.

****

Rayner pulled up outside the oak door in his dark blue BMW. As well as visiting on two previous occasions in the interim with boxes of Benson's, he'd also promised to return me to the so-called real world, travelling the four-hour journey back to Bristol together. This time, I sat beside him in the front and we smoked and chatted. Rayner possessed more than a healthy serving of gallows humour and was never short of a rock 'n' roll story. During his younger days, he'd served as a roadie for Thin Lizzy and most of that journey home was spent laughing as he recalled some of his bombed-out antics.

He commented that I was looking 10 years younger. That my face was no longer red, that I'd lost weight and that I'd obviously washed that day and even brushed my teeth. Most of all he asserted that I should have gained enough understanding by now of how to 'stay' clean. He'd still help me but treatment was over.

All that was true, but in the sunshine standing outside my new flat near The Downs, I had to bite back the tears saying goodbye. My stomach churned and the words stuck in my throat. Life without being out of it? I'd already tried this before and it had been a nightmare. I didn't trust myself and at the same time I didn't want to let him or anyone else down.

As a parting gift, Rayner handed me the poem on the wooden plaque from his office and I discovered that Nick Cave hadn't written it after all. In fact, he said he didn't know where those words had originated. He'd purchased the plaque from a homeless guy in L.A who was making and selling them on the streets. Watching Rayner drive away, I waved him off like a little kid again. Standing there lost till he'd completely disappeared before walking back into my flat.

Having moved in a few weeks previously to the Maker Shaker Tour all my possessions remained in the cardboard boxes I hadn't bothered to unpack as yet.

Turning the wooden plaque over, on the reverse side Rayner had scrawled in red marker pen.

NEVER FORGET
WHY YOU CLEANED UP
I AM ALWAYS THERE
RAYNER

I'm looking at that writing now as I write these words more than 25 years later, and despite the fact that Rayner is now dead as a result of his own alcoholism and drug addiction, I still believe those words as much as I ever did on that day I first read them. Because Rayner remains in my heart. He went on to help me so much in the years to come and his subsequent relapse and death were one tragedy from which I've never fully recovered.

Chapter 23

SONGWRITING

On arriving home, there was a month or so of this continuing reflection accompanied by a slow acclimatisation to life 'on the outside'. I began to go to bed at a reasonable hour and wake up early the next morning and prepare myself three healthy meals a day. I'd left Farm Place with a long list of actions they said I'd have to implement in order to maintain my new way of life and I followed these instructions with a pertinacity I wasn't previously aware I was capable of. In fact, it was close to obsessional. For a while, I believed you had to do absolutely everything they'd suggested down to the letter to avoid relapse and remained terrified of making a mistake. I lived like a monk and was prepared to do anything however banal in order to stop myself going back to where I'd come from. Still in my 20s and immediately spending most of my time alone it nevertheless remained slightly embarrassing, even in front of just myself, to be living like such a square.

However, life did slowly change as Rayner had promised and, walking in Leigh Woods, I found solace from the loneliness as my imagination began to spring back into life. Bright-eyed and miles from anyone wandering around in the dappled light underneath trees, noticing as if for the first time. Being properly clean was a bit like being on acid for a while. I began to read poetry and meditate too. Making friends with Rilke and Dylan Thomas and W.B. Yeats as my grandfather once had. Listening to the sacred choral music of Abbess Hildegard of Bingen and watching dust particles spinning in the sunlight as I lay on my sofa. Slowly beginning to rediscover the world and what made me tick.

Human interaction on the other hand took a lot longer to figure out. I needed to re-engage with the rest of the band and attempt to convey to them where I was at. It was hard to get the courage up because I wanted to get that right. Trying to make amends for the previous years and assuring them that Strangelove was what I wanted and that I was more than happy for us to continue if they felt the same way. Understandably, things were slightly awkward for everyone at first. I suddenly didn't drink or take any drugs and turned up to everything on time and was keen to engage in a way I hadn't before.

Their faces appeared to me in a new light and I noticed expressions and peculiarities that I'd not witnessed previously and became highly attuned to the atmospheres they carried into a room. Without knowing it, I was still very much in my own world. The others had been through a lot of changes themselves, as we all do in our 20s. With so much to come to terms with, in such a chaotic situation. They'd managed to grow up in front of my eyes without me truly noticing before and now appeared slightly suspicious of me, and who could blame them. To make matters worse, I remained withdrawn. In truth, I'd have been delighted to tell them who I was now if I'd have had any kind of a clue myself. Those first few rehearsals were like an awkward family reunion with all kinds of unresolved emotions in the air that, as always, we refused to acknowledge.

****

I began to spend days at home writing songs. Longing to come up with something that would encapsulate the moment – whatever that was. To shake off the past and find expression for a present that was as yet unclear. The world was full of other artists creating all sorts of music that appealed to me in one way or another and it was easy to be pulled this way and that.

Songwriting is a natural process and it's important to fall into step with it. Back then, I had no conscious idea about how it actually worked and this was just the beginning of what was to become a lifetime's contemplation. *Wellington Road* was the first song that ever came to me sober and it was most certainly one of these natural songs. It came about as a series of walks, the sound of the birds, the quiet hours, memories and flashbacks of a more difficult time and yet the sense of being loved and held despite all the chaos.

The song came rising up from a deep place within me and when it was ripe arrived on my fingers and lips at exactly the right moment. Sitting on my bed with an acoustic guitar, sensing something was about to come through. I was more fully present now and that meant I was present for its arrival. I'd written songs like this before of course, but previously I'd been far less conscious and far less grateful for the actual process.

These kinds of songs came in their own time and carried a meaning that you didn't quite understand but nevertheless *knew* about. Far more like falling in love than writing musical notation. I played it out, sitting on my bed, listening to the way it changed the feeling in the room; recognising that the song meant I could never be the same again. Those songs began to teach me something about myself, not the other way round. They flowed out and grew on me and started to carry me somewhere that I wasn't aware of at the time. The place where I'm living now.

****

On other days, I'd try to force songs. Driven by ambition or fear or the nag, nag, nag of having something to prove to the band and the rest of the world. These songs didn't have the same kind of life in them but I was still slightly too insensitive and determined to fully recognise this. Don't get me wrong, I know those motivations work wonders for many people and some great music has come out of all that and I certainly do not consider the way I have ended up writing to be any more worthy than anyone else. And I say that with the utmost sincerity. But 'ambition' and 'fear' and 'what the latest thing is' are not my way. I have all these motivations within me but they simply don't convert well into my particular songwriting. I've written songs driven by these urges for sure and have observed that they just don't work as well.

That's what I was beginning to find out: My Way. All songwriters have to discover this and also to recognise that 'My Way' changes through the years too and you have to remain sensitive to that if you don't want to die as a creative or end up another sullen copycat. Through trial and error, and staying sober, I was growing closer towards the source of my own creativity. Recognising that you have to be patient and to feed yourself with the right ingredients and wait for them to travel down into your bloodstream and be rearranged by your talent. Then you have to be able to wait till they are ready to re-emerge as an expression of who you really are.

I discovered so much by making all sorts of mistakes. But finally, and with a growing acceptance of my limitations, I began to live the life that I'd always been destined for. Learning and expanding and steadily becoming more alive each day. Sobriety isn't just the absence of alcohol and drugs. If you give it time it begins to possess a quality all of its own. Sobriety has grace, it has depth and weight and, at the same time, can be incredibly subtle and compassionate. Sobriety has its joys and its crosses to bear. And from sobriety, if you will only allow it, a new kind of song begins to flow out. Naturally, like honey from the rock.

****

Our first comeback concert was in one of those dives in Camden. We'd been off the scene for a while and I don't recall a particularly large audience. The gig was so loud that I could barely hear myself through the stage monitors. As usual, we hadn't rehearsed properly and sounded rusty.

Standing there with no chemical rush to put between myself and the crowd, you could only protect yourself by sinking deeper into the music. Closing your eyes and trying to stay in tune when there was little to pitch to. Cymbals being smacked hard about 10 inches from your ear and muddy guitar sludge wobbling back off every greasy surface. It was so much more ramshackle than I'd remembered. Back to where we'd started. In a club in Camden with my head down and my hands behind my back. The only other time I'd ever done a sober gig was that very first one.

However, this chaos was relatively short-lived and after a few more concerts the momentum that had been interrupted by my incarceration in treatment, began to return. The band quickly shifted up through the gears. The arrangements they'd come up with on *Love And Other Demons* were breath-taking and when those songs started coming together in a live setting a new band emerged into the spotlight. A band that seemed to spit a different kind of venom. The kind of venom that woke you up out of a coma.

'Once upon a time, Strangelove were a disaster. Their first album may have been a damaged masterpiece but they were too mired in singer Patrick's alcoholism to stagger to their feet. Tonight however Strangelove stand up to show they have finally emerged from the umbra of self-destruction. And they are positively luminous. No longer chemically cluttered, the new Patrick with his impeccable haircut and skinny (boy, is he!) black top, pogos around stage. This could be a completely different band.

Even the older songs shimmer rather than whimper, each of them injected with re-invented and inspired gusto. The crashing *Time For The Rest Of Your Life* sounds life-affirming rather than doom-laden and the paranoid shriek of *Human Machines* is now a gargantuan technological aria with whirring Moogs and squalling guitars.

This is a message to the skies. Strangelove have scaled the heights of their potential at last. Let's hope they don't fall down. '

Written by April Long for the *NME*

****

We were back in Eden studios recording B sides for the upcoming release of our next single and on arrival there was a new member, Nick Powell. Alex had invited him in firstly because of our use of various keyboards during the recording of *Love And Other Demons*. Nick was a talented piano player as well as having the ability to work with synthesizers and sampled sound. His flair provided us with many more colours to play with onstage and we immediately began to transmit a more sophisticated picture. Unlike many bands, this actually suited us. There was a grander feel now especially to the melancholy tracks and the sense of singing over these new arrangements reconnected me strongly to the origins of our music. Nick also had a fair sized helping of rock 'n' roll attitude and we'd sometimes go to a screaming three-electric-guitars thrash out too.

I also believe Alex wanted to invite in someone who he considered at that time, relatively speaking, sane. In truth, it was refreshing to have a new person around. So much was changing and it was helpful to assimilate somebody who hadn't been through the particular lunacy of the last few years and therefore carried a natural exuberance without our baggage. Nick fitted in quickly and everyone appeared to accept him. I personally found his presence uplifting. He came across as gentle and clever and he liked having a laugh. He looked like one of us too. Skinny, nervous, socially awkward with carelessly dyed hair. He rolled cigarettes with one hand while he was still playing with the other and he liked to drink and take drugs. Because funnily enough, just as I'd finally got my act together, the others slowly but surely descended more deeply into their own dalliances with the rock 'n' roll lifestyle.

****

The second single to come off *Love And Other Demons* was *Beautiful Alone*. We were up in London doing a Radio 1 session when Kevin McCabe, our plugger, strutted into the live room as we were packing away the gear.

"Get ready for this boys," he said. "*Beautiful Alone* has just gone in the charts at 34."

I honestly don't know who was more surprised, him or us.

"Bollocks!" said Joe, always suspicious of a wind-up.

"Honestly, I've just heard it from the charts. You're in."

"Fucking hell!" said about four voices at the same time.

Watching the Top 40 countdown on *Top Of The Pops* in Shepherd's Bush on a small television set, there it was. Coming up over that stupid drumbeat.

"And at number 34, Strangelove with *Beautiful Alone*."

"And at number 33…"

It's hard to convey to a younger generation what *Top Of The Pops* actually meant if you grew up in the 70s and early 80s. As a kid, I watched it religiously every Thursday evening with my family. Quite simply, *Top Of The Pops* was music back then. At the time, I would never have imagined that one day I'd actually be in a band on that countdown. Even though the show was undoubtedly past its heyday in the 90s, it still meant 'something' sweet to witness that moment. Something that had its roots in my childhood.

Now that I was sober, there was a growing sense in our camp that like some of our contemporaries, maybe we could make it properly big. That sense was exhilarating and terrifying in equal measures and registered as an almost permanent lump in my throat for the next two years. Whereas beforehand I possessed only a wavering ambition and was basically happy so long as I was out of it, now my desire for success, which began as a spark on the Suede tour, was turning into a personal conflagration. All stoked up by the sense of desperately wanting to put things right.

Our popularity was growing. From that first gig back in Camden to a handful of diehards, we were now pulling hundreds of people in London and the bigger cities and we also began to play headlining tours in Europe. Our next single *Sway* was a hit in Poland and we were immediately booked on to their biggest TV show and flown over to a television studio in Warsaw.

That programme was called *Lucky Hearts* and had a viewing figure into the 10s of millions. The show centred around acts of heroism carried out by the Polish general public. After endless enquiries, it was finally explained to me in broken English by a kind of policewoman that the story on our particular show featured a little boy who'd fallen down a disused mine shaft and a middle-aged man (with a Lech Walesa moustache) who'd climbed down and carried him back up in a feat of inhuman strength which had saved the boy's life. The boy and his mother were initially invited on to the set of cosy sofas and the story unfolded, incomprehensible to us, until we were waved on to an adjoining stage to play *Sway*, covered in make-up.

As soon as the drums kicked in, women in military uniforms hit clipboards against their wrists (off camera) and encouraged the audience to clap along to every single snare beat of the entire song, which every person in the studio dutifully obliged with. Although I was singing a live vocal, the band were miming. The television company had also provided a string quartet made up of some young people in tuxedos, who'd touchingly memorised the entire score by heart despite the fact they were only miming too.

Halfway through our performance, a 'ballerina' dressed in skimpy underwear suddenly emerged from the side of another empty stage opposite us and started a melancholy modern ballet interpretation of the song. Some of the cameras turned in her direction. We had not been consulted in any way regarding this and whilst undoubtedly very attractive she was also blatantly attempting to steal the limelight with the 'over the top' nature of her performance, which grew more ridiculous as the seconds rolled on.

However, you'd have thought it was *Swan Lake* in St Petersburg by the look of the band's open mouths, relinquishing almost any attempts to concentrate on their instruments and secure the illusion of the mime. The sudden urge to laugh forced me to close my eyes where the out of time clapping became only the more obvious. I had insisted on so much makeup from the old ladies backstage that I could feel it coagulating over my face.

Closing my sticky eyes and singing *Sway* and giving it everything. Trying to find something real to transmit to the millions at home, and at the same time praying. Please, please can it always be like this. Because for a moment in the midst of this most appalling situation, I suddenly found myself the happiest and most at peace I'd ever been on a stage. I really could do it, totally straight.

The song finished to rapturous applause, that was admittedly initiated and further incited by the joyless women in uniforms. Then, the heroic man with the moustache came on stage left, it has to be said, to even more applause. Telling his side of the tale and then receiving the gift of a golden Lucky Heart from the boy, to an even greater rapture.

Thinking we'd already done the job, without realising, we were then waved back on to finish the show with another number which turned out to be *Beautiful Alone*, our previous single. Second verse in I walked out into the studio audience to try and do 'something' to draw attention away from a second ballerina who'd now emerged from a third stage to do a pole dance dressed in even less. I sang the last verse sitting on the lap of an old woman who I'd picked out at random as possibly the most unsuitable person to sit on. Anyway, every eye and every camera in the room was now on me and not the ballerina. Apart from the bands'.

****

Afterwards in the dressing room the people from EMI Poland burst in incredibly excited, without any reference to my singing, yelling,

"Did you know who she was? Did you know who she was, Patrick?"

"Who?"

"The old lady whose lap you sit in?"

"No, no, of course I don't." All anxious.

"That is the old mother of the man who is head of the whole television network in Poland, and she loves you now. She absolutely loves this sitting. It is so great for you. So great!"

Maybe we should move to Poland. I suggested in all seriousness later to Joe and Alex following a long silence as we idled around in possibly the emptiest Mexican restaurant in the whole of Warsaw.

Since coming out of Farm Place, Simon, our press officer at Parlophone, had been finding it far easier to procure column inches for Strangelove, and not just because of our growing popularity. A lot of these interviews now centred around my addiction problems. This was back in a time when rock 'n' roll 'recovery' had only just hit the news and had a novelty value, long gone these days. *The Guardian* even asked me to write a piece about alcoholism, which I had the naive confidence to dash off whilst travelling back in a van midway through our latest U.K tour. But on reflection, it wasn't the best time in my life to have been talking to the press about all this. Leaking years of pain and madness and having recently been encouraged in treatment to open up as part of the healing process, it was too easy to be spouting off to journalists like they were some kind of counselling service. Mind you, thinking back, many of them did encourage me shamelessly. Although in truth, I didn't need that much encouragement.

This fresh out of treatment voice is often the one that stands in place as the sober point of view in our world. Whereas the recovering addict 10 or 20 years down the line, often forgotten or more discerning, is overlooked once the sensationalism of those early years of getting clean, and being willing to dish the dirt, have died away.

These highly personal interviews started to give the band a new identity. One which I hadn't thought through. Still incredibly impetuous at times, especially in the spotlight, I was prepared to hold back nothing. We began to be identified as the band with the alcoholic singer who'd got clean and with all this attention, I was now starting to feel a sense of importance as an individual rather than part of a collective at exactly the time we needed to be healing the distances. That willingness to open up so easily also took the focus off our music to a degree it didn't warrant, and at the time I was unable to consider with enough clarity how this might affect the others. Especially as their contributions to *Love and Other Demons* had been so inspired.

Down their end of the sleeper bus, every now and again it would go suspiciously quiet and soon afterwards you'd hear laughing and shouting and corks popping and then the sound of *The Police* being blasted out at ear splitting volumes and everybody singing,

"Ay O. Ay O. Ay O. Ay O." Really, really loudly.

Because Alex hated Sting.

Behind the scenes, all through this period they were getting more and more off their tits.

The first journalists I met were sympathetic and supportive. Interviews carried out at the EMI offices in Hammersmith. With smiles and handshakes and underfloor heating and cups of green tea and sparkling water. They'd been arranged by Simon, our press officer, a man with a good deal of tact and sensitivity.

Unsurprisingly however, we eventually came to experience a darker side to all this newfound recognition. This was the height of Britpop lad culture and I soon became a target for certain other coke-sniffing journalists who were not in any way enamoured or impressed with what they considered my sob story or my recovery.

****

The *Melody Maker* review of *Love And Other Demons* felt like such a scathing attack on my fledgling sobriety that the band and Cerne tried to hide it from me initially. Worried that it might start me drinking again. But a so-called friend of mine let the cat out of the bag. A piece only thinly disguised as a musical critique, the vitriol of the words severely knocked my newly found but still fragile sense of self. Even though I now recognise that this was in the post and I'd been careless in talking about my vulnerabilities *so* frankly, to be on the receiving end of that amount of scorn when you're nowhere near developing the psychological wherewithal to cope with it was challenging to say the least. In fact, in my secret heart, it was crushing. Thank God I didn't drink or use on it. But that typewriter fist was the closest I ever came.

Mercifully, I had Rayner to confide in, and he was without doubt the person who pulled me through. His contempt for this kind of journalism was like a vintage draft fermented for decades and so infused with world weariness and cynical humour that even in my confused state he was able to turn it all around. Continuing to support me in my attempts to change my life with a fierce solidarity like I'd never known before. Days later he drove down to Bristol so we could talk face to face. With a slightly crazy glint in his eye recalling that in defence of Nick Cave, who'd also been taunted and insulted in the press after he'd first come out of treatment, Rayner had posted an actual dead squid through to the *NME* with a note saying.

'Why are music journalists like squids - because they squirt ink everywhere and they've got no backbone.'

The dark glee he expressed in recounting that particular tale was so uplifting to witness that there was no way I could carry on being self-obsessed and miserable with him on the other end of the phone every day. Knowing I didn't possess that extra layer of skin they say you need in order to survive in the music business, he was somehow able to sympathise and make me laugh at myself at the same time.

CHAPTER 24

KING OF THE
SINGING TREES

Eventually, it was Cerne who suggested we go away, spend some time together, and start work on a new album. Parlophone had recently decided to renew their option and good old Mike Smith at EMI Publishing was also continuing his support. Both these decisions amounted to clear endorsements of our future and paid for the band to keep going for a few more years. Cerne found us a suitably large and remote house somewhere in Carmarthenshire, West Wales, and we set up our equipment in the lounge, pushing the sofas into the corner of the room and forming a loose circle of chairs, amps, keyboards, and drums.

We sat in the circle each day and jammed out ideas with the tectonic plates of the band grinding away underneath. In all honestly, I hadn't bargained for quite that amount of tension in the air as all sorts of complicated feelings continued to dance around in the shadows. Somewhere else in the background was also the knowledge that this was probably our last chance. That we needed to eclipse the Top 40 success of *Beautiful Alone* with an album to consolidate our position with the record companies and the press, as well as reach out to those people who had not as yet connected with us.

As a result of these somewhat subterranean pressures, I started to take long rambling walks in the surrounding countryside to let off steam. John had given me a tape of *The Lark Ascending* by Vaughan Williams and I started to listen to that cassette on my Walkman every day. Most mornings whilst they slept it off or smoked the first dooby of the day, I was up bright and early and out into the sunshine, scrying the natural world for messages and signs regarding our future.

No clear idea of a way forward, I was waiting for inspiration to make its next move. Hanging on for an intervention. At the time my mind had become virtually mediaeval, and the world responded in kind with all manner of potential portents. Always more of a fan in the hope of some strange miracle than in the dreary, complicated negotiations of resolving the issues of a long-term dysfunctional band. I put much of my effort into wandering around daydreaming.

One morning, lost in yet more of these reveries, I walked further still along the small road that ran past our remote house and for the first time spied a place name in the distance. Having always refused to wear glasses, on approaching I was unable to decipher this village and squinted at the blurry letters on the sign as they emerged into focus. Finally, when it became clear, I ripped off the headphones and stopped dead in my tracks with the sound of the flies and the sheep suddenly flat against my ears. For a good minute or so staring straight ahead just to make sure I wasn't hallucinating.

Bethlehem.

****

The funny old man in the post office filled me in. This tiny village had been named after its chapel during the great Methodist revival in Wales during the 19th century.

"They still come by yer in coach loads at Christmas. Just to get the post mark see. Bethlehem Post Office," stamping it down hard and fast onto a postcard of a robin, which I immediately felt obliged to buy.

On my enquiring he also evangelised, in a high-pitched voice, about Carn Gogh, the nearby hillside I'd been climbing on a daily basis. There'd once been an Iron Age hillfort on the summit, he informed me.

"That's where my ancestors are see," he said. "Up there on that bloody hill."

It was true. Standing on the top of Carn Gogh you'd often come to experience an eerie stillness. The Iron Age ramparts towered over the rolling valleys of Carmarthenshire. A huge pile of stones on the crest of a steep hill that had once served as the battlements of a fort. Standing on the bones of the dead from thousands of years ago was just the tonic I needed for the constant talk in my head. We were a long, long way from anywhere up here and for a few seconds the relentless interpretation ceased.

The long green hills, the songs of the birds, and the wind over my face revealed themselves, in an ordinary mysticism, as I peered over Bethlehem. Its toy-town post office and cluster of little houses, the empty chapel with its graveyard and, further in the distance, desolate farm buildings with piles of tyres and defunct machinery outside in the yards. I had no idea that in those few brief moments of peace my life lay waiting and not in the dreams and schemes that shifted around my head all day.

I'd experienced a moment of truth and something within me had recognised it. The natural world was talking back and I might have stayed longer but for the bracing wind and the fact that I couldn't quite hear what she was trying to tell me.

****

However, this 'new world' kept calling and I eventually became familiar with the whole area. One afternoon, approaching Carn Gogh from the side nearer to our house, I jumped a gate and ran over some farmland. This was a steeper ascent to the summit and gentle rain began to fall. About halfway up I took shelter under a small, gnarled hawthorn tree, sitting in the rough grass and stones with my back against the trunk. As the raindrops fell against the leaves and the wind shifted through the branches, I settled down to meditate and almost immediately heard a softly spoken feminine voice.

"Hello..."

"I've been on the side of this hill for many years," she said. "In the wind and the rain and the sunshine and the snow, but no one comes here. No one notices me."

This voice revealed itself to be the spirit of the hawthorn tree.

"I've stared out across this valley, across these fields, and I have longed to reach out. To reach out and touch the tree that grows beside me. Look, can you see, I love him."

Close by stood another tree whose name was unknown to me and whose voice I couldn't hear. Nevertheless, you could still sense the springtime's early love radiating out from the hawthorn. Sitting with my back against the trunk and listening into the longing. The sweet world was alive and every movement in the air and every raindrop fresh with the sense of an old song which had whispered for thousands of years across these slopes. My Celtic blood was singing along and with the rain falling I found a patch of brambles and pulled up a great long swathe of them. After fashioning and pruning the brambles into a single length of green, hands all prickled with spikes and hair damp with drizzle, I tied one end to a branch in the hawthorn and the other to a branch in the nearby tree so that they were connected physically, and I sat down once more. Staring out over the fields and down into the nearby badger setts.

"Thank you," she seemed to murmur. "Thank you"

I remained with my back to the trunk and the words of a simple poem flowed into my mind. The melancholic atmosphere of that hillside and the singing in the wind and the voice of the tree ringing in my ears.

****

The next day, I bought a ball of string from the post office and cut 12 long pieces. Tying them from branch to branch and connecting the two trees at 12 more locations. Writing out the poem and popping it into a see-through polythene cover and hanging it in the thorns. The poem told the story of the two trees. How she'd lived for years on the side of the hill, longing to reach out and touch the one she loved. And how the bramble had come to connect them along a bridge of thorns.

As I walked back to the house, the wind was blowing strong and it was as if all the other trees were waving their arms and showering their blessings down upon me, returning from some long, endless war. King of the Singing Trees, like a six year old child roaming wild through the hillsides of Carmarthenshire.

Suddenly, I looked up across the fields to see a hare approach. Bounding over the greens, returning with my soul in its mouth. I stood motionless, suspended in anticipation before experiencing the rush as it re-entered my body intact. Familiar but altogether changed.

The hare told me that my soul had a wound that would never heal and that it would bleed for the rest of my life because of what had happened. But from out of the wound, songs would flow and because of this, I would always have songs to show where I'd been.

Then, without waiting for thanks, the hare ran away. Running and turning back to look at me. Running and stopping. Running and turning to look at me once more until it disappeared into the distance and I knew in my bones that it was waiting for me somewhere over the horizon.

****

Back in my bedroom in the rented house, I lay puzzling over these changes. Changes that would have been difficult to explain and yet seemed to me as real as my own hands. Downstairs, the band were fooling around and playing a kind of spontaneous joke music to entertain themselves. As they often would. A kind of joint rehearsal. A musical stream of consciousness. Even in the midst of all that crazy melody you could hear each individual's contribution to the mayhem. How the differing personalities shone through their instruments especially when they were just messing about. How at times, one member suddenly fought for domination and tried to drag the music in his own direction, how they would reach agreements and disagreements. How ideas would break out and break down and reassemble and how they complimented one another without a word ever being spoken. It was fascinating to lie there and listen from a distance. At times like this, I would long for us to resolve our differences. To wipe clean the years. You could hear their talents blaring out so brightly. Raw potential, like the big bang beginnings of some new cosmos. All we needed were the right songs to focus all this crazy rock 'n' roll and the worlds would spin toward us. I tried to open my eyes wider, longing for inspiration to strike when it already had on the slopes of Carn Gogh, but in such a curious way that I didn't yet connect it to songwriting.

****

Around the circle we all agreed that Paul Corkett should produce this mushrooming record and hoped he would agree after the insanity we'd been through on *Love And Other Demons*. Happily, he remained up for it and as luck would have it travelled down to Bethlehem almost immediately. To listen and to talk and to help us make decisions moving forward.

Paul's own career was taking off and he was growing in quiet confidence, chipping in with ideas and challenging too. He'd never previously arrived at such an early stage of our process and his presence was helping to settle and further re-enliven our collective. We jammed away and focussed and then jammed and focussed more. He sat, listening, in the circle like another member. His head bowed and his fringe hanging down across his face. When he became excited, he'd suddenly draw stronger on his cigarette and breathe it right down into his lungs and hold in the smoke and start running his hand through his hair. You knew you were on to something when that happened and slowly but surely some new songs started to materialise and evolve.

Many of our mealtime conversations outside of this music centred around Paul and the projects he'd worked on of late. He'd recently been recording with Nick Cave, engineering *The Boatman's Call* at Abbey Road and one evening he suggested that we should record there too, promising that Studio Two and its golden past would inspire the very best out of us. Everybody in Strangelove was immediately fired up by that suggestion and having just been signed again we were in a position to make it happen. Although it was costly, Cerne also agreed that this was the best way forward and as a result of his approval it wasn't long till Parlophone and Food were on board too. After another couple of weeks jamming and with some new music finally beginning to take shape, we travelled across to London. Abbey Road. Studio Two.

CHAPTER 25

ABBEY ROAD

On the first day of recording, I went out of my way to walk over the zebra crossing and then to read some of the graffiti outside.

'We love you Mr Ringo – Love Ang from China.'

Or 'John, you live forever in my heart.'

Almost every inch of the road's white stone wall and its black top plate were covered in layers of personal messages to Beatles both dead and alive. Scrawled in coloured marker pens and signifying beyond doubt that this place was rock 'n' roll sacred ground. I wandered up the steps and under the EMI sign and through the invisible hand that stopped most other people at that wall outside. Mind blowing to be walking into all that musical history. Through the front door and past the reception desk and along a small dusty corridor with old tape machines shoved to one side and framed gold discs leaning up against the other. You turned right into the control room where there were black leather sofas to lounge around on and a window by the desk overlooking the spacious live room. The control room was connected to the live room by a set of stairs that descended into it. Walking down those stairs, the band had already been there for a few hours setting up.

As a 14-year-old I'd been obsessed with the Beatles. They'd been the first band who had truly captivated me. I'd saved my dinner money, going without food every lunchtime, until I had enough to buy the next album. All of them, one at a time, in random succession. From *Please Please Me*, all the way to *Abbey Road* and *Let It Be*.

Descending those stairs into the actual place where almost all that music had been recorded was reminiscent of the unsettling confusion, as a four-year-old, of suddenly glimpsing the bald-headed *Punch and Judy* man at the end of the show. Coming up from beneath the stage with a flustered red face. Completely taken in by the performance you couldn't quite believe the whole thing was real but in a totally different way. As I walked down 'those' stairs, into 'that' room hundreds of light bulbs went off in my mind, I could actually see flashes. Experiencing my brain chemistry being altered by the act of it. I'd spent countless hours listening to their music as a teenager and Alex had always loved them too. That love was one of the things that had bonded us most in our beginnings and coming down the stairs I immediately caught his eye. He looked happier and more relaxed than I'd seen him in a while and he beamed a smile back at me.

"What do you think, Pad? Abbey Road."

Having been there most of the day they'd already settled in and he mooched over to the piano, which the Beatles had left there, and played the opening to *Lady Madonna*. That sound was the exact sound. It actually was *Lady Madonna* and the precise resonance sent a chill through my bones.

****

The live room at Abbey Road was far larger than any we'd experienced previously with a dark brown, slatted wooden floor like a school gymnasium. White walls with cheap looking panels and a towering ceiling. Hence the staircase down from the control room which was built into the upper portion of the wall. It was the most perfunctory room you could have imagined without any of the cosiness or clean and precise air of a modern-day studio.

Mercifully, they'd left it exactly the same so you didn't even have to imagine. Even the psychedelic lights that The Beatles had brought in to try and vibe up the place were still hanging there, high on the walls. The room, so large and echoey that everybody's amps and the drums sat hidden behind large screens with windows in them. Paul had built me a little vocal booth too, under the control room window with all the old mics inside, allowing us to record completely live.

The days and nights passed by in a kind of daze. As well as being a dream come true, the band were fidgety because in light of all these momentous yesterdays I don't think we were entirely convinced by our new material yet. We worked long hours and the intensity of imminent success or failure seemed to loom over our every move. At times, I would long for some relief. For some great inspiration to break through. One evening in particular it wasn't happening and they all decided to take time out and go to the pub with Paul. For obvious reasons, I wasn't asked and stayed behind in Abbey Road. Paul assured me it would be fine to hang out there on my own and so I lounged on the control room sofa in the dark listening to *Thursday Afternoon* by Brian Eno.

****

Half asleep. Deep into the 60 minute meditation, I suddenly experienced another flashing of brainwaves. Springing up as if from nowhere, a strange flower began to bloom behind my eyes and all at once I knew what I had to do. Born of love and born of ambition and born of confusion and born of admiration and born of vanity and born of hope and born of desperation and born of self-importance and born of the wasted years looking for a hand to hold.

So many curious things had happened. Ghosts on recordings and voices in my head and sudden influxes of light leading to synchronicities so unlikely that the flight path of my life had been changed forever. Pulled from the gutter and almost certain death and into some kind of recovery. Naturally I had started to wonder where all this pointed to and what the spirit could do if you engaged with it in a more conscious way. Without an experienced spiritual advisor around me at that time, I'd began testing out whether you could somehow initiate and then swing these experiences to your own advantage.

Turning off all the lights, including the ones in the mixing room, the huge live area looked more like a cathedral now. I'd pushed some of our gear to the sides, clearing a space and marking out a large circle of tea lights on the wooden floor. Between 30 and 40 candles alight, shadows dancing over the walls and ceiling. The band would be gone for a few hours more. Such a strange opportunity. To be here, alone. With the timeless glitter of all those Beatles songs darting across the corners of your eyes like shooting stars.

Looking down from the top of the stairs, the circle of candles against the pitch black of the live room looked evocative of some ancient pagan ritual. I descended the staircase naked and stepped into the middle of the circle. My sister Catherine had recently taught me how to call in the elements and the angels of protection. Each invocation draws the moment closer.

Fingers tingling. Abbey Road appeared gigantic in the candlelight.

I stood still in the circle and I called upon the spirit of John Lennon, my childhood hero, and waited for the stardust.

Because he was here. He'd spent many days and nights in this exact location and in fact almost every time I'd ever heard his voice on any recording by The Beatles, this is where he'd been standing. Every time he sang. Every time I'd listen to *Strawberry Fields* in my room at night aged 14. Every time we'd listen to *A Day In The Life* round at Alex's. These very walls were full of the splinters of his voice. Trapped in the chemicals of the paint and in the bricks and in the dusty old carpet and the perforated ceiling. He was here and you could experience that presence in every cell of your body. I was calling him. Waking him up out of his death sleep. I called again with my chest rising and falling from the sheer effort of breaking through the taboo and the sheer youthful impertinence. Finally, opening my eyes to wait in the ensuing hush.

All at once, that silence caved in and the flickering room was filled with a sense of laughter. A manic laughter that echoed around the walls and the ceiling. An intense madcap laughter. A laughter that came bouncing back off every surface. Shifting and rearranging the ground you stood on so that it seemed to be giving way. Arising again and again in overlapping waves. Washing over you, drenching you in an invisible sea of laughter. Coming in from above and below and from all sides. Filling your ears and eyes, your mouth and your nose with its rushing sound. Roaring. Like a freefall. And from the heart of that laughter came a voice. A distinct clear voice from inside its pulse.

"You don't know what you're doing. You don't know what you've done. You've called upon forces more powerful than you can imagine. You don't even know what you've done."

The laughter of the trickster. The laughter that comes over people high on LSD who are suddenly struck for the first time by the absurdity of the human condition and by what fools we are to believe in anything we imagine about ourselves and our vanities. Laughter that recognises its own futility and is laughing out a lifetime of self-reverence and seriousness with a delirious relief. The laughter of the laughing buddha, the laughter of the cosmic joke, the empty laughter at the end of time. It was terrifying to stand there naked and to be washed over in it again and again. Drenched. Out of my depth. Struggling to breathe. Drowning.

"You don't know what you're doing. You don't know what you've done. You've called upon forces more powerful than you can ever imagine."

The charge of those words seemed to be circulating over me in ever quicker patterns around the room like a mad comet that had strayed off its path and burst in through the studio walls.

Quickly, breathlessly and without following the protocol, I blew out all the candles one by one till Abbey Road was plunged back into darkness and the sudden silence stuck to my ears and eyes like a cloth sack over the head of a man who is about to swing. Kneeling on the floor uncertain. Hesitating. Scampering up the staircase and into my clothes I lay on the black sofa in the control room with my heart beating in my chest like a fast, fast song. Staring at the flickering little lights on the mixing desk and on the compressors. Not knowing what I'd done.

The rest of the band returned an hour or so later and I said nothing. Whereas once I might have told them and they would have laughed or just dismissed it – now I was in a world of my own. Somewhere too personal and forbidden to admit to. Because I knew beyond question that something had actually happened down there. Something real. Something I once again could never have explained. And I was afraid. Because I could still hear the ghosts of that laughter and I didn't know what it meant.

****

The overriding conclusion of that session at Abbey Road was that we needed more songs and decided to return to Bethlehem with Paul. Things were starting to disintegrate in my relationship with the ITN newsreader Jennifer Nadel and after a particularly difficult phone call, I walked into the rehearsal space, picked up my guitar, and wrote *Freak*. Straight out, in frustration. Words and chords and melody. By the end of that evening, they'd nailed a super cool arrangement and suddenly out of nowhere we had a new song.

"That's the best one you've done yet," said John and my heart went zing because we rarely if ever praised one another.

The next day, I wrote the beginning of *Superstar* using the first chord from *Time For The Rest Of Your Life* and going different places with it. Again, the arrangement came easily to the band and we were on a roll. Alex had chords for *The Runaway Brothers* and I came up with the lyrics upstairs in my room.

Continuing with my walks, it wasn't long till one afternoon I found myself back at the hawthorn tree on the slopes of Carn Gogh. It was late spring now; the earth was fully awakening and the smell of damp moss and soil heightened on the shadowy side of the mountain. I soon discovered that the two trees had both sent out small green shoots from the tips of their branches that were growing around the pieces of string and bramble that I'd strung up to connect them. Thin green stems curling and winding their way along by a few centimetres. The fairy tale was coming alive, the two trees growing out to touch one another. No discernible voice this time, she'd spoken nevertheless. In the form of shoots that you could see with your real eyes. I was sure it was a good omen and sat once more halfway up Carn Gogh with my back against the trunk. Recalling the words the hawthorn had first spoken and sinking into a peace that had eluded me for a while. The ghostly laughter was fading now as I wandered back to the house. Music papers scattered over the kitchen table. Miles and miles away in another world Blur and Oasis were fighting it out against each other to be heralded as Britain's best band.

****

After returning from Bethlehem, for the next recording sessions we went to Richmond to record our remaining songs. In between we'd been working hard. Gigs and press and local radio tours, management meetings and photo sessions. The unspoken pressures were starting to get to us. I rarely travelled with the band anymore because of their increasing partying and their hangovers and we'd stopped talking about the direction of the record and our objectives. Unthinking, I'd told Cerne and the record company that I wanted to call the album Bethlehem before I'd even discussed it with the rest of them. Probably on reflection because I knew they wouldn't like it.

Which they didn't. And they were pissed off to find out about this without having been consulted.

A drunken Nick was the one who eventually confronted me in the control room in Richmond and I threw a glass at the wall just left of his head and it smashed, casting hundreds of shards over the desk and the floor. We went on to mix the final record with tiny pieces of broken glass everywhere as a constant reminder of that best forgotten incident and what had initiated it.

CHAPTER 26

THE STRANGELOVE ALBUM

We eventually named the new album *Strangelove*. The first single, music written by Jazz, was called *The Greatest Show On Earth* and once more went Top 40. The record company was upbeat and we had stylists come into the studio and lay hundreds of outfits before us to choose from. I spent time in trendy hair salons in the west end refusing the champagne they offered while you waited to be snipped. I ate in posh restaurants with my friend Dilly Gent, Parlophone's creative director, and we plotted and giggled. Strangelove performed on some TV talk show, made expensive pop videos and toured Europe and the UK as a headlining act and started to pull even larger audiences. Still slightly unsure of who I was supposed to be onstage, I wore too much makeup, made self-deprecating comments between songs, and told half jokes as I battled to try and discover some true confidence within myself. Kissing Nick onstage high on adrenaline to try and say sorry instead of just saying sorry.

Around this time, we played on the mainstage at the Reading Festival and immediately afterwards Steve Lamacq, who was doing the stage introductions, invited us to go live on his Radio One evening show.

We were geared up for *Freak* coming out. A song that captured the intensity of our moment. Direct and brooding, it was going down a storm at our live shows. I waited in the vocal booth at Maida Vale knowing we had a new kind of vitality to spit out into the country. People in cars, in kitchens and bedrooms who'd be listening, their imaginary faces shuffling through me. As a young man, it was so exhilarating to have the illusion of that kind of power. The power of going out live on Radio One. The power to shout

'Fuck You All' to millions of people, if you wanted to, was terrifying when you already found it hard enough to trust yourself as it was.

"And here's the moment I've been waiting for. We're going over to Maida Vale where Strangelove are waiting to play live for us. It's their new one, and this is called *Freak*."

The band launched in. The simple repetitive riff. Alex said he wanted it to sound like a 16-year-old kid was playing it. I remained cut off in a soundproof vocal booth and things started going wrong from the start. There was nothing coming down the cans and there was nothing I could do to alert anyone. Couldn't hear the music and had to watch Alex's hands playing the chords to get my place and try to pitch against the vague musical sludge coming from outside the booth. Like drowning in a submarine. All the others so deep in their playing, the engineers couldn't see me either. Unable to communicate my distress and having to sing a vocal by guesswork, live in front of millions of people.

"There was nothing coming through my fucking ear goggles. Nothing. Fucking nothing.

Fuck all. aARHHGGHHHH!" I screamed immediately afterwards.

None of the technicians in Maida Vale studios could understand how it had happened and although I'd managed to pull off the semblance of a vocal, it wasn't the career-defining performance I'd been waiting those past years to deliver. We drove back home to Bristol in yet another confused and slightly awkward silence.

****

With the new album coming out there was all sorts of press, and one morning I got a phone call from my sister Bridget.

"Paddy," she squealed. "You're on the front of the *Big Issue!*"

"What, we are? Strangelove? Fucking hell! Amazing!"

"No, it's just you. It's a photo of just you."

"Just me. Fuck! What photo is it? Do I look good?"

"Yeah of course you do, you look great."

"Honestly? Explain the photo, Mocky. Have I got my black leather jacket on?"

Bridget, or Mocky as I'd always called her, tried to explain and after she'd hung up, I had to lie down on my kitchen floor. Having recently rented a large flat in Clifton, I'd never have imagined that I'd be living on Apsley Road in my own place.

"Oh my God. Am I actually going to be famous?" My heart was beating fast now,

"Am I like, actually going to make it? Fucking hell man? Have I already made it?" Round and round in my head. I eventually jumped into bed and listened to *Ram Dass* tapes, trying to calm down and get some perspective while the sensation of ants crawling all over me only intensified.

If I really was on the front cover, I'd better get out and see if there was anyone selling it. There was often a guy by the local Tesco.

****

Spring had blossomed into summer and it was a drawn-out evening just before another late sundown. The scents of honeysuckles and roses burst out of the front gardens as I walked along Apsley Road towards the shops. But more than all that, my hands were clammy and my throat was itchy as I turned the corner and strained my eyes up Whiteladies Road to Tesco. Yes, he was standing there, that same guy as always, matted hair and unshaven, slightly stooping with his *Big Issues*. And as I approached, plain as day there was my face staring out from the cover.

'Shit, man. It was that photo. Cool.'

Would he recognise that the guy on the front cover was the same guy who was approaching? No, he looked weary and totally distracted by the long hours of rejection. Lost in a sad and complicated dream. Like some kind of weird holy man. It seemed rude to interrupt his thoughts and so I didn't try. There's a strange, almost unapproachable purity about a certain kind of homeless man who's being humbled into selling a newspaper that reveals his plight. I was walking too fast anyway and too self-conscious to buy one at first, so I ducked into the shop.

'It's true, it's true. I'm on the front cover. Oh my God!'

Roaming the aisles of brightly coloured wrappers in a state of semi-terror, semi-excitement, my whole body seethed with adrenaline. I waited a while for the right time to go back outside. When no one else was around, just in case it appeared like I was attention seeking. Not wanting anyone to witness the embarrassment of being the one on the front of the magazine who was buying that same magazine from someone who had to sell it because he didn't have a roof over his head. The shock of what greeted me outside was impossible to assimilate and I've been swallowing it piecemeal ever since. The vendor had collapsed to the floor and was lying on his back. The copies of the *Issue* were scattered around him and about 20 of my faces flapped around in the breeze across the pavement. Flapping in and out of sync. My face. My face. My face. My face. My face. My face. My face.

Almost inconceivably one of the magazines was resting over 'his' face. My face on the cover of a magazine was on top of the face of a man who'd just collapsed from a drug overdose and was lying on the street. The image burned its way into my retina to remain there as a permanent fixture. So startled, so appalled, so dreamlike was the experience that I didn't even think to help the guy. Instead I walked, almost half ran away. Turning back over and over again to see the sight of my own face stuck to the face of some poor casualty. My face superimposed over his face. My face. My face. My face. My face. Scattered all over the pavement.

Fleeing now, as if I'd done something terribly wrong. Something that I might even be held to account for. I didn't even think to take my own copy.

There I was, running away. And there I was too, collapsed on the floor in front of Tesco on the front of the *Big Issue*. Time stood still again.

****

Weeks later, we played a sold-out show at the Shepherd's Bush Empire as the headlining act. With no idea it was the penultimate gig of our career, I waited in a room at the Hilton Hotel, plastering make-up onto my face and listening to Leonard Cohen's first album. We'd recently sold out The Astoria too and there'd been a stage invasion. With *Freak* playing, I'd walked down the catwalk at London Fashion Week, a model for *Red Or Dead*. The news footage of me ripping off my shirt and throwing it into the cameras had been used by the Labour Party for their Cool Britannia election advertisement and they'd run that on *News At 10*. At that very moment we were Radio One's Breakfast time single of the week. We were in *The Times*, *The Guardian*, *The Independent*, even *The Sun* and *The Mirror*. With supportive pieces about our upcoming single.

Earlier that day, from the back of the huge hall in the shadows, I had watched the band sound checking *Sway*. It remains for me one of the most powerful and moving spectacles I ever witnessed on a stage. Their instrumental, that afternoon, was a kind of perfection to me. Having no idea anyone was watching them, I kept my face hidden in the shadows. My stomach full of foreboding and my feet nailed to the floor by the subtlety and growing intensity of the arrangement. Nick on a synth playing the sampled strings and Alex on piano. Jazz on acoustic and Joe and John, both with their eyes closed and lost in concentration, on bass and drums.

The band had grown beyond anything I could have imagined when we'd started all those years ago in Dave's bedroom. The music blaring out of those huge speakers at Shepherd's Bush Empire sounded so grand and so accomplished that I started to well up. Because I recognised in that moment that I loved them in a way I had never been capable of expressing and that because of my hang ups I'd never truly appreciated them in all their glory till that moment. It was heart-breaking because at the same time their faces looked sad. We had drifted apart and the expanse between us had become impossible to bridge. And even if I could do it justice with words, it was too late, because it was over.

****

The moon was full that night and staring out from the hotel window waiting for the taxi to the gig, there was a moment's stillness to recall that afternoon's sound check once again. The same moon that I'd seen when I'd been homeless 10 years previously, before any of this had begun. The same moon that had shone the first night Strangelove had jammed on acid. The same moon that had blazed the night we'd recorded *Is There A Place?* That had raged over the desert outside Granada. The same moon that had carried Elin away from me. The same pregnant moon that I'd stared up to when singing *The Sea Of Black*. The same full moon that Jim Duff had looked up to back in Tipperary at the beginning of the century. I was sober. I'd finally got myself together. But the growing intuition continued to whisper, and I pleaded with that moon not to take it all away from me. Not now. Please, not now.

As I jumped up onstage that night, before we went into our first number, people were shouting my name.

Patrick. Patrick. Patrick. We love you. Patrick. Patrick.

Those excitable laughing cries rang out around the auditorium just like the flash bulbs going off down the stairs at Abbey Road. The gig, a celebration, a kind of party. Uplifting and full of noise and excitement and goodwill towards us. Finally, we were one of those bands that we used to support. With the roadies and the set lists and the light show and the backdrop and the hits. But unlike them, something else was with us in the shadows of the stage. However wild the cheers became, you could sense it there. Something darker, pacing in the wings.

****

Later, I sat in the dressing room listening to Leonard Cohen again. The others had gone to the after show party and with no drugs to keep my rush going, like all rushes the gig adrenalin was dying away. In that moment, I saw myself in an out of body experience. Sitting in front of the mirror alone in the dressing room at the Shepherd's Bush Empire.

I imagine we all have a dream of some sort. Whatever that might be. Something we are trying to attain, a goal we are trying to manifest as yet out of reach. We tell ourselves that once we arrive at this place our insecurities will disappear and that we will finally be able to stand up fully alive and at ease with ourselves, satisfied and justified and ultimately fulfilled.

I'd just arrived at that place. We'd done a vibrant show to hundreds of people. Who'd called out my name. Who were excited and evidently inspired. People who transmitted genuine love. A great crush of love that poured out from the darkness of the crowd and onto the stage and straight into your body like a spiritual transfusion. Lifting you far out of yourself and allowing you to shine back something so radiant in return that you'd never have been able to manufacture it alone. Something so luminous and timeless that you could never be the same person again. That night onstage I had finally experienced a flashing sense of achievement and the rush and exhilaration that comes with it. But the rush was disappearing now and looking into that mirror I suddenly needed it again.

My spirit, floating over me. Like you hear about with people in hospitals who've had near death experiences. I looked down upon myself. I actually saw the top of my own head. The hairspray and the make up on the table. Back to being me again after the transcendence of the gig. Alone and anxious and lost and already needing another audience and needing their applause so that I could feel alright again. Just 30 minutes after the curtain had gone down.

But this time I caught myself and I saw through to some truth, with that precious distance I'd finally won over myself. That same distance which had grown into a recovery from alcoholism and addiction.

Success was the ultimate high, another kind of glass I was reaching for that was never going to fill me up. It was no great eureka moment and there were no lights or voices. But I knew it at that moment. There was nothing wrong with success. It was exhilarating and exciting and entirely innocent. Success was actually the greatest high of all. But success wasn't the answer to the way you felt about yourself. Success wasn't the answer to the riddle I'd been wrestling with inside myself since a boy. I'd already heard so many people say it of course but there's nothing like truly knowing a thing like that for yourself. Not because someone told you but because you went there and tasted it for a while. There is no substitute for that.

****

Freak didn't make it into the Top 20. It got to number 42. Neither did *Another Night In*. That got to number 46.

****

Waking up in the middle of the night, it came on the radio World Service. Lady Diana was dead. Killed in a car crash, chased down by photographers in Paris. I was in a hotel in Kensington doing press for a couple of days so next afternoon, I walked down to the nearby palace. There were thousands of bunches of flowers laid by the gates and over the grass outside. A floating platform of colour and see-through plastic. Through the never-ending rumble of London a great hand had reached down through the clouds and ripped out a giant hole of silence that clung around the palace like a huge, ever-collapsing barrage balloon.

As you approached, the sense of grief hanging in the air was like walking through quicksand. All the grief that lay under the concrete surfaces, everybody's personal grief had found a place to gather. Filled with flowers, a great polythene whale of grief had beached itself outside Kensington Palace. And just for those moments the world seemed to be dying into something more contemplative. I stood there for as long as I could bear it, trying to assimilate the moment. A moment in history for which by chance I was present. Standing there with slow tears pouring down my face. Knowing something had changed forever. Because just for once they weren't my tears and somehow against all the odds I was beginning to grow up.

CHAPTER 27

THE END

When the phone finally rang, it was Alex. We rarely spoke outside hours back then and you could sense what was coming. In the end, it didn't take long. Having woken up the previous night, he'd dreamed that the band was over. He came to my flat on Apsley Road. I knew he was right and the whole conversation lasted 10 minutes.

Suddenly, the shifting sands I'd been standing on for almost 10 years had disappeared, leaving me stranded in mid-air. I was perched on a tightrope, miles high in the sky, with no sense of balance, having not paid attention to the real world for almost a decade. My footing was going. Nervously looking down I could see the hills and the city and the tiny buildings that made up what I knew must have been Bristol. It was decidedly shocking to realise I was going to have to somehow get back down there to the dole office and it was far, far too high to jump.

✳✳✳✳

Over the following weeks, I floated over the Downs almost every night. Across the long stretches of grass to peer over the gorge that dropped down into the river Avon. In the distance further along that same river was Brunel's Suspension Bridge. Hanging in mid-air with its car headlights and taillights crossing back and forth, connecting the neon glow of the city to the dark expanses of Leigh Woods. On the first full moon since the band had split three weeks earlier, I looked into the sky again. Up into another moon, so ripe and clear.

Turning away, I walked back across the grass with the coat I'd bought from Uncle Sam's in my arms. The same coat which had looked so cool when I'd first put it on but had ultimately turned against me. Turned me into a hungry ghost who could never swallow enough booze and drugs and money and love and applause to fill up that God-shaped hole inside. A hungry ghost whose entertainment value was the fact that he was dying right in front of your eyes. A hungry ghost who had survived and come back to life.

Unsurprisingly, the coat was still, even now, whispering my desires. Trying to seduce me with the same old promises. Trying to frighten me that nothing would ever be the same. That I was lost without those dreams. But tonight, I wasn't listening, as I hung it into the branches.

Stepping away to a distance in the moonlight, it was still moving like rock 'n' roll royalty but desolate too, like the hanged man. Thin tailored body, wide lapels, thin tailored arms, shiny bright black buttons, the swish swish of Ossie Clark in the wind. Watching it sway. Scenes from the previous years flashed before my eyes. Gigs and recording studios, record companies and tour buses. I walked back and squirted the lighter fluid into the lining.

Whoosh! The initial jump of the flame managed to singe the small hairs on the back of my knuckles and inspired an intuitive step back. With the stink of my own hand in my nostrils I remained slightly in awe of the coat's power. Walking 20 paces away again to turn and watch it burn. At one point my heart was in my mouth because some of the twigs started to crackle yellow and red and I feared it might get out of control and kill the tree, but it didn't catch on. Finally, it was just the coat. The coat and a few burning twigs.

I stood in stillness watching the flames.

Over the nearby stone wall, you could hear the lion in Bristol Zoo grumbling in its cage and the voice told me straight,

"You don't have what it takes to be one of those people walking around in a leather jacket and sunglasses as they start getting older.

"You have to walk out somewhere less chartered.

"Not through choice but through necessity.

"The necessity of you having unwittingly asked for this."

As the flames died down out there in the darkness of the Downs, the voice continued to speak in clear pictures that sailed across my mind's eye.

"Society is like a well-lit circle of light. People who live inside that circle tell you, 'Stay here. Stay here in the light. Stay here, where you can see what you're doing. It's safe. Do this, do that, you'll be alright. There are simple rules you have to follow to be happy and successful. Just do those things and it will all work out. Live out your days. It's easy'.

"But sometimes, certain people, and truthfully not through any choice of their own, have to take whatever is left of their own star and leave that circle of light behind and walk out into the darkness that surrounds it. Using only their own star to light the way. Not truly knowing where they are going but leaving a little trail of light behind themselves that leads out through the darkness. Sometimes what they find out there might even increase the diameter of the circle of light they leave behind. If they can create something that sings back of what they discover. But that doesn't always happen and there are no guarantees."

However much I didn't want to see, I knew what those pictures were trying to say. The voice was leading me away. Beyond my dreams and schemes, beyond the flames, beyond the circle of light. Out into the darkness. Something was calling me. The same something that had carried me this far. The same something I had experienced all my life that I was now being asked to follow and to trust. Something that knew me. Something more powerful than myself. Something more mysterious and more elusive and truer than the prolonged and empty thoughts of youth.

CHAPTER 28

MOON

At the very beginning of that journey into the unknown, I spent a few months lying on my bed witnessing a kaleidoscope of Strangelove in my head. If nothing else, failure gives you time to think and I gradually came to accept that the band had always been a plane that was going down. But walking out of the flames, I also had to face the fact that on getting sober, I'd tried to grab the controls and fly us out of that tailspin and up over the peaks only to steer us smack into the side of the mountain instead.

Apsley Road was a spacious apartment on the top floor of a handsome Victorian House and decorated with wallpaper of such a sombre shade of purple that you couldn't see clearly into the upper reaches of the rooms. Unbeknownst to me, the previous summer a rabble of red admiral butterflies had flown in through an open window and landed just above the ceiling rail in the bedroom. 30 or so of their brittle black corpses remaining clotted high up on the wall. For a while after the band split, I slept night after night with mummified butterflies above my head without ever noticing it.

The first winter when I turned the heating on, one of them came winging back to life. Fluttering around my Christmas candle before spinning out of control to fall down dead on the dark-green carpet. That's how I'd first discovered their presence and eventually decided to leave them up there as some kind of silent paean to transformation.

While gradually becoming accustomed to a far quieter life, one morning I received a postcard from the rest of the band, who'd stayed together for a while, hiring themselves out as a backing band for record company singer/songwriters.

'Fuck You Patrick. Love from Paris!'

They'd all signed it and also written Ha! Ha! Ha! Ha! many times in an ever-decreasing spiral. We'd had no contact through this intervening period and it wasn't till a long while later I discovered from Alex they'd never written or sent that card.

Someone else had forged their signatures and either knew or had tracked down my address.

1998 was a strange time. Getting used to not being the singer in Strangelove was more uncomfortable than I could ever possibly have imagined, recognising the mistakes I'd made and having to soak them up alone in silence. What was I now, if not a rock singer in a band? Despite the vision I'd experienced on the Downs, for a long while no clear answer materialised.

****

Almost a year later, the phone was ringing again.

I'd had to vacate Apsley Road and move to another flat on housing benefit. This time near the suspension bridge in Clifton Village. At the end of a long and windowless communal corridor leading from a street door were two cramped rooms. One a kitchen and the other a bedroom (with a tiny en suite bathroom) connected by a spiral staircase and squeezed in behind a bridal gown shop. You could barely swing a cockroach in there.

One small window in each room looked out onto a brick wall about a foot away. As a result, it was dark and we lit the place with candles because the spot lighting, which you couldn't dim, was so penetrating that it was like being interviewed by the East German police. I was living there with my new girlfriend, Stephanie from Leipzig, whom I'd previously met when Strangelove were touring. Thinking back, this probably wasn't the glamorous lifestyle she might have imagined after approaching me backstage in Switzerland a year or so earlier.

Stephanie was cat-like slender, tall, and in her 20s. Peering out through light brown eyes full of wonder. Clever, sensitive and elegant, she dressed in black and walked slowly like a model. When we mooched along the street together, I often witnessed other men gawking at her, which she was completely oblivious to through years of having become accustomed to it.

She didn't understand why I was struggling so much with self-confidence and self-esteem. She loved me and thought I was great and regularly said so. In her mind, it was all so simple and in my own way I loved her too and knew beyond doubt that I was blessed by her presence. But I wasn't in a place within myself to be able to appreciate her in the way any other sane man would have. So lost was I in the puzzle house of my recently-restored poverty.

I still couldn't face even glancing at the music papers and purposely avoided newsagents and anyone who talked about bands. Pulling Stephanie away from the magazines she liked to peruse in WH Smiths. Thom Yorke's eyes followed me around from the front covers wherever we went. I couldn't think straight. My world suddenly emptying out into this domestic never-never land was confusing and with no idea of how to begin again I was trying to turn my back in the other direction.

"Honeyz!"

she called to me, up the spiral staircase in her German singsong.

"Zer is a guy on zee phone for youz. He sayz hiz name izt Donz."

As was often the case, I was upstairs worrying away about the spots that had continued to appear on my face with gruesome regularity since giving up drugs. Staring at myself in the warm, golden reflection on the back of her metallic pencil case. The phone hardly ever rang these days.

"What?" I retorted.

"Donz Jenkinz," she insisted.

"Don Jenkins," I mumbled to myself, absentmindedly correcting her pronunciation.

Down the staircase I flew. Without touching the stairs once with my feet. Hands sliding down the white metal handrails and simultaneously supporting the weight of my body. Zoom. This at least I was a success in and had it down to one impressively smooth and fluid motion. Completely instinctive. Now, if there was a Mercury Prize for speedily descending small spiral staircases …

Whoosh!

"Hi, Don?"

"Look man…" There was a slight pause as I sensed him collecting his words. But he soon cut to the chase. Don never did polite chit chat, not even that first time.

"Look man, I'm not being funny or anything, but basically what the fuck are you up to?"

"What do you mean, Don?"

"Why aren't you doing music? I've been asking around. No one knows where you are. You never go out. You never go to gigs. What are you doing with yourself?"

"I don't know. I'm writing songs, man," I lied in my defence.

"Well, that sounds promising. What are they like?"

"Ughhh. I dunno."

"Look, man. Can you get down to Park Street? I want to meet you."

"Yeah, I suppose. OK, man," I said before I could stop myself.

I didn't know Don that well to be honest. He was just another one of the faces in a long line-up of the Bristol music scene. The very same lot who I'd been trying to avoid. I'd heard people say he was a crazy bastard (a sort of compliment when used by a musician to describe another musician) and an even more intense drummer. He was also a mate of Alex's and as a result of that, his old band Moorhaven had supported us a couple of times a few years previously. All those combinations spinning through my head were just about enough to get me to agree. That and the fact I had absolutely nothing else on.

****

We convened a few days later in a coffee shop and once again he launched in, immediately.

"Look, Patrick. There's no other way of saying this. I want to be in a band with you."

"OK?" I replied, looking up briefly to catch his eye.

Don was staring straight back from under a dark-haired fringe. He was handsome and unhealthy looking, in a Mediterranean kind of way. With olive skin, brown moles on his face, and dark rings under his eyes. Despite the fact that underneath it all he was actually Welsh.

Accepting my somewhat uncertain response, he presented me with a large book of glossy photographs, which he pulled out from a black bag underneath the table.

The photographs were black and white. Stark images taken of the post-punk scene in Britain around 1979. While I turned through, Don waxed lyrical about PIL, Siouxsie, Magazine, Joy Division and Wire. He handed me a home-made mix cassette saying he wanted to form a band inspired by this kind of music and wanted me to be the lead singer and songwriter. He said he'd found an amazing young guitarist called Jimmy (who no one knew about) and that we could easily find some "fucking bassist". The songs were going to be short and full of energy and catchy and we'd be clean shaven. This was early 1999 and a good few years before The Strokes and all that scene and whilst he talked Don's eyes grew full of wildfire. Looking back, he was undoubtedly channelling something already in the air that hadn't found its full expression yet.

It was Dave Francolini all over again and despite everything I'd just been through I was a fully paid-up believer within minutes.

Don was complimentary about the Strangelove gigs he'd seen and said there was no one else 'he' knew who could do it. In truth, it was a tonic to be on the receiving end of all this froth having been exclusively listening to myself on the demise of Strangelove for far too long. Even though Stephanie was regularly trying to boost me, I secretly believed that she was just biased because of her love.

****

I showed Stephanie the photographs and that same day we wandered the second-hand shops to arrive at our own version. We'd sorted the outfit before the band had even played a note. An array of skinny ties and a skinny grey suit jacket and some born skinny drainpipes that went out a bit at the bottom because I couldn't quite let go of the flares. I also found a big plastic silver badge that said SHERIFF on it. On arriving home for the final fashion show of everything together, she remained unsure. So next was a purple shirt from her side of the clothes rail we shared. Annoying to have to stand there. Like some horrible band photo session, but this was my girlfriend and she didn't even have a camera.

We also didn't have a mirror in the flat (hence the pencil case) and all I could get out of her was umming and ahhing as I waited for her verdict to fall upon me like a new wave sword of Damocles.

"Bloody hell, Stephie. What?"

After having me spin round a few times in the narrow kitchen.

"Do I really have to do that again?"

"Yez honeyz, youz do."

She started laughing and enunciated in her best Nico voice,

"Youz look amazzzing, darlingz."

We'd been shopping for less than an hour.

****

Jimmy was as good as Don had promised. Sporting a big, old brown semi acoustic and playing out of a youthful swagger but combining it with razor-cool economy. When he wasn't plugged in, he was modest and calm and we were comfortable around each other from the start. Jimmy owned an expensive bottle of champagne that his mum had gifted to him on his 18th birthday. Quietly asserting that he was only going to open that bottle after he'd signed a major record deal. Like Don, Jimmy had his eyes fixed on the only prize we knew back then for musicians. The champagne bottle glistened in the sunshine of his window. A talisman that emanated pure green destiny. It felt such a blessing to have become part of something which appeared so utterly clear. Jimmy also began wearing the thin ties and the new wave gear and dyed his hair gold.

We started rehearsals. Kindly, Andy Ross from Food Records funded the whole thing for us and we played together three or four times a week for eight hours at a time. Jimmy had found us a bassist. His real name was Simon but I couldn't be sure about him at first because he was about seven feet tall and I thought that might make the rest of us look short on stage. He also had an uncanny resemblance to the mass murderer Fred West.

Once you got to know him though he was actually just a friendly, down-to-earth guy and I became drawn into agreeing with Jimmy. Simon was content playing simple lines without complaining or trying to put in extra bits that we didn't need for the kind of band we'd envisaged. After a few more rehearsals, we both felt sure it couldn't be anybody else and Don finally agreed too. Suede had Matt who was about 10-foot tall for fuck's sake, and as we pointed out to him, Don was sat down anyway.

We were going flat out. Writing our first songs and then combing back through every section over and over again. Don channelled a potent intent and his single-hearted pursuit of perfection was almost alarming at times. Weeks in, if Simon made even the smallest mistake or hesitation on the bass Don would spit at him from behind the drum kit. That Fred West face cringing and hoping he'd gotten away with it whilst every eye was instinctively drawn to his side of the room to see the streams of white spittle that were already flying a split second before you could even look. I had to turn away at times to hide the nervous laughter but luckily Jimmy and myself never messed up because all we did was live and breathe the band and it wasn't long till it was exactly the same with Simon.

Don was like some kind of a tsunami. A force of nature and inspiring to make music with. One afternoon, as the conviction began to get out of control, we all cut ourselves with a steel blade from the kitchen in our rehearsal rooms and did blood-brothers.

Stephanie would occasionally wander in too and lie on the big black sofa sucking lollipops. Occasionally opening her eyes to say.

"I love zis muzic, boyz. Great drummingz, Donz. Great riffingz, Jimmyz."

It was obvious to me that everybody fancied her and this could be kind of infuriating, even though as she correctly pointed out it wasn't exactly her fault.

****

We composed a lot of the songs with Don playing rhythms and building up from there. He came up with catchy, hooky drumbeats. We'd jam over the top and then later that night I'd turn those jams into songs or write new ones in the style that was emerging from them. Scouse Norm and Big Merv, the people who ran the rehearsal rooms, loitered in to hang out with us because they were getting into our music through the walls. That seemingly small gesture seemed like a massive sign and the talk afterwards was always about the big time.

Don would rouse us all into a kind of frenzy with his furious rhetoric and we'd often be cheering and laughing as we floated out into the cold nights. There was a ruthless purple flare around everything. We recorded some demos at Moles Studio with Paul Corkett. Wrote a whole set of songs at breakneck speed and played our first Bristol show at the Fleece to a large audience. Afterwards, my best friend Rich B said we were so ridiculously tight that it seemed almost rude to applaud.

We also invited Vicky in on keyboards. She was playing in a young stoner band who practised in a smaller rehearsal room along from us. This was another shrewd move from Don because she was an intuitive musician and a songwriter in her own right and gave the band an expanded, more early 80s sound. Vicky had powder-blonde hair, pale skin, and smoky eye liner. She was melancholic and sexy and looked dead cool on stage.

We played on the main stage at Bristol's Ashton Court Festival and got in trouble for smashing up the monitors and stands. On finishing our set, the crowd were cheering for an encore but our time was up. So, we carried on anyway and they pulled the power on us. After the band had flounced off, I stood there, fronting it out, refusing to leave the stage for about five minutes whilst the compere tried to slag me off as an example to young aspirants everywhere of what you must never do if you want to get on in music. Whilst the crowd hurled abuse back at the compere. It was an unsettling, exciting, out-of-control moment.

Once I'd simmered down, just long enough to actually think, I realised I didn't know how to end this stand off without it looking like a defeat. A moment of punk inspiration struck and I disconnected my microphone and lobbed it high out into the crowd. Walking off through the festival cheers into a torrent of abuse from the organisers and more rowdy cheering from the rest of the band and our friends backstage. As a result of Don's uncompromising vision, we were channelling increasingly intoxicating Fuck You energy. Later on at home, I got all nervous and embarrassed and self-deprecating and Stephanie had to reassure me many times in her slow drawl.

"Listen, it doesn't matter if your parentz find out, honeyz. You are 33 yearz of age for heavenz zake, and maybe zee other bands after you didn't even care. And if theyz did, well so whatz. And who cares about organisers anywayz, honeyz. Don't you know that theze organisers are the ones who fucked up zis world anyway."

****

We taped our rehearsals in a rough way using a portable cassette recorder in the corner of the room. Poor quality distorted blasts of the songs that were really just reminders. But Don would stay up all night long listening to them. Becoming increasingly convinced of their genius as the small hours crept by. Over the years, he'd managed to get the telephone numbers of many of the major players in the music business and hypnotised by these tapes he'd call them up, yelling down the phone to anyone who picked up.

"Wake up and listen to this. This is Patrick Duff's new band Moon. We are going to be the biggest thing since the fucking Pistols"

****

It was time to go to London.

I still had contacts through Cerne and Andy Ross at Food and all the cool people I knew at Parlophone. They did a great job booking us Dingwalls in Camden and promoting the night so that it was rammed. On Cerne's suggestion, we gave away 100 vinyl singles, featuring a couple of our demos and Andy generously paid for that too. There was continuing interest from Strangelove fans, as well as a kind of speculative industry presence. *NME* and *Melody Maker* were around to review the concert as well as many other suspects from the 90s music scene.

The short, punchy gig was charged with nervous angst and furore as we tore through our set of hastily written minimalist songs. There was a lot of upbeat, babbling talk backstage afterwards. Plenty of good-natured faces from my past crowding into the dressing room. On the way home in the van, Merv floored the pedal and we drove back to Bristol listening to *Never Mind The Bollocks* and *Unknown Pleasures*.

It took me days to come down. I remember walking around the streets of Cotham feeling jittery and high. Jimmy got recognised in the launderette and it was the first time he'd ever had to sign an autograph. He was freaking out. Going on and on about it, far too often, repeating how much he'd hated the experience. It seemed to me like there were good omens like that coming from all directions. People phoning Don and saying how much they'd enjoyed the gig. He was regularly on the blower relaying every scrap of good news to me.

"So, say that again, Don. He said what?"

I never got tired of listening, making him tell me the exact same things a hundred times over just for the buzz. Never weary of hearing what Don thought it might 'mean' either. He had an astute business head on his shoulders and I loved to be mesmerised by his never-ending, ever-changing speculations that in all honesty, despite the thrill, made no real 'sense' to me whatsoever.

****

We were pretty sure the reviews would come out the following week. As anyone who has experienced this dubious honour will tell you, the expectation is both nerve-wracking and exciting. Walking into Kingsdown newsagents and then down St Michael's Hill with the *Melody Maker* and the *NME* fluttering in my hands and my stomach turning somersaults. Maybe I was going to be somebody again. Opening the *Melody Maker*. Hands tearing through pages trying to find it. We'd spent close to a year of our lives working and working and giving it everything.

'Oh my God. There it is.'

Melody Maker: Reviews

Moon: Dingwalls

'Patrick Duff is either back on drugs and if so, he needs to get off them, or he is still off drugs and if so, he needs to get back on them.'

Those opening lines went through my solar plexus like a steel lance. Back out and back into my heart as I read on. Electricity streamed up into my throat and down into my fingers and back up into my skull and dissolved into white nothing. I came round lying outside St Michael's on the Mount collapsed on the paving stones by some steel railings. It had been on and off drizzling all that morning and the ground was cold and wet.

The severity of that opening line and the review that followed had shocked and disturbed me to such an extent that I'd fainted. Broadsheets tangled up all over me struggling to escape in the wind and the remainder of them blowing away down the street into the road and caught up on the fronts of vehicles.

The *NME* was no better and the white heat of my life turned blue.

****

We met back at the rehearsal rooms a few days later. Don said we were fucked. This wasn't like when Strangelove suffered a bad review. Despite blood-brothers, Moon simply hadn't grown the roots to withstand such an attack.

Don came back outside where the rest of us stood skulking in the car park. I couldn't face playing. In fact, I couldn't face even looking at them anymore, after all the effort we'd put in.

"I've wiped my arse on 'em," he said.

And indeed, it was true. He threw the shit-stained reviews down in front of us, got out his zippo and burnt each of the papers in their entirety. Throwing page after page on to the flames. We watched our dreams go up in black and white smoke and that was the end of Moon.

We never rehearsed or played a gig again.

A few months later, Jimmy ended up drinking his champagne coming home pissed from the pub on some nondescript Wednesday night. I bumped into him a few years later walking home from his day job on a sunny evening. He'd lost his gold hair and was married with two kids. He smiled a gentle, happy, tired smile. Don started up a company to promote bands online and within a couple of years was employing 30 staff with posh offices in Clifton and driving around in a brand-new BMW. He eventually ended up managing The Damned and does so to this day. Simon disappeared into the long night and Stephanie left too. She'd found a job as an air hostess. Got married to an airline pilot and moved away to Brazil.

There was no more Strangelove and no more Moon. No more gigs and no more reviews. No more money and no more attention. No more drugs and no more booze to kill the pain or fuel some fierce determination to win again. No more Stephanie either. But I'd stayed clean and sober through it all. That was all I had left now. Sobriety. Rayner and sobriety.

Without knowing it at the time, it was only then that I was able to start walking out into that darkness I'd experienced on the Downs.

CHAPTER 29

GALLOWS CROSS

Towards the end of 1999, I began to rent a single room in a vicarage near the centre of Bristol, arriving soaked to the skin with guitars and suitcases in the cold November rain. The landlord and sole occupier of this house was the Reverend Neville Boundy, vicar of Cotham Parish Church. As the millennium wound down, he found himself in his mid 60s after a lifetime as a priest, seeing out the final year of his official working life before retirement from the Anglican church.

Neville was tall and thin with a wide, smiling face, unruly white hair, and he usually wore a threadbare, rainbow-coloured jumper with his dog collar popping out over the sagging crew neck. He was a natural non-conformist, relaxed and understanding and went out of his way to make me comfortable from the beginning. Regularly repeating world-weary jokes at God's expense as well as his parishioners'. On getting to know him, I came to recognise that beneath those jovial surfaces he was also engaging in the bigger questions which had taken up permanent residence within him, and he was no longer looking for mere answers. Philosophical by inclination, he was enmeshed in politics and current affairs as well as religion and spoke to me at length about humanity's brokenness and its relation to the gospels. After I'd settled in and we'd become accustomed to one another, this cultured politeness remained but he relaxed to a greater degree and I soon came to witness his fiery temper. Meditating in my room one morning when all of a sudden from downstairs the hush of the house was shattered.

"For fuck's sake!"

That first time, my spirit jumped about 10 feet out of my bones.

On the next occasion, a few days later: "Jesus H. Chriiiiiiiist!!!!"
And then towards the end of the week, more succinctly: "Bollocks!!!!!!"

****

There was a short cut from the vicarage to the church next door that saved walking 40 yards along the pavement to the main gate – turn immediately right out the front door; leap up onto a pile of paving slabs; leap again on to the garden wall; jump a gap on to the church wall opposite; go down into a tiny yard; up three steep stone steps and straight in through a backdoor that led into the church hall.

Between the wall of the vicarage and the wall of the adjacent church was an eight foot drop into a cramped disused passageway cluttered with broken masonry. The leap between these walls required a confident bound and Neville, who had already slipped once and broken his hip, still took the risk, even in the rain, a good few times a day. I'd sometimes accompany him on this foolish exercise to help out in the church or hear him speak to his elderly congregation. Sitting as part of these geriatric gatherings and witnessing his grey-haired flock drifting off into cloudland, I would in stark comparison sit there riveted to my seat.

In my estimation, he was clearly expressing the wisdom of a lifetime of decided contemplation and his words afforded me endless insights. He also introduced me to the poet R.S. Thomas, who remains a favourite of mine and unbeknownst to me at that time was the priest who had preached to my mother from the pulpit when she was a girl attending a parish church in Manafon, mid Wales in the 1940s and 50s.

The rooms in our house were dusty and full of old books and framed pictures of actors and dilapidated furniture. Situated on the top of St Michael's Hill. We were living on the exact site of what was once called Gallows Cross, where a few hundred years before, the public hangings in Bristol had taken place in what was then known as Gallows Field.

'James Covey: Stealing from a warehouse, hanged Friday 15th 1737'
'John Price: Stealing from a shop, hanged Friday 8th September 1758'
'Robert Slack: Hanged for horse theft, Friday 9th June 1769'
'William Dillon Sheppard: Hanged for sodomy, Thursday 4th June 1761
- Mr Sheppard behaved very penitent, and with surprising composure and

declared to the spectators he was innocent of the crime for which he was going to suffer.'

In Bristol central library the long lists of these executed souls and the accompanying perfunctory descriptions of their deaths infected my imagination. Following further investigation, I also became intrigued to read that Britain's popular press had originated in the 18th century around public hangings. At these events, which were popular spectacles, unscrupulous hacks and printers would sell leaflets or pamphlets containing the confessions of these condemned men and women, which were often works of complete fiction.

****

Neville had a fiendish enthusiasm for the theatre and our time together also developed into something of a cultural education for me. He was the chaplain at the Bristol Old Vic and continued in that role many years beyond his retirement. There was no other subject he spoke about with more passion and as a result of this devotion to the stage, over the next few years I accompanied him on numerous trips to Stratford-upon-Avon to watch Shakespeare productions. *Hamlet, King Lear, Romeo And Juliet, The Merchant Of Venice, The Tempest* and *Othello*.

Daily meditation had granted me the gift of being able to concentrate to a far greater degree than I'd ever known and much to my surprise I was easily able to follow the unfamiliar Olde English. Sitting in my seat spellbound. After each performance I was eager to take in Nev's expertise and the praise or disdain he expressed in discussing the various merits of the production and the actors. Combined with the encouragement he afforded me I also began to share my own insights and slowly but surely without actually recognising it, I lapsed into the process of being reinvented by life.

****

It was New Year's Eve 1999. The last day of a millennium. Clean for almost four years now, I still hadn't fully established many new relationships and continued to shy away from old friends for the sake of my sobriety. December 31st and I'd absolutely nowhere I wanted to go, having instead planned to tidy my room and stay in, which is what I'd successfully accomplished the previous three Hogmanay. Using it as a day to reflect upon how far I'd come. Retiring to bed early and listening to the drunks singing *Bohemian Rhapsody* and *Last Christmas* in the streets below with a certain satisfaction that 'I' was free.

It was about nine a.m. I was bumbling around, up and down the stairs, from kitchen to bedroom tidying away and sensed Neville unusually conscious of my presence in the house. He had come to witness my manner of living and how few people I actually saw at this particular time but to my relief had always been too tactful to ask questions. However, with a rare day off himself, that morning a natural curiosity suddenly got the better of him.

"My dear boy," he intoned. "Tell me, surely you must have something on today? It's New Year's Eve for God's sake."

"Uhhh. Ummmm. I'm all right," I offered. "It's cool, I'm just going to hang out here. I'm cool, man."

"You're seriously expecting me to believe you're staying in on your own today as well? That's ridiculous. For the whole day? I've never heard such nonsense."

He looked almost irritated with me for the first time,

"Uhhhh."

"My dear boy, you're coming with me."

****

We were soon hurtling along in his clapped-out car to Salisbury Cathedral, where at midday a service was being held in honour of the last day of the millennium. Readings and music.

As a result of Neville's breakneck driving, we arrived early. It was about 11.15 a.m.

"Let's nip over to the Bishop's," he muttered, half to himself.

We drove a little further along the close and pulled up outside a grand old house. Knocking on the wooden door, a housekeeper led us into a light, spacious kitchen. Where seven or eight people were enjoying genteel conversation over breakfast tea in china cups and saucers. Finger sandwiches with the crusts cut off. One of these apparently blessed souls stood slightly apart, leaning on a sideboard, staring out of the window. That was the Bishop and whilst the rest of the company loitered about the food table chortling in posh voices, he seemed to search for something within himself beyond the clouds.

Neville appeared well known to these people and was soon commanding proceedings with non-stop jibes at the expense of the Church of England. The atmosphere in the room was made livelier by his presence, but in my shyness and lack of familiarity with such a situation I backed off and found myself drifting over to the Bishop's side of the kitchen to lean against the wall. Before long though, through his politeness, we'd begun a conversation ourselves.

Having already been introduced by Neville as a musician, the Bishop began by asking me questions about bands and in trying to get the focus off myself, I in return asked him questions about being a Bishop. This tactic worked wonders with most people but not with him because, completely undistracted, he continued to pose his enquiries with what appeared to be a genuine interest. For some intangible reason, we hit it off almost immediately. He listened to all my replies with a considered self-assurance and his eyes appeared full of thought and a peculiar sensitivity. I couldn't put my finger on it but it quickly became apparent that I'd never met anyone quite like him before. In fact, the conversation flowed so naturally between us and Neville's diatribe on the other side of the room was so entertaining that the Bishop's wife suddenly entered with a slight alarm in her voice.

"It's nearly 12 o'clock. For heaven's sake, you'll be late!"

All of us grabbed our coats and were back out the front door in seconds. Half running up to the cathedral across the close. Nervous the ancient clock might begin to strike at any moment. This end of a millennium event was set to commence at midday precisely. Hurrying along the Bishop turned to me,

"Come up the front and sit by me if you like, Patrick."

At the main door of the cathedral, we all paused to gather some sense of decorum. Creeping in but remaining caught up in the rush and moving rather more quickly than if we'd been on time.

It's a long, old walk up the aisle of Salisbury and every seat in the place was occupied. Walking alongside the Bishop, many heads turned to fix their eyes upon us as we hastened to our VIP seats. Surprisingly, this sudden elevation in social position was something of a buzz. Even though it definitely wasn't *Top Of The Pops*, at least it was 'some' kind of attention. Still intent on playing the rockstar and even though we'd left Neville's in a rush, I'd managed a tiny black leather jacket, stick insect flares and platform shoes. Eyeliner, pale foundation over the spots, the merest hint of a dark purplish lipstick, dyed black hair, nervous walk, nervous grin, the pupils of my eyes dilated in self-consciousness. In fact, if you'd pulled a tarot card for this time in my life it would have to be a new one called The Popstar. Every step up the aisle, now briefly turned catwalk, a sacred marriage of bravado and shame.

I imagined I saw many mouths preventing themselves from falling open in the congregation. Registering by their appearance to be Salisbury's finest assortment of old-school establishment families. Whom by their restrained expressions couldn't seem to quite believe what the Bishop was doing with 'that'. You could sense a tiny rustle of surprise spreading through the pews.

****

Safely in my seat beside the Bishop, and relatively anonymous once more, an expectant silence settled down and the cathedral clock began to strike a minute or so later. Midday, New Year's Eve 1999. The end of a millennium. Clang! Silence. Clang! Hundreds all listening together. Time rushing onwards because of us and despite us and brought more fully to our attention by that bell.

Every one of those 12 clangs seemed to be separated by a little stretch of forever. Suddenly, the vulnerability of being human rushed in and collapsed across the entire gathering and my heart rushed out to everyone there and to everyone everywhere. A blue-eyed planet singing a wide-eyed song. The whole assembly hung in stillness. All the way till the end of the retreating wash of that 12th bell. Spinning out of its lingering highs and back into noiselessness. The end of a millennium.

Gravitas held sway for some further intense lingering moments and then, with what appeared to be a slight sigh of relief, the recital was introduced by Michael Mayne, the once Dean of Westminster Cathedral;

followed by Simon Russell Beale announcing the first of T.S. Eliot's Four Quartets.

"Burnt Norton."

Unaware of these poems or indeed of T.S. Eliot before that moment, I was nevertheless captivated from the beginning. In fact, the depth and at the same time the simplicity, subtlety, and economy of those lines are still unfolding in my heart and mind to this day.

In between each of these *Four Quartets*, musicians played passages from Olivier Messiaen's *Quartet For The End of Time*. Written in the captivity of the prisoner of war camp Stalag VIII, it features the only instruments available to the inmates at that time. Clarinet, violin, cello, and piano.

The haunting, transcendental quality of the piece lifted me far out of myself and as each slow round note followed on in *Louange De L'éternite De Jesus*, I was struck by a growing awareness that I'd waited for this moment always. Never had I listened with such rapt attention and comprehension. By the end of that presentation, the combination of Messiaen's music and Eliot's studied inspiration and the manner in which they complimented one another had completely silenced me in my seat. Rarely in my lifetime could I recall having been so profoundly moved by any concert.

Afterwards, I wandered alone into a side chapel confused. Listening to the sound of my own breath. An inner voice whispering,

"You have to change your whole life."

****

I walked back out into the main cathedral searching through the swirl of unfamiliar faces and came across the Bishop who was being treated like some kind of a celebrity. Surrounded by shoals of elderly couples whose enquiries echoed around in the stones reverb. As soon as he saw me, he broke away.

"I'm going to a party across the Green – fancy coming along?" he grinned.

"Yeah, man, definitely. Thanks."

As we walked outside, I was grinning too. It was that excitable, nerve-wracking feeling. Like when you're first starting out and it's the last gig of the tour and you're being asked to the after show by the lead singer from the main band. But in the same moment, my jangling pop star clothes suddenly seemed redundant and I felt almost absurd as the Bishop, Neville, and myself wandered across the expanse of Salisbury Green.

Deeply affected by what we'd just witnessed, I had no idea how to effectively express what I'd experienced or to whom I owed the tremendous sense of gratitude pulsing through my blood.

Later, I discovered that Messiaen had written in the preface to the score of a *Quartet For The End Of Time* that it was inspired by a passage from the *Book Of Revelation.*

'And I saw another mighty angel come down from heaven, clothed with a cloud: and a rainbow was upon his head, and his face was as it were the sun, and his feet as pillars of fire… and he set his right foot upon the sea, and his left foot on the earth… And the angel which I saw stand upon the sea and upon the earth lifted up his hand to heaven, and sware by him that liveth for ever and ever… that there should be time no longer: But in the days of the voice of the seventh angel, when he shall begin to sound, the mystery of God should be finished…'

****

As soon as we entered the party, at the Canon Presenter's House, Nev and the Bishop were swamped. The whole place was zoo'd out again with more pensioners who also wanted to engage the Bishop and were not in any way too embarrassed to totter up and begin. I stood there ignored and at the first opportunity he turned to me once more and said,

"Sorry. Why don't you grab yourself some food, Patrick."

"Yeah, yeah, OK, thanks, man."

****

Even against the loud clamour of exchanges you could still hear Nev making people laugh in a distant room with his bad-taste jokes. But as directed, I walked away through to the dining area and stood in line at the Christmas dinner buffet which was steaming away in bright metal trolleys. Already knowing that there wouldn't be an option and to just go for the vegetables without even asking.

Directly in front of me in this orderly queue was a smartly dressed elderly gentleman in a dark-blue suit. He was a deal shorter than me because in my heels, I was easily able to inspect the top of his head where wisps of white hair stubbornly remained swept across in the old school way. Disguising a bald scalp encrusted with a variety of scabs that looked like a nasty dermatitis of some kind. I also noticed his right hand reaching furtively but at the same time almost absentmindedly towards a stainless-steel chafing dish to his side which was filled with steaming pigs in blankets. Popping the greasy spoil straight into his mouth each time.

This buffet was not self-service and we were expected to pass by the steel dishes and wait till our arrival at the front of the queue where people in chef's outfits and flushed faces were dishing out the dinners. As the queue inched on the old man continued to pilfer from the dish. Having to turn further and further round in my direction to accomplish this as we moved forward in the queue. Eventually, revealing the entire profile of his face as he reached back further for more mouthfuls of pork. I recognised him immediately. It was the former Conservative prime minister Edward Heath.

"Mr Heath," the words jumped out of my mouth.

Turning himself fully around now to look at me directly through two sizzling beady eyes. The skin on his face, a keen, mottled pink.

"Edward Heath," I blurted out his name again. Like I was on one of those game shows for the masses where the questions are dumb-down easy and we'd got to the round where you had to recognise faces.

He continued to size me up with an aloofness of surprising intensity.

"Did you enjoy the event today then, Mr Heath?" I suddenly enquired.

Trying to settle and develop the exchange. Genuinely intrigued by what 'he'd' made of a presentation which had inspired such awe in me.

He paused for a few seconds and appeared deeply irritated.

"It's not a case of enjoyment at an event like that," he eventually boomed. "It's a case of being there."

Morsels of partly masticated pig splattered across my face and the impish grin on my lips vanished. You knew that voice so well but it was peculiar to hear it in all its glory, not coming out of a radio or television set speaker. Even more resonant and somehow more impressive here in the flesh and yet even more perplexing to have become the focus of such a seething contempt. In response to what was for me such an innocent inquiry. Staring back at him without a retort of any kind. The initial tickle at finding myself in the same place, same time, same party as a once prime minister scorched into yet more confusion.

With the bad vibes still crackling between us, he turned on his heel and the conversation was over. He did not reach back for any more pigs in blankets.

'What?' I thought to myself, baffled.

I found Nev and asked if we could leave. I didn't bother having a New Year's Eve dinner or even saying goodbye to the Bishop, who I never saw again. As we stood by the front door searching for Nev's coat, I turned back briefly and looked towards the dining room.

"I just met Edward Heath," I said. "He's horrible."

Nev paused too and looking back into the room himself said in hushed tones through the side of his mouth,

"Oh, Edward Heath," rolling his eyes at me in mock exaggeration. "He's an awful man, a truly awful man."

****

I'd pretty much forgotten about Ted. It was a few years later and we were on holiday. My dad's side of the family had organised a reunion. Something that had never occurred before in the history of The Duffs. We were in a damp, coniferous glade in the New Forest where you could rent a caravan for the weekend. There were hundreds of these caravans and chalets nestled in the shadows around a clearing where the entertainment took place inside two long, wooden huts in a mock Scandinavian style. One of these downtrodden looking buildings was full of fruit machines and video games and the other boasted a bar that catered for a sizable, scuzzy carpeted interior of tables and chairs – reminiscent in decor and character to a rugby club from the 70s, or Lakeside where they do the darts, and reminding me of the places we used to be taken as kids. Where we watched my dad get drunk in the distance on weekends whilst we sat at small, round tables guzzling bottles of Coke and salt and vinegar crisps that took the lining off the roof of your mouth.

All my uncles and aunts and cousins had turned up and the proceedings soon turned into a big, old Catholic/lapsed-Catholic piss-up. They stayed in the bar from late afternoon onwards; dribbling back to the caravans at closing time for more drinks and seasick Irish sing-songs that could suddenly turn into fiery confrontations. Resentments and grievances that had bubbled under the surface for decades, washed up on the tides of whiskey, which once back on dry land the next morning were swept aside and not mentioned further. Until the wee bobbing hours of the following night.

****

After a few days, I needed respite. When you aren't drinking, and other people are drinking around you for days on end, there comes a time when you need to collect yourself. But in truth, I didn't seem to be able to recognise exactly when that time was for myself. Fortunately, Mum picked up on it on my behalf and over breakfast suggested that I should take a bus into Salisbury and not worry about being involved with any family activities that day.

It must have been getting to me more than I'd realised because after agreeing I moped off like some overgrown teenager who still believes it is his divine right to be chauffeured around in a car. The bus stop which she had insisted was just around the corner turned out to be about an hour's walk from the caravan park. The following stomp through the drizzle left plenty of time for some seriously self-indulgent black sheep sulking; conveniently brushing aside that it was me and only me who still hadn't learnt how to drive.

****

When the bus finally rumbled into Salisbury, I decided to visit the cathedral in search of some much-needed perspective. I still hadn't put two and two together - as for some reason, it had slipped my mind that this was the same cathedral I'd attended for the millennium a couple of years previously. It was a warm summer's day and passing in through the door at the south transept, I was immediately hit by that familiar hush of stones. Conscious of the sweat on my brow as it cooled and I stepped past a number of railed side chapels to my right-hand side. Graffiti on the walls and tombs that whispered back to mediaeval times.

I continued to wander into the main part of the cathedral where the ceiling began to open out into its full majesty but it wasn't long till I found myself rooted to the spot. Life has given us a sixth sense and since I'd stopped drinking that sixth sense had been flourishing within me and gathering in sensitivity. Without explanation, a gentle intensity began to spread over my body and my heart started to speed up and my skin began to prickle. I knew about all this by now and recognised that 'something' was happening.

"What's going on?"

I asked that question to myself like some kind of a mantra, as my eyes searched in vain across the vault of the vast ceiling and then into each of the stained glass windows. What was it? I couldn't move. I couldn't take another step. Breathing in the cool stillness. I waited patiently, eventually with my eyes closed, but no realisation arrived in words or pictures. I was left with only swirls of intuition. Some kind of mystery that seemed to be nailing me to the ground.

On opening my eyes again, I aimlessly looked down at my feet to recognise that I was standing on a grave.

EDWARD

HEATH

KG   MBE

Statesman

Musician

&

Sailor

MEMBER   of   PARLIAMENT

1950   -   2001

PRIME   MINISTER

1970   -   1974

REQVIESCAT   IN   PACE

I had no idea that Ted was dead or that he was buried here and those stone words immediately sent a shock through my nervous system. I'd been standing directly over him for a number of minutes. Exactly where he lay was the exact spot where I'd been forced to come to a halt and before I could engage in any way with the faculty of reason, two impressions flashed across my mind like bolts of lightning.

'Last time I saw you, you were spitting pigs' blankets in my face and now you're dead and I'm alive and I'm standing on your grave.'

And:

'People like you are on the way out and people like me are on the way in.'

****

Around the summer of 2000, Nev retired and moved out of the vicarage, leaving me there alone for a few more months to work out what to do next. On departing, he'd said it would be cool to live rent-free for a while but just a couple of weeks later there was a knock at the door. The church warden stood there with various members of the congregation and they lost no time in stripping the place bare. There and then. Every single article of furniture, all the beds and all the carpets were gone. I slept on an old mattress now and despite what Nev had promised the church expected me to pay rent at an increased rate. Luckily, Jimmy moved in to help me out and took an upstairs bedroom at the front of the house. However, it wasn't long before he began to complain of shuffling noises coming from the room below him at night and late one evening, a couple of weeks afterwards, he called me into his bedroom.

We stood on the bare floorboards listening to a series of distinct bumps that were emanating from the equally empty room downstairs. Jimmy remained pale and frowning and after every one of these thumps his face twitched and he looked directly at me as if to say, 'I told you. I told you.' Having previously experienced such things, I'd never imagined he was lying and on the contrary was filled with only a relaxed curiosity (verging on bluster) that soon had me nonchalantly strolling down to investigate.

"I'm not freaked out," I called back to Jimmy. "I'll go and see what it is. No worries, man."

The bumps continued as I descended the staircase, growing only louder as I reached the downstairs hallway. My heart was beginning to beat a little faster now and at first I opened the door slowly with just enough space to feel for the light switch with my fingers – only to discover later that the church people had removed the bulbs and so it remained dark in there. With what sounded like furniture being moved around, despite the fact we already knew it was empty, I stepped inside. Yellow light poured in from the streetlamp outside the window and into the small square lounge, now deadly silent and full of the sense of some disembodied entity. It was the sense of standing in the same room as a huge, black, bristling dog whose territory you'd stumbled into. But there was no dog you could actually see. No barking you could actually hear. Instead, the room continued to smoulder with an increasing sense of malevolence and my eyes hallucinated a kind of swarming mist against the yellowy glow.

It's peculiar how your brain buries all kinds of information below the surface and then delivers it when needed. Because suddenly, out of nowhere, I recalled exactly how my druid friend Adrian Rook had once confided in me that on encountering such a presence the best response was to stand up straight and confront it with a question.

"Are you for the light?"

Adrian said if you asked that question three times and the entity was malevolent then it would have to leave.

"Are you for the light?"

I stood my ground fighting the urge to flee.

"Are you for the light?"

The final time I announced those words, my mouth was dry and my voice had been reduced to somewhat of a whimper such was the surrounding intensity. Adrian must have been right because the terrible animosity did appear to lighten somewhat after that third inquiry, but not enough to stop me from turning my back to slam the door and run upstairs to Jimmy's room. I paced back and forth and we looked at each other.

"This is not OK, man. There's something actually fucking down there."

We were living over Gallows Cross and on reflection it shouldn't have been so surprising an incident. For the second time in my life I'd found myself in a haunted house, but this time with a far darker presence. There was no doubt about it in my mind. Something wanted us out. Jimmy had also sensed that darkness and he wasn't hanging around to find out anymore and left soon afterwards.

Over the next few weeks, there were no more of these visitations, but I eventually left too and went on to live alone. This nomadic existence has continued and to this day I've still never settled in one place for more than a couple of years.

CHAPTER 30

LEIGH WOODS

My next flat was cheap and slightly claustrophobic but in a great location near the edge of a forest outside Bristol called Leigh Woods. Forced to sign on the dole again, throughout this latest period of adjustment my head went round and round with self-rejection and I soon found myself wandering around in those woods on a regular basis. At first simply as an attempt to gain some respite from the sense of failure I was carrying - which always appeared to be made more acute around 'other people'.

Whereas in my previous life I'd mostly walked the streets, where chance encounters were far more likely, I now hid out under the trees. The forest welcomed me with open arms and it was here that a deeper healing began to unfold. I walked in there for hours at a time almost every day for the next two years.

As a result of all this loafing, my morbid preoccupation with the past and worrying about the future appeared to drift away for longer and longer periods of time and I became more present to the surroundings. Not because I'd read about it in a book by Eckhart Tolle. I had not. But more simply as a natural response to the place itself.

Concrete is not alive in the same way as a forest is alive and I'd never fully grasped that before. Unlike the buildings and billboards I had grown up with, the atmosphere of the forest changed more subtly. Every day it came out singing a slightly different song, and slowly but surely I began to appreciate that music more clearly. Just as the atmosphere of the forest changed each day, I eventually came to recognise that at the same time the atmosphere within me was changing each day alongside it. In developing this sensitivity, I became more conscious of those corresponding changes.

Developing a relationship with a landscape that was more fully alive began to wake me up to the subtlety and complexity that life has seeded within my own inner world.

The dappled light flickering through the canopy far above your head and falling in bright pools of leaves at your feet. A stag raising its antlered head further up along the trail as we stood staring back at each other. The birdsong opening up cathedrals inside your ears. In the afternoons, lying in the openings where yew trees had traced dry brownish circles around themselves with their poison needles. The odour of the dead leaves and the damp soil lying with your face to the ground. Bulbous fungi that smelt like underground caves and streams of red ants. Some carried severed leaves back to their nest in one direction whilst others ran out empty handed in the other.

I found myself tearing tangles of poison ivy from the trunks of trees so that they could breathe more easily. Or I found myself carrying heavy mottled stones from out of the shadows and arranging them in bright circles in the sunlight. Sitting on these stones and sinking into the sun rays at the end of the day. At dusk, owls followed the open pathways, flying so silently that you instinctively held your breath. Lighting fires with dry twigs and brambles. Burying dead crows in holes in the ground I'd dug with my own nails. Covering them over with the earth and in my imagination floating their bodies back into the same cool breeze that blew over my face. Picking up a dead holly leaf and pressing the brown spikes into my finger until the blood ran out and spilt over the makeshift grave. Because suddenly, I cared. I cared about life and was letting my own blood because I wanted life to know that I meant it. Under the spell of all this richness I found myself acting out all kinds of these spontaneous rituals inspired by the voices of the forest. Actions that arose from impulses which had no particular reasons but at the same time seemed to pulsate with some deeper dumbstruck wisdom.

I began to write songs for specific places which had become almost sacred to me through these rituals. Places that sustained all manner of restless moods that I had grown to treasure. Bringing my nylon strung guitar and playing till it was dark. Music that no one else ever heard. Gigs where no one came and where there was nothing to be nervous about and where you could do exactly as you pleased. Playing for hours as the trees joined in alongside me and the birds joined in too and you played back to them and they sang back to you and every sound suddenly became a part of the music. Feeling like I was playing the greatest concerts I'd ever played.

Breaking through again and again into the most profound moments of my musical life up till then. Lying on my back in the leaves with the rain seeping through the branches and falling in splashes upon my face. Droplets drumming on the roofs of the broader leafed trees rising and falling, filling the air with avant-garde rhythms that developed on through spiralling movements. A kind of ancient music that was suddenly imminent and that would never play again in the same way.

The rain and the wind knew what they were doing more fully than I ever had, so I followed along. They knew when to whisper of their arrival and they knew when to fall away and they knew when to stop and open up into emptiness for more soft breezes to spring out of nowhere onto your lips. Showing you what music could really be. Sometimes, as these concerts deepened, the forest would start to go wild and get so loud with swishing excitement that it seemed to be breaking at the seams. Promising to sweep you off forever and then trailing away like the end of some great symphony and on into the dumb silence that was always waiting in the end. These moments were my true beginnings as a songwriter.

****

Late at night, the forest was different again. An intense whispering darkness from out of which all kinds of primal fears arose. Fears that I became increasingly determined to conquer. These musings led to a notion that as a challenge to myself I'd walk to a particular yew tree and arrive there at midnight on Halloween. I'd discovered this old tree on one of my daily meanderings and through the proceeding weeks had made the effort to rediscover it, making many attempts to return until I finally knew the way without faltering because it was far off the beaten track. I'd carved my initials into the maroon trunk and the atmosphere standing beneath those branches was one of the deepest and most forlorn expressions of the forest.

With Samhain arriving, I left the road where a last streetlamp shone out the end of the city's neon yellow. It was 11 p.m. and the air was cold and still and clear. Walking slowly into the forest on nerves like tightropes, with my eyes nailed to a path revealing itself only blurred feet ahead at a time. The veils between the worlds are thin at Halloween and the darkness and restlessness primed your body to every rustling sound. With my heart pounding, I'd been walking in for about 10 minutes when through this heightened awareness I discerned the sound of a man muttering to himself further along the dirt track. Stopping for a minute or so, although you couldn't see clearly, something or somebody was most definitely up ahead. Cautiously moving onwards, I eventually made out a crumpled bag of rags slumped down at the side of a tree. You couldn't discern a single feature but, with your eyes accustomed, in the glow of the purple sky he was pale and bearded in a filthy fisherman's coat. A collapsed heap of bones. Closer now, I could smell the alcohol as his mumbling grainy incantations passed through my body and I stopped before him.

"What are you doing out here, man?"

The old man's grumbling stopped for a few long seconds.

"Talking to the trees," he grizzled.

"Talking to the trees," I repeated. "OK, man. OK."

On I walked, hardly able to draw a breath. On through the darkness, deeper into the trees, trying to reason with myself to resist breaking into a run and further expose my panic. Stumbling on for 15 minutes more with no relief from its physical tyranny. With the whole black forest trapped in my throat, I suddenly disturbed a huge gathering of roosting crows. All at once sending them up into the night. Miles from anywhere, the lament of their cawing haunted me to the core of my being. The terrible frenzy of their cries circling through my bloodstream and their flapping wings dragging the sky down upon my head.

I was still breathing heavily by the time I reached the old yew. A colossal specimen with a great gnarled trunk and knotted arms. I lit a thin white candle and secured it in dripping wax to one of the lower horizontal branches. Daddy longlegs and moths sizzled and fiddled around the flame and its glow cast my body in a flickering circle of light that glimmered across the dry needles scattered over the ground. Bringing a candle to this place on such a cold clear night and seeing my own shadow in the circle of light suddenly lifted the oppression and I was able to breathe freely again. Halloween and the presence of the dead of my own family around me. The ancestors who'd gone before and whose lives had informed mine. They were alive once more and had called me here and there was a palpable sense of their presence. It was midnight and in the middle of the dark forest, a startling love began to pour into my awareness. A love that seemed to hold dominion over the dead and over the generations of fear.

After an hour or so, I slowly walked away. Most of the other trees had shed their leaves and you could still see the candle shining out through the forest from hundreds of metres away. There was such a sense of elation in witnessing that light. Knowing what it had taken within me to set it there. My ancestors seemed to remain behind for a while longer, waiting in the candlelight as I returned along the path towards the tree where the old man had slumped only hours before. Striding on through the blackness with a growing assurance. On reaching the place, there was no sign of him. The candle blazed on through the trees and the madman was gone.

Me and my sister Catherine bought suits from charity shops and we cut the bottoms off the legs.

(picture Gavin Evans)

'Too nervous to look up I stood, hands behind my back, and head down into the microphone'.
(picture Gavin Evans).

'Would my hands and voice really stop shaking once we got on, like they'd all promised?'

Alex was often a source of strength to me. (Picture Sébastien Bepoix)

Patrick, 1994. (picture Phil Nicholls)

My sister Catherine also cut my hair. (Picture Sébastien Bepoix)

THE BIG ISSUE

COMING UP FROM THE STREETS

JULY 21 – 27 1997 No.242

STRANGELOVE

EXCLUSIVE INTERVIEW WITH PATRICK DUFF

At the hideout. Brecon Beacons 1995.

Nick Powell became the sixth member of Strangelove around the time of *Love And Other Demons* in 1996. From left: Joe, Patrick, John, Nick, Jazz, Alex.

Backstage in Paris with Adrian Utley before our gig together.

Rayner Jesson: 'I am always there…'

Our manager Cerne Canning with road manager Gary The Geezer in the background.

Jonny Greenwood, Thom Yorke, Janet Jackson.

Moon, 1998. From left: Don, Simon, Patrick, Jimmy.

Patrick with Adam Coombes.

Madosini. (Gallo Images / Getty).

On Table View Beach with Vuyo, Madosini and the 'black feathers of a king'. (picture Rouvanne).

In the Healer's shack. From left: Rasta, Vuyo and Tera.

Yoneli and Yolanda on top of Table Mountain.

WOMAD Festival, Reading. The first day I saw Madosini. (picture Pete Trill)

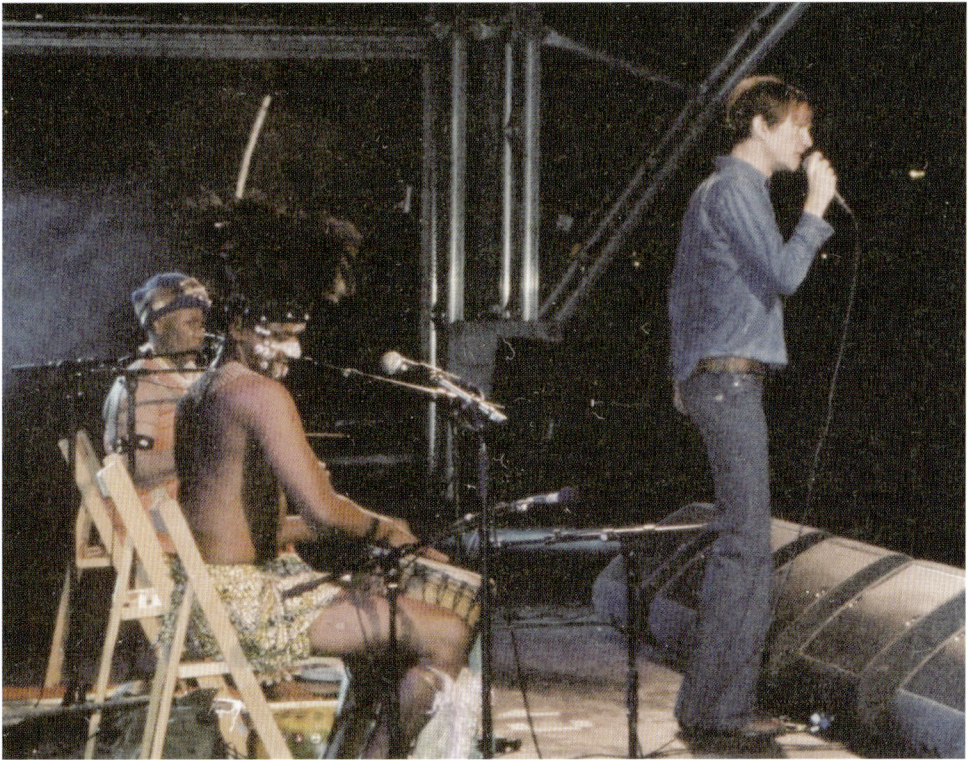

With Madosini and Vuyo in the Canary Islands.

CHAPTER 31

THE GIN PALACE

'Be patient towards all that is unsolved in your heart and try to love the questions themselves, like locked rooms and like books that are now written in a very foreign tongue. Do not now seek answers, which cannot be given you because you would not be able to live them. And the point is, to live everything. Live the questions now. Perhaps you will then gradually, without noticing it, live along some distant day into the answer.'
Rainer Maria Rilke.

After a couple of years of drifting around in Leigh Woods, the wonder I experienced as a result arose from within me almost continually. Leaving the forest paths behind every two weeks to sign on at the Jobseekers Allowance Office in Nelson Street was becoming more and more disconcerting. The sensation of where I ended and where the world began was now way beyond the boundary of my skin and whilst this out of body sensation was uplifting when wandering under the trees, on edging along Bristol's pavements, every car was driving through me.

The noise, fumes, and particular chaos of the city, which I'd once relished, started to strike me as alarming, and the sight of the many faces who appeared so troubled was equally unsettling. In fact, those strangers appeared to correspond with a sense of some open wound in my own psyche. Because on returning to the forest for days afterwards I would clearly see their faces again – arising in my mind and presenting themselves to me over and over like a Rubik's Cube I had no idea how to master.

As chance would have it, one sunny Wednesday morning dole day I bumped into Big Merv at the bottom of Park Street.

"Fucking Hell! Patrick, me babber! You're not dead then!" he joshed in his best, boisterous Bristolian.

"Woah, Merv! Hey, man!"

"Fucking hell! Well, well, well!" he cooed as the vehicles continued to zoom by a mere few feet away from us.

Merv worked at the studio in Bedminster where both Strangelove and Moon had rehearsed and after Strangelove's split he'd managed some solo shows for me. However, on our return from London, Merv had disappeared off with the proceeds, and although he always swore blind to me he'd lost the money, it remained something of a testimony to what a good bloke I considered him to be that despite the fact I knew he was lying, it made absolutely no difference to our friendship.

"I haven't seen you for ages," he challenged, opening his arms.

Drinking was having an effect on Merv. It was before opening time and he left a streak of sweat down the side of my face from the withdrawals. Whilst in the hug you could sense the trembling deep down in his body as it tried to deal with the colossal sweltering he was giving himself. As if his internal organs were trying to communicate with me. Pleading with me to talk some sense into him.

"Why aren't you doing any gigs then?" he scoffed instead. "Come on and play at the Gin Palace. I'm the manager down there now and we're doing acoustic gigs. Come on, for fuck's sake," he insisted. "You need to play. People still want to hear you. What are you doing? Think you're too good for us, do you?"

Because he prized himself as a cynical pub-drinking alchie, I'd always listened to Merv's encouraging words far more than I might otherwise have – and in that moment despite everything I'd told myself about performing in public, I found that there was still some part of me that just couldn't resist.

"Yeah. OK, man. Thanks, Merv. Let's do it."

He pulled a piece of paper from beneath a nearby car windscreen wiper. A glossy unappetising advert for various cut-price pizzas. He tore it in half and scrawled a date on the blank side and then disappeared up off the road with a sheepish grin.

Over the next few months, I was to grow intimately familiar with the wobbly brag of his handwriting. Because I must have looked at that date a hundred times wandering around in the trees as it slowly began to dawn on me. I hadn't played in front of 'people' for almost two years.

****

One evening a few weeks later, I had an occasion to stroll into central Bristol again. Brown's cafe bar at the top of Park Street. Arriving early for that meeting my ears were drawn to the piano playing and on searching for the culprit, I saw a tall young man in a suit with messy brown hair. Long fingers that twinkled up and down the ivories. A Beck number. *Tropicalia* off *Mutations*. He was turning the song upside down on its head for his own amusement and the skill he possessed in being able to bend and stretch the melody soon had me smiling and tapping my feet along. Musing about what to do for Merv's gig, I suddenly swallowed my more usual pride and walked up to him outside on his next fag break.

"Hey, man. Do you want to do a gig?"

His face looked uncertain.

"Because of the Beck thing," I continued,

"Patrick," I offered my hand.

"Adam," he looked briefly into my eyes and then just as quickly turned away.

"OK, man. Yeah, why not?" chuckling to himself.

"It's gonna be pretty chilled out though," I warned, and he laughed again. Louder this time.

That was it. A few days later we started rehearsals down at his flat in Stokes Croft.

****

Adam Coombes was about 20 years of age and lived in part of an abandoned building in Stokes Croft where he acted as a sitting caretaker. As a result, he paid next to nothing in rent and was able to survive by playing piano in restaurants and bars. His dark rooms were filled with dilapidated instruments from second-hand shops. An out of tune piano he'd 'rescued from outside someone's house'. Busted-up trombones and saxophones and even an old tuba. Fucked up electric guitars he was in the process of sanding down. Basses with wires hanging out of them that nevertheless wobbled through similarly destroyed amplifiers that hissed and crackled and spat away. Through the laughter we both testified to loving the distress of these sounds and immediately clicked over it. There were zithers and plinky plonk kids style xylophones and melodicas too. All of which he'd taught himself to play to a maverick standard.

Every time he picked up one of these instruments, he'd spontaneously go into a self-composed number that usually started out with a melancholic air and then developed into something way too complicated for the instrument's decrepitude; eventually messing it up and bursting out laughing again. When you walked between the rooms there were drowsy rats in the process of dying from the poison he'd put down, who couldn't even get it together to scarper.

We rehearsed there twice a week till the concert.

****

Around this time, I also began to experience intense, vivid dreams on an almost nightly basis. The various atmospheres expressed in them were so unfamiliar to me that I imagined they must be pointing towards some kind of inner transformation. In one of these dreams, I found myself face-to-face with a pale girl of about 13 years of age with blonde hair in plaits. She stood staring at me through blue eyes and despite her youthful appearance was able to read my insecurities to the point where I grew increasingly puzzled. Yet at the same time it gradually became clear she held no judgement over me – and didn't appear to want anything either – and instead just continued to look into my eyes with an extraordinary sense of her own inner peace.

Even in the dream, I recognised how rare it is to be seen. To be loved and accepted because of who you are and not despite who you are. Her face was only a few feet away and she stood on a red road that ran away behind her. A red road that wound through an entirely black and objectless landscape to the sides of a large black mountain on the horizon. The whole scene played itself out under a red sky which was the same colour as the red road. In fact, apart from the girl, everything else in the dream was either red or black.

I listened as she spoke out five verses still staring into my eyes – and on awakening I immediately had the sense to scrawl them down in a mad flourish. Those words of hers went on to become…

SONG TO AMERICA

Every man has a song he is singing or a song he is trying to sing,
But the man who has chosen to sing his own song is the man who will sing like a king,
For he don't dance to the tune of another or call the tune of another his hymn,
And he's not about to crawl to the pilgrim but the pilgrim is about to crawl to him.

Every man has a place he is leaving and a place he is trying to go,
But the man who has chosen to take his own place at the place he does not as yet know.
He will drink from a cup that is heavy but a cup that is filled to the brim
Cause he's not about to die in a prison cell but a prison cell is about to die in him.

Every man has a hole he is digging or a hole he is trying to fill,
But the man who has chosen to dig his own dream he must climb to the top of the hill,
For although he has sacrificed nothing he has nothing to sacrifice him,
And he's not about to trade for eternity but eternity is about to trade for him.

Every man has a love that is dying and a love that is coming to birth,
But the man who has chosen to lead his own love to four corners of the earth,
He will stare through the masks of creation down a road with no horizon but him
Cause he's not committing suicide in America but America's

> committing suicide in him
> No he's not committing suicide in America but America's committing
> suicide in him

I held back the fifth verse – but the rest were almost exactly as she'd spoken them in the dream. I found simple chords around these words and the sense this new song gave me was nothing less than exhilarating. I'd never written anything quite like it before and strangely enough (for those who know the song and its unusual last lines) it was a few months 'later' that the planes went into the twin towers.

****

The concert arrived. The Old Market district of Bristol was full of shabby cider houses, massage parlours, and pole dancing clubs, and the Gin Palace was squeezed in between them. A tiny bar filled with people from here and abroad who'd been into Strangelove, and others who'd climbed onboard at Moon gigs and who sat around on the tables at the front; with other Bristol music types loitering at the back on barstools, who I initially began to worry had only turned up hoping to see me take a dive because they'd heard rumours I'd lost it.

Julie Of The Rose, Fucked and *Song To America* all got played that night. Complete silence all the way through. The first time I'd experienced that spooky hush which has now become the mainstay of my concerts. This was such a different experience from the loud rock gigs I'd played up till then. You could discern a subtle reverberation from the very start which grew as the performance continued and looking out into all the faces, it began to register within me that perhaps Adam and I had entered a musical world we could trust. After each song, there were encouraging rounds of applause and at the end, two and then three encores.

CHAPTER 32

WOMAD

After the concert I met Thomas Brooman, owner of the Gin Palace, who lived above the premises and who'd allowed me to use his living space upstairs as a dressing room beforehand.

Immediately after the last song, I'd gone straight back up there whilst Adam remained downstairs chatting for us in the bar. The walls in Thomas' quiet rooms were crowded with festival posters and framed photographs of musicians I didn't yet recognise. Fela Kuti, Nusrat Fateh Ali Khan, Youssou N'Dour, and Salif Keita. As well as the more familiar Johnny Cash, Elvis, the Beatles, and the Stones. In fact, his whole house was something of a shrine to music, and I sensed a particularly strong presence in the living room. A hushed reverence that seemed to preside over all these names and faces.

30 minutes later, Thomas knocked softly on the door and I rose from the sofa to thank him. He had a wide, open, welcoming face and in describing an appreciation of our gig chose his words carefully due to what I later came to understand was a great sensitivity on his behalf towards every artist he ever met. Thomas spoke and listened back with a considered mind that flickered away brightly behind his blue eyes and when I asked about the numerous photos it came to light that he was the artistic director of WOMAD and had started the festival back in the 80s along with Peter Gabriel. In fact, many of the faces on his walls - captured in the wild transcendence of performance - were taken at events that 'he'd' put on all over the world.

Despite these achievements, he came across as a modest and courteous man and there was something touching about his sincerity when talking about all these musicians that put me at ease. This was a short conversation, but I was also visited by the strange feeling that somehow I'd met Thomas previously in some other time or place. Certain people say we have lived many times before. That we have acted in many dramas. Lived and died upon the earth on countless occasions and carry within our deepest selves the outlines of these previous existences. I don't know whether that is true. Perhaps somehow we do carry the life lessons of our ancestors. But whatever was happening, I *can* say with certainty for me, that even though we'd only just met, there was an immediate connection and a comforting sense of familiarity.

We walked back along the dark corridor that led from his living room to a set of stairs that carried you down past the pub below and out into the Old Market night. You could feel the doors opening before you even reached them.

****

A few weeks later, a letter arrived. It was from WOMAD inviting me to be a part of that year's summer festival, as a speaker on a songwriting panel with, amongst others, Midge Ure.

I blew nearly all my dole money catching the train to Reading and a taxi that took me to a hotel outside the festival where WOMAD were housing some of the artists. They'd laid on free mini-buses that were running in and out of the site every half hour and the reception area was full of musicians from far flung countries who wore brightly coloured clothes and were singing in large groups accompanied by acoustic guitar players and gaggles of percussionists. After listening for a while to the happy banter in between songs, it began to register with me that a lot of these people had only just met and they were improvising. The scene, noisy and chaotic and joyous and so unlike the more sombre rock 'n' roll daytime vibe I was more accustomed to.

****

I spotted Midge standing by the side of a stage which had been set up at the end of a basketball court. Part of the Rivermead Centre – the grounds in which the WOMAD festival was held. Midge was the chair of the songwriting panel and I walked over to introduce myself. Approaching in platform shoes, my footsteps echoed far more loudly than I felt they should have and that clatter eventually stopped me in my tracks as I waited for him to finish a conversation with a middle-aged woman. She had a prominent, aquiline nose, a big, blond 80s hairdo, and was staring way into his eyes with intensity. It was unsettling to stand there only 10 yards away still carrying my guitar and not knowing where to look. Both of them engaged in a whispered exchange full of pregnant silences that grew longer as time passed.

Even though I felt sure they were aware of me, neither of them acknowledged my presence in the otherwise empty court. It was a perfect reflection of my relationship with the music business as it appeared to me at that time. I waited, uncertain of what to do and unsure of whether I should retreat or try to stay. I kept at what I hoped was a polite distance and tried not to look overly eager. I sat down on the hard case of my guitar and peered in the other direction. Too uncertain to step away into the empty reverb of the court in the disintegrating pop star shoes I'd pulled from a dusty box in my room at home. Too uncertain to continue and possibly interrupt.

Eventually, I heard and then saw 'her' cream high heels clicking past me and out of the sports hall. She was wearing a matching cream mac with shoulder pads. Like one of those women out of The Human League. Maybe it even was one of them?

"Hello, Midge," I said.

Like many famous people I've met, he appeared preoccupied, nervous, and distracted. Unsure of me or what was actually going on. He couldn't hold my gaze and you could sense his restlessness.

"Are you part of this songwriting thing then," he said. "Who's you?"

"My name's Patrick."

"Oh, OK," he replied in his immediately identifiable Scottish twang.

"What's this all about then?" he continued.

I laughed at that, but 'he' didn't.

Then the other musicians on the panel turned up. A protest singer from Northern Ireland, who was a punk from the first time around. This was 2002 but the ghost of '77 remained clearly in his aura. Everything he had grown into since had its roots sunk in punk and you could feel 25 years of sticking-with-the-cause fermenting inside him like a vintage rough cider. Next was a female singer from Australia with manicured dreadlocks. The smell of various essential oils. A vegan, a hippy, and entirely different from him and his contrary intellect. Full of exaggerated laughing positivity sunshine.

I'd been in a forest every day for almost two years and my heart was racing from the uncertainty of where I now fitted. Where I might have been rising above it all and concentrating on the sound check for some reason all I could register within myself was the tyranny of what it's like to have an Adam's apple when you can't stop thinking about how weird that is. Nervousness moves in mysterious ways and I half-choked my way through the introductions.

****

Later in the afternoon, the basketball court was half-filled with mostly middle-aged people in green Barbour coats and Wellington boots, whom I surmised enjoyed listening to *Late Junction* on Radio 3. From the side of the stage peeking around, you could sense the tired, wired aura of a festival thrown over them like an invisible soggy blanket and I fancied I could perceive some small part of each one of them that secretly wanted to go home because of the 'appalling inconvenience of camping'.

On the stage, we sat on plastic stools and my skin began to tingle. Midge opened proceedings and chaired the panel with a charming down to earth aplomb. He'd totally snapped out of his distant mood and was funny, relaxed, and inclusive. He got the audience laughing and generously brought the rest of us into the conversation as if we were long, lost friends. When it came to my turn, I could hear a low voice galumphing around the room courtesy of large PA speakers and I knew that particular sound was at that precise moment being generated in my Adam's apple. As a result, my attention faltered again and again back into the mystery of throats and away from the meaning of the words I was conveying with amplification to an audience of about 200. They stood before me in lines that seemed to join up in all directions like a crossword puzzle filled out beyond my comprehension. My Adam's apple kept going regardless as did the bla-bla-bla of whatever it was I might have been saying about creativity.

We all got to 'play' a song too. One that would lend support to our words of wisdom. The guy from Northern Ireland made an impassioned plea for the beaten generations to rise up out of their boxes one more time whilst strumming a steel string acoustic with gusto.

Hooray!

The Australian woman stopped at one point just before her second chorus and soon had everyone singing along in a call and response. A happy, sad message loosely based around the idea that love could save this big ol' beautiful world if we could only just get together and 'be one'. I saw the audience smiling to themselves in response to her genuine hopefulness and there was a charming little buzz in the room.

On the spur of the moment, I played a song that I'd started to write a week previously and wasn't properly finished called *Lazy Satellites*, which had no particular meaning whatsoever. Even though I'd already penned some amazing solo songs, I cast them all to one side for the sake of the one I was working on. Typical. I sensed the audience intrigued up to a point but not exactly with me and a polite round of applause collapsed on the basketball court almost immediately after I'd finished.

Midge courteously thanked me before stepping up to play *Dancing With Tears In My Eyes* and it immediately became apparent why the people were there. His guitar playing was rudimentary and the song obvious and although that's not something that has ever bothered me – I noticed that it was hard not to take the huge round of applause he received at the end as some kind of personal insult. This wasn't the Verity Sharp fan club at all. These were posh 80s kids on a kind of nostalgia trip to the fountains of *Vienna*. My chance to make a splash was over and though I wanted to get humble and say thanks and goodbye to Midge he was being mobbed and I could see the woman with the mac way ahead of me in the line – re-awaiting her moment.

****

Stricken with self-doubt, I wandered back into the anonymity of the festival crowd relieved and forlorn. This was the first real chance I'd had in years to get my head above water and certainly my first as a solo artist. I'd got my hopes and expectations up and now the savage ravings of that old inner voice were tearing in.

'That was a real chance to do something cool for yourself, man, and you – Fucked – It – Up.'

'Midge Ure just blew you off stage.'

On and on the choir sang. It was like going home for Christmas.

After an hour or so of wandering around and surrendering without appeal to this self-indulgence, those voices started to lose their grip. By now the forest had given me some distance from my troublesome self and I'd learned the hard way that at times like this it was best to stop listening as soon as you'd caught yourself and go and do something less boring instead.

MADOSINI

This was the WOMAD festival and there were plenty of opportunities for distractions. On a small outdoor stage stood some drummers from Morocco. Tall, thin men in brown robes whose agitated rhythms were the precise remedy I was searching for. Mesmerising Brian Jones-type voodoo madness. Relentless counter rhythms that insisted on the timeless moment until you were wiped clean. Afterwards, I headed back towards the Rivermead sports centre, the sun shining through the clouds. All the music from various stages blurred into one slipshod bass-heavy rumble and I warmed to the families with toddlers sitting on the grass eating ice creams. Young teenagers skipping around babbling to one another. Older couples drifting off together into groovy silences and mouthfuls of festival food.

Suddenly, I was seized with a strong premonition. An inner voice that commanded me. Go through that door there. Go through that door and out of here. It didn't look particularly promising. Just a fire door 50 yards away, ajar at the side of the sports centre.

Nevertheless, I went through that door into a drab corridor and another series of doors. Go through that door there. Go through that door there, go through that door there, the voice insisted.

****

The small, panelled, windowless room was warm and muggy and a handful of sleepy middle-aged festival goers laid on the floor staring into space. On a tiny makeshift stage sat a buxom African woman of about 80 years of age dressed in traditional costume. With a bright orange shawl wrapped around her body and elaborately beaded jewellery hanging from her neck. Upon her head was a blue blanket with white spots, cleverly sculpted into the shape of a bicorne which she wore side on like Napoleon. Her lips were drawn inwards and clenched around a mouth bow called the mhrubhe and her wide face crumpled into the frown of art's concentration. The sound engineer crouched before her trying to position a microphone that squealed feedback into the room. The old African lady looked sceptical but continued to play her mouth bow with one ear cocked to the electrical interference.

The eerie scraping and whistling that emerged simultaneously from the mhrubhe and her mouth were too faint to be easily amplified by the small stage equipment. A clash of worlds. Eventually however, the feedback was brought under control and the soundman hesitantly backed away to leave the old woman alone on the stage. Her instrument had a crinkled metal string that ran from one end of the wooden arc of the bow to the other – and with a thin wooden reed she scraped the metal string back and forth. At the same time, with the bow clutched between her lips, sucked in, she used her mouth as a resonant chamber whilst whistling strange trembling melodies alongside the scraping. She fretted the string between her thumb nail and index finger playing fluttering two-note melodies. The effect was haunting and immediately provoked a sense of deep stillness that brought me from standing to my knees.

The concert progressed slowly as Madosini moved through a series of roughly hewn instruments which she played with tantalising dexterity. Between songs she appeared awkward and intensely serious but as soon as she re-entered the music a solemn grace emanated from within her. Like a swan ungainly on dry land but as soon as it hits the water gliding with a faultless dignity.

I remained dumbfounded upon my knees, and before long fat tears began to well in my eyes and then fall down my face. All the despair I had ever known and all the truth I'd ever been able to wring from life was screaming at the magnificence of this old woman whose majesty sat before me on a wooden chair playing to an audience of less than 20 people.

Later on, I witnessed her again on a larger stage where she charmed an audience of hundreds. This time accompanied by an African man, also in traditional costume, who played percussion; between songs, translating the stories she told about the village where she was born in Transky, a remote district in the eastern cape of South Africa.

"*Here Comes The Motor Car* – a song about the first time she ever saw a motor car driving towards her village."

After that tune, she sprang up and danced and woohooed into the air, stamping her feet and laughing. The audience clapped in time to her stomp. She played train songs on a Jew's harp and also sang more ancient compositions accompanying herself with another larger single-stringed instrument called the uhadi. The concert was a triumph with many people rising to their feet at the end to applaud – and afterwards I wandered around the festival distraught. All the raw emotion she'd drawn from me was so confusing and so unexpected that I could no longer face all the faces around me. So I hid myself under the huge folds of some white tarpaulin that lay to the side of one of the giant marquees. Lying prostrate in the darkness with the smell of dead grass and plastic tents and the muffled confusion of the festival hub-bub in my ears. I cried and cried in the blackness and I didn't even know why. And when I finally emerged and dragged myself back to the hotel and stared out the window, it was like a brand-new star was shining in the night's sky.

CHAPTER 34

LUXURY PROBLEMS

Back in Bristol, it was high time to begin recording a new album. I'd composed more than enough material but without someone like Alex or Don around I wasn't coming up with solutions of my own as to how to go about accomplishing this. Without realising it, I'd spent most of my life relying on other people to come up with plans and still hadn't developed the muscles you need. However, I *was* starting to make many new friends and beginning to learn how to socialise without chemicals. Learning to talk straight, stand up for myself, and stay safe around all sorts of people in all sorts of situations. Slowly but surely, re-entering the social arena. One of these friendships, which had a lasting impact on me, was with a poet called Annie McGann.

Annie was in her 40s and dressed in black every day. There were high ceilings in the four-storey house where she lived in Clifton and where we'd while away the afternoons in her spacious back room. Red carpets, red chaise longues, red curtains, and dark wooden shelves with hundreds of poetry books. She wore gothy make-up and hated housework and didn't get up till past midday due to an overactive imagination which kept her awake most nights till dawn. She complained of headaches and we talked about Sylvia Plath and Anne Sexton and drank fresh mint tea from a golden teapot. The mantlepiece and ledges overflowed with candlesticks, snow globes, and plastic spiders. Glass gas lamps and statues of pagan goddesses. Icons of Our Lady and lockets that opened up on Jimi Hendrix.

Annie had eyes that could see straight through you and a mocking cockney voice that exposed and then encouraged you to burst into laughter over your paranoia. Over the next few years, we laughed a lot. Through the winter months, there would be open fires and tiny twinkling lights and stories about the punk scene in Soho during the late 70s and in the summertime she'd shout all manner of instructions out the window at a nervous looking gardener. While we talked, she played cool, intense music in the background and when I commented on this she immediately made me a mixtape cassette she called 'We Slash Our Wrists So You Don't Have To'.

****

Annie threw regular parties in her sumptuous home with many of Bristol's glitterati music scene in attendance and held court around the kitchen table with a kind of good-natured witchery. Effortless put-downs flying from her mouth and continuing to command the conversation even if she wasn't talking. Usually, these parties began late in the afternoon and musicians from Portishead and Massive Attack and Spiritualised forced down plates of smoked salmon and salad as she stood over them, insisting they needed feeding. As a favoured friend of Annie's, I was lucky enough to meet them all and this signalled another turning point in my musical life.

Annie was married to the actor Paul McGann and occasionally his smiling face would pop round the door too. *Withnail And I* was a film my friends and I had watched many times back in the drinking days and it was difficult, at first, to separate him from the character he'd played. In real life however, Paul was friendly and full of enthusiasm with a mischievous grin and would often make you laugh out loud, but 'he' had his edge sorted too. Because sometimes his face would darken and without explaining, he'd take off whatever quirky music was playing mid-way through and put on one of those long Dylan tracks like *Sad Eyed Lady Of The Lowlands* and the whole room would go quiet.

The fact that Annie had taken me under her wing and believed in my songwriting was one of the great gifts of this particular time in my life. She encouraged me to believe in myself too and helped me re-emerge into the social world of my contemporaries – while still feeling safe enough with her around to begin to let go of some of the ideas I hadn't quite grown out of yet. Like you couldn't possibly trust anyone who didn't wear eyeliner.

Her get-togethers went on all night long and everybody apart from the musicians danced till dawn. They remained in the kitchen instead, getting drunk and making 'knowing' comments about the studio production techniques of the same records that Annie's other friends simply boogied to in the front room. They made increasingly unhinged jokes and later on in the wee hours moaned and slagged off other bands and the music business in general. It was familiar and comforting to be there, partake in all the fun and, at the same time, know I could stay clean without getting weird about it. With much encouragement from Annie, I also started to make friends with Adrian Utley from Portishead.

****

One afternoon, a few weeks later, I found myself aimlessly wandering the streets of Redland listening to Annie's tape on a Walkman. Down one of the terraced streets, I came across a house with smoke pouring out from its chimney. In fact, the density and intensity of this smoke was so over the top that I stopped in the middle of the road to savour it – whilst listening to Rod Stewart singing *In A Broken Dream* with Python Lee Jackson. Huge white clouds were blowing down from the rooftop and into the street, swallowing whole cars like a dry ice rock show. In fact, it eventually became apparent that something wasn't quite right and in an unprecedented act of good neighbourliness I approached this same house and rapped on the door with alarm.

When I saw Adrian's face appear it was a shocking double take and my brain hotwired as the probability numbers span round into their millions. Two separate worlds colliding inside my head. I hadn't seen him since the party and had absolutely no idea that this was his place. For a few seconds, we stood staring at each other.

"I think your house is on fire, man," I finally heard myself say from a million miles away, realising I still had the headphones on and Rod was blasting in my cars.

Thankfully, on further investigation, his house was safe. This was his first fire of the year and it had uncovered a particularly vehement chimney problem of some kind that he said he would get someone else to sort out pronto.

Afterwards, we swapped phone numbers; and sometime later, Adrian invited me to his birthday party.

****

On the night of the party, a few minutes after leaving my flat, it began to rain and I walked on for half an hour, having not thought to bring an umbrella – too lazy to turn back once I'd started. On arrival at his house, I walked upstairs to the bathroom and discovered my hair and clothes were completely dry. Not a drop of water on me in any form whatsoever. I could make no rational explanation to myself and stared into the mirror in disbelief. The excitable chatter of the party suddenly seemed far off and irrelevant as I began to wonder what the hell was going on. Back downstairs and dry as a bone, I soon found myself chatting to Adrian and not long into that conversation he asked me what I was up to with my own music. We got on well that night and by the end he'd suggested producing a solo album for me. We'd go to a cottage on Dartmoor which he promised would be perfect for recording as he'd already done something there with P.J. Harvey.

****

Over the coming weeks, we got together at his house in the daytime to play through the various songs I was considering. I'd sing with my acoustic guitar and before getting to the end, even if it was the first time I'd played the song, he'd be accompanying me on his silver Gretsch, coming out through an Orange amp, playing with a screwdriver or a rusty nail or a plastic fan in his hand. From the very beginning, everything he came up with was drenched in a mysterious atmosphere that made me see spirits.

I also learned something about myself from Adrian. He was a guitarist extraordinaire who'd been playing since he was 14 and had developed a technical ability which allowed him to perfect anything he wanted on his instrument. But when I was with him, he always played the most simple and yet challenging lines. Usually with an impediment in his hand and going through some retro psychedelic effects pedal on max. In battling with whatever he was holding in his hand he'd reintroduced a tension into his effortless playing and was never smug or self-satisfied in the way he approached what we did. There was an intensity to even our rehearsals that was consoling to be around and you could talk to him about a feeling rather than chords and he would nail it with imagination. His restless artistic nature presided over everything and he moved us on quickly through the songs. Nothing was ever the same and he recorded everything on Dictaphones, including parts of our conversations he was intrigued by.

One afternoon, watching him struggle with some chisel as a scream from Dante's *Inferno* came creeping out of his amplifier, it suddenly struck me that creativity arises out of tension, and without this tension something of its essence dies. Give a rat everything it needs and it gets lazy. Place it in some maze where things get difficult and it naturally gets creative. Adrian was so technically proficient on the guitar that he was missing the struggle, so he'd reintroduced it. Scraping it out of the strings. Whether or not this was consciously intended on his part I never asked, but witnessing him got me thinking and I soon began to recognise that so much of my own creativity had arisen in tension too. Not the tension of having to play a guitar with a rusty nail but the tension of having to deal with my personality. I'd always struggled with myself and my place in the world – and much of my songwriting had come about as a consequence of this. The things I cursed myself for were the reasons I wrote songs. A destabilised personality was *my* rusty nail and without that the music I wrote may never have even arisen.

If I really were the self-confident person I'd always longed to be, perhaps none of my songs would have mattered enough to me and Adrian made me see that. Not through words in a conversation, but by watching him and realising. The difficulties I'd encountered in staying alive were exactly what I'd needed. It was comforting to imagine that perhaps they'd even been introduced into me by my own creative spirit in the same way he'd introduced the rusty nail. Whatever the truth, that afternoon in Adrian's house was a breakthrough moment and the beginnings of some further kind of self-acceptance.

****

If anyone on the scene began proselytising about some new band, you could guarantee that soon enough Adrian would have bought their CD. On numerous occasions, I witnessed him listening to these purchases as we drove along in his posh jeep with its blacked-out windows. Him, further removed behind sunglasses. If the said music did not capture his imagination within a few seconds he'd fast forward and then again and again. Watching the numbers go spinning up on the digital track read out on his car stereo. If he wasn't satisfied, he'd then pull the album out of the player and lob it out of the window as we speeded on. Sometimes frowning without comment or more often with a kind of embarrassed laughter at his own audacity. Once, slightly blushing, he told me it was actually Geoff Barrow who'd taught him this particular method of disposal and that it was all his fault.

If, on the rarer occasions, there was something that grabbed him about a song, he'd play it once again through the studio speakers immediately on re-entering his house. Listening like his life depended on it, his face wide and almost frightened. Afterwards, he'd genuinely want to know what *you* thought too and when we talked, he listened with great openness. But his mind was never at rest for long and seemed to seethe at all times with the unfettered neurosis of art.

Once, I went over for a jam to discover Mark Linkous from Sparklehorse in the back room. Adrian and I on guitars and Mark on an old radio thing he'd found in Brighton, going through an amp and dialling up feedback loops from outer space. The ghostly music went in and out of phase and eventually when we'd got way into the trance, I understood enough to be able to open my mouth and sing. For hours. Right at the end, Mark and I sang *Candy Says* together.

On leaving, I shook his hand with a great, spaced-out satisfaction, but in all my life I honestly never saw a man so sad looking back at me. His face was drawn and his skin looked ill and his eyes couldn't lift themselves out of himself. There was no life in them to greet you and I suddenly didn't know where to hide my enthusiasm for our jam. He was carrying the weight of a heavy world on his shoulders and it felt like something of a crime to walk away without having been able to carry off even a little of the burden for him before he flew back to America.

****

A few weeks later, we left Adrian's house in a big blue van loaded with a

24-track recording desk, copious amplifiers and microphones, drums, bass guitars, more guitars, a Wurlitzer, a Hammond organ with its giant Lesley speaker, and rows of 60s and 70s synthesisers. This was the beginning of *Luxury Problems*, my first solo album. We drove down to a village called Postbridge on Dartmoor and then further still, along narrow country lanes where wild ponies stood on the road and you had to wait in the van for as long as it took. We finally arrived at a remote cottage with five or six bedrooms that smelled of coal and wood burners and where there was no signal or phone line.

Adrian had organised the other musicians for this session. Mike Mooney and Damon Reece from Spiritualised.

Damon set up in the front room and started to play the drums with dampening pads from the 70s over his snare and toms. From the second I heard him warm up, I was a fully paid-up believer. His playing was reserved and accomplished yet so full of life and enthusiasm that it was perplexing to work out how he actually did it. We jammed through the songs with me on a Spanish guitar, singing into the air and him following along – and immediately ended up laughing about how cool we sounded together. Straight after that he looked me straight in the eye and said with a sudden seriousness.

"There's really only two things that fuck bands up, man. Girls, and publishing."

Damon also owned an original full-sized Mellotron from the 60s, heavy as a cow, which he'd dragged along, and you can hear it over quite a few of the tracks on *Luxury Problems*. That prized instrument was on its last legs, the reels struggling and the crinkled tape emitting a stoned, wobbly sound which was out of this world when you played chords. Mike came up with many of those parts. He was a scouser who increasingly had us falling about laughing with his dour and debauched rock 'n' roll lifestyle. He was a total natural when it came to music too and could conjure a catchy melody absolutely every single time he could be bothered to. We worked through the afternoons and late into the night and ate together each evening around a big kitchen table.

Would we be able to get a record company on board to fund the project onwards? All the faces gloomed in the candlelight and you could feel the pressure again. It raised its head most days.

Every time they started to talk about money and the music business, the atmosphere in the cottage changed. All the happy-go-lucky music making was forgotten and a soon familiar darkness settled back down. The three of them were dealing with significant pressures as a result of their successes in music and had to regularly make all kinds of decisions in an attempt to keep themselves afloat, move forwards and remain relevant in a world that was rapidly changing. In listening, you could sense how much intelligence and candidness it took to be able to survive at the top. On witnessing these conversations I experienced somewhat of a secret admiration for them – but all this agitation also unsettled me. Because, unlike when we were playing music together, I suddenly felt out of my depth and would slope off. Excusing myself to walk out onto the pitch-black moors where an hour or so away there were stone circles that had seen millennia come and go and where I stood staring at the star-spangled heavens till my neck hurt.

Out there one time, I came across a tame brown-and-white pony and went back to the very same spot the following night hoping to feed her an apple. She immediately came walking towards me out of the blackness and when you touched the mane it was rough and tense. Streams of juice cascading to the ground from the side of the monster teeth. Suddenly, in that strange moment, it was like I was floating high above it all looking down on Dartmoor. Miles and miles above the ground, where you could see to the horizons. Here in the middle of nowhere in the pitch-black, something primitive was eating out of my hands whilst far away back in the cottage they schemed like outlaws to secure their futures.

At the end of that week, we had four tracks we felt happy with. *Song To America*, *In My Junkie Clothes*, *Mother Nature's Refugee*, and a song that never made it on the album called *Deep Beneath The Waves*. The conclusion was that on the strength of this material and with our contacts we'd be able to find someone to get on board and fund the rest of the project. Adrian had kindly paid for the cottage and for the services of Rik Dowding our engineer – and for all the food too. I'd reimburse him when something happened, he said.

****

In my efforts to find this money, I contacted some of the people I'd known around Strangelove to no avail – and then went out to Real World Studios to talk to Thomas.

Whilst out visiting Thomas, I also mentioned how profoundly moved I'd been by Madosini's performance at WOMAD that summer. Something of my admiration must have struck him because we were soon wandering over to another office at the Real World site where I was introduced to Annie Menter, the woman who'd discovered Madosini in Africa and who had subsequently brought her to the UK.

Annie seemed so full of positive energy that day. She showed me black-and-white photographs recently taken in a mud hut in Transky. Madosini telling stories to her grandchildren as they sat around her in a circle. Their pure, open concentration and Madosini's expressive face started to bring it all back and I tried once more to convey my admiration. As those words trailed away, a hush descended upon us there in the office and Thomas suddenly spoke up.

"You need to work with Madosini, Patrick."

"Yes," said Annie immediately.

And she was straight on the phone to Cape Town to ascertain whether Madosini might be interested in meeting a rock musician from the United Kingdom with a view to collaborating.

Speaking no English herself and not possessing a telephone, Madosini's contact in Africa was her percussionist Vuyo. You could hear his babbling enthusiasm bursting out of the receiver, saying he'd be delighted and was sure Madosini would be too.

Before I had time to take another breath, Thomas was on the phone to the PRS, who at that time had a pot of money for the purpose of supporting live collaborations between artists on different continents. "Yes," they were interested and all I had to do was write a letter explaining why I wanted to work with Madosini.

With some help from Janine Kelly, Thomas's personal assistant, in filling out the forms – along with my letter the proposal was sent and accepted by the PRS. We had a few thousand pounds at our disposal as well as the promise of some WOMAD festivals around the world to showcase our as yet non-existent collaboration.

CHAPTER 35

CAPE TOWN

After the money came through, Thomas invited me and my then girlfriend Sophie to his house in Old Market to discuss moving forward. For some reason in my imagination, I had always seen Madosini and I in the practice rooms at Real World, working on songs together. We talked for a number of hours and it was well towards the end of the evening that Thomas said,

"It seems to me that if you are to create new work with Madosini, you need to experience her environment too. I must say, you need to go to South Africa, Patrick. I'm sure that's where you should write this material. Going to Africa, if you've never been before, is life changing."

Thomas was someone who made things happen. He wrote things down in biro on pieces of paper and then weeks or months later they would be a reality. I once saw him sketch out a festival site that then took place in Spain and looked almost exactly like the drawing. Using that same simple formula over the next few years, I would come to witness him accomplish so much. But this was the first time I'd actually sussed who I was sitting around a table with.

The expectation of going to South Africa blotted out everything over the next few weeks and the night before leaving I woke up at four a.m. with intense vomiting. I'd seen the illness in my dream. A huge jelly clown dressed in a green suit, laughing and opening all the doors inside me and slamming them shut again for kicks. My head was still spinning with that laughter in the doctor's surgery at nine a.m., as I lay there trembling and where much to my relief Dr J.W. Walsh said I was fit to fly.

Poet Annie had lent me a big backpack which I'd stuffed full with clothes and books, a CD player, and discs and a few hawthorn berries from my favourite tree on the Downs. The same tree from which I'd hung and burnt my coat after Strangelove split.

I dragged the heavy bag along with my guitar down to the bus station. Clearly recalling the years I'd spent busking on that same spot. Drunk without a penny to my name. Passers-by throwing coins into the folds of my jacket.

Now l was travelling to Cape Town to meet and work with an 81-year-old master musician and storyteller, and as the coach pulled away there was an incredible sense of wonder about it all. At the beginning of this journey, despite being ill and very weak, a profound sense hit me that I was on some kind of mission to discover something – and all the way to London my imagination kept showing me a big white pearl.

****

On the flight, I sat between two businessmen. The one on my right was called Charl and he was tall and gaunt with a full head of grey hair. He relaxed and stretched his long legs into the aisle, buzzing the stewardess again and again for liquor. Charl's face was flushed and he spoke loudly in clipped Afrikaans. Hellbent on telling me his life story, he was soon drinking himself stupid and as the plane flew onwards into the night he gradually quietened and lent his head in towards me in a gesture of increasing confidentiality.

"The greatest advice of my entire lifetime came from a multi-millionaire," he grumbled,

"He was a very, very fine man - and I can tell you that for nothing, Patrick. And if you've got the ears to hear I'm going to tell you right now what he once told me. Any 'tru-u-u-u-ly' successful man must attain bankruptcy at least three times in his life before he can 'tru-u-ly' say he has tasted success. That's the recipe, Patrick. Success AND failure, together. That's the Ju-Ju."

After this confession, Charl continued to spill his own story in the way a drunken man will sometimes offer great intimacy about himself to a stranger. The divorces, the children's names and their subsequently chaotic lives, the sumptuous houses and the vast sums of money that had gone astray. He trotted it all out with a careless passion that lacked the decorum quietly expected in the hush of an aeroplane. The window screens lowered; most people were trying to sleep in their chairs. Only a few reading lights remained on, illuminating seats dotted further up the carriageway. Whiskey fumes evaporated from his mouth and writhed over my face as I weighed a stifled intensity coming from the other passengers nearby, who pretending to kip were in fact listening to the slurring tale where over and over again he attempted to regale himself as some kind of misunderstood hero. But because of his belligerence and drunkenness it was impossible not to fill in the gaps for yourself. Eventually, without any prevailing conclusion he drifted on into less and less meaning, mumbling dream-like imagery until he passed out with his head thrown back and his mouth still open for business.

In stark contrast, the balding businessman on my other side had as yet muttered nothing. Dressed smartly, all in black, he had remained steadfastly focussed on an academic paper to which he was adding notation, but as the red sun rose, blinding through the gaps in the window shutters, he began to tell me his tale too. An alcohol and drugs councillor from a treatment centre in Cape Town, he specialised in the trauma sometimes suffered by alcoholics in early childhood. His deep, thoughtful voice came across all comforting and, unlike Charl, he showed interest in me and my journey too, listening with quiet thoughtful attention to my strange tale. Suddenly, I didn't feel so sick and sat between these two strangers, I knew which direction called me now without even having to think.

****

I arrived at Cape Town airport in the morning sunshine with no one there to meet me. The other passengers whose faces I'd contemplated back in the queues at Heathrow drifted away with their luggage and the stories I'd made up about them, and I was left alone with the drones of the air conditioning and the empty luggage rack continuing its perambulations. Standing for an hour or so in the deserted lobby with no one but the occasional cleaner ambling by with faraway eyes.

Finally, a man in his late 20s arrived, striding towards me, laughing with a few gold teeth. Vuyo Katsha. Tall, black, and skinny with a shaved head and dressed entirely in white. We had never met or even spoken before this moment.

"Hello, my brother, Patrick."

He made no reference to his lateness and instead insisted on carrying my bags. I was far too tired and relieved at his arrival to care about this protocol and responded by attempting, to no avail, to wrestle back the luggage and carry it myself. This back and forth became almost heated until by nodding gestures we agreed to share the burden. It became apparent that we had to move quickly as our lift was waiting at an unpermitted parking spot right outside the main airport's revolving doors. The car we bundled into was welded together from a number of vehicles. Two blue doors, one red door, one brown door and a brown chassis. All of which were covered in an ominous-looking rust. Grey smoke curling from the exhaust pipe. I flung myself into the back seats with the smell of old leather and cannabis in the sunshine and off we juddered.

Cape Town, the old city, is surrounded by ring roads, and beyond these are the black townships and the squatter camps. Vuyo was intent on giving me a tour of these townships so I could begin to accustom myself to 'life' there. Firstly, driving towards Gugulethu. We were soon way off the main roads and pulled into a garage where a loud speaker in the courtyard barked out instructions in a clipped English accent and two scruffy black men flung rocks into a wheelbarrow. Everything left standing in Gugulethu was either wobbling or broken.

Our driver said nothing as we trundled along but grinned as Vuyo talked-on incessantly. As if the sound of his voice was all that enabled this junk heap to keep on rolling over what were surely its last few miles. We drove around the townships all day until our journey took us to Montana. The township where I'd be staying with a member of Vuyo's family.

****

Vuyo's brother Patrick was a teacher and married to Orianda. Their bungalow was more familiar in outer appearance to anything I'd seen from the car window. Together they'd two daughters, Yolanda aged 11 and Yoneli aged six. The small bedroom into which I was ushered had been abandoned on my behalf by the youngest girl and had a threadbare brown carpet beneath a child's single bed. There was a striking absence of any kind of comfort in the room and the sound of what I had already been informed were gunshots clacking out through the night. A ripped-up picture of Tupac staring out from the back of the flimsy plywood door.

I lay on the bed exhausted, head spinning round with images of the townships. Blocks of brown tenement flats, derelict squares, broken down cars, oil drums with fires burning inside them, groups of people standing around the flames cooking and warming themselves in the glow, chickens and skinny stray dogs, miles of tumbledown shacks cobbled together from wooden fences and corrugated iron, plastic sheets and cardboard. Haunted black faces moving slowly through the streets that spidered out in every direction like forest pathways. I lay there awake in the kaleidoscope of what I'd just witnessed with the remnants of my illness lingering on into the small hours. With my own eyes, I'd never witnessed such poverty before and eventually through the curtainless window dawn arrived like a bad headache.

****

Mid-morning and Vuyo was back again. In order for us to move around more easily, we had hired a car using some of our PRS money and he was noticeably pleased to be driving this relatively posh automobile. Over the first few days, we visited many deadbeat looking houses so that he could show off his new wheels to a variety of young women, or alternatively score weed. At first, I was not invited into either of these places and I had to learn to wait (first thing you learn) in the passenger seat outside.

"Keep the car windows down whatever happens, my brother," he laughingly informed me before disappearing inside where faces quickly appeared at the windows and then at the windows of the neighbouring shacks.

The atmosphere intensified and the humid vegetation on the dealer's street seemed to be growing in front of my eyes and stealing the oxygen from my lungs. Vuyo eventually returned with a seriously bloodshot grin, needlessly fiddling with the dials on the car's air conditioning for everlasting minutes before we moved on. Back down the beaten-up roads. On the third day we drove to Langa, the township where Madosini lived when in Cape Town. Up to this point, all the arrangements seemed disorganised but I was far too unsettled to voice concerns.

There were yellow stones outside the tenement flats of brown concrete where Vuyo said she would most likely be staying. He appeared agitated as we continued to circle aimlessly; eventually winding down the window of the car and shouting up to where two young women were leaning over a stone balcony two floors high above us. They shouted back down to him in the Xhosa language, laughing in the prickly sunshine.

"Madosini is here, my brother," he turned to me with a manic grin.

****

We knocked on the door of a ground-floor dwelling and were shown inside by a 10-year-old boy. Immediately down a deep step into a dark rectangular hole made of grey concrete. Even though a bright sun blazed outside, it was cool and gloomy. We stood entombed by a concrete ceiling and bare concrete walls. No carpets, no rugs, again nothing resembling comfort apart from a single bed over at the far wall with its legs raised up on some concrete bricks and the mattress covered in thick plastic sheeting. The sole article of furniture in the apartment.

Two stout washing lines stretched the longer length of the rectangle and five black boys aged between five and 10 crouched around a Calor gas camping stove burning blue on the bare concrete floor. The faint, uneasy smell of gas permeated the dark room as they worried away together, playing some game with small flat stones. A woman's red coat, again covered in a plastic sheet, hung from one of the washing lines and for some reason the floor was covered in black bowls full of water.

It was a terrible struggle to take in even as your eyes adjusted to the light. There on the tall bed she sat. The Queen of Mpondoland, Madosini. Her grave face transmitting an unsettling charisma. Laying down her umrhubhe she rose to greet me, limping a few steps in my direction and taking me in her arms, her low guttural voice blowing away in my ear a thunderstorm of Xhosa, as Vuyo excitedly translated.

"She is pleased to see you. She says she is pleased you are here."

She spoke four or five times quicker than Vuyo translated; her words filled with the clicks that inhabit the Xhosa tongue. 10 words to every one of his in retort.

"She is giving you blessings from the ancestors. She is thanking the ancestors. She is going to play a song in your honour now."

Madosini sat back upon the bed and clicked her stout fingers. Without a further word or gesture from her, the boys' game ceased. Their wide dark eyes glancing around the room, quickly back and forth, sizing me up in flashes, before lowering their collective gaze to the ground. Their tongues silenced; their quiet-breathing bodies held completely still in obedience. She picked up the uhadi, an instrument with a dried gourd tied, using torn lace, onto the upper half of a four foot wooden bow. She loosened her dress revealing the upper portion of her bosom and rested the hollowed-out gourd against the exposed flesh.

She began to strike the middle portion of a crinkled metal string that was attached to either end of the bow's arc, tapping it with a thin dried reed. Towards the lower part of the bow, she fretted the string between her thumb nail and index finger playing two-note melodies a tone apart that jumped back and forth in complex rhythms between the string fretted and the string opened. She held the reed with relaxed dexterity and flicked it back and forth against the string. These two notes were the only ones the instrument offered and the grandeur of the melodies relied entirely upon their complex rhythmical appeal and the fact that at the same time as she played these melodies, she rocked the bow and therefore the hollowed-out gourd back and forth over her flesh.

The frequency of sound coming from the gourd, which acted as the resonant chamber for the string's vibration, was thereby altered and the frequencies of each note ducked and dived as she played. Something like the effect of a flanger pedal. She evoked strange cross rhythms using this phasing as it danced in artful patterns through the notes being drawn from the string. At the same time, she sang a swooping melody, which rode the waves of her two-note accompaniment.

Her voice stretched and reinterpreted the complexity of their potential over and over again. She utilised two distinct styles of voicing. A higher, mournful cri de coeur and a lower, stifled, guttural yelp that came entirely from her throat. The atmosphere continued to cook as she performed and the character of the concrete hellhole was slowly transformed into the quality of something like a holy shrine. A feeling of awe resounded in me throughout this exploration of her song and on finishing the silence answered her back with a dark reverence which thickened the mood of the room even more, like a funeral.

I stared wide-eyed and watched her sit back in repose upon the bed surrounded by the vast ghost presence of her song. We waited there in the gloom but in no way did she allude to this atmosphere. However, its influence remained strong and held me suspended in a kind of daydream until I suddenly understood.

She was waiting for me to respond.

****

To follow such an awesome experience I might have easily felt overwhelmed, but on closing my eyes to find the words you could still feel the heat of her music on your face. I sang *Evergreen* as an acapella. Two years previously this particular song had come. Channelled through in one pure wave late at night in my bedroom, as I sat listening to a drone I'd created on a synthesiser.

In that moment, there in the darkness with Madosini, I reconnected with the depths of where that song had arisen. The notes that rose and fell so naturally with the melancholy of the story and the cry of my *own* bloodline.

When I finished and opened my eyes, she spoke slowly from the bed.

"Madosini says you have a gift that comes to you from your ancestors and from God. She now knows this project will bear fruit and be successful."

In the blacked-out room full of bowls of dark water and dusty fruit, I stood before her and her five young grandchildren. Almost like I was disappearing.

After such an auspicious beginning, it was with great expectations that I approached our first rehearsal, which began the next morning in the front room of the house where I was staying with Patrick and his family.

****

Madosini played uhadi, Vuyo percussion, and me on guitar, as we began in an upright formal spirit, trying to find common ground around one of Madosini's more familiar sounding compositions. The elaborate rhythms played so effortlessly were not so apparent to me and the tuning on Madosini's instrument seemed to morph in and out against my guitar creating a dirge like combination unpleasing to the ears. As a result, it became tricky to keep in step with her and at the end of every attempt they both turned to look in my direction, as it became evident that I was supposed to supply every suggestion on how to go forward.

Each time I offered up the latest idea, it had to be translated to Madosini and there would be a lengthy exchange between the two of them incomprehensible to me. These frequent negotiations would always end in Madosini giving one serious nod and picking up one or other of the various instruments at her disposal before waiting to begin again on my count in.

Was it just me? The good nature of our initial encounter appeared to be changing into a far more complicated emotional landscape. Madosini's mysterious aura now entirely focussed into a frown which she wore more and more petulantly across her face as the morning's work meandered into dead ends. I tried everything inspiration afforded me to wrestle some resolution from the air – even to the point of acting out between us, in simple theatre, a childhood story from Madosini's village, in an attempt to try and create some sense of connection through humour. But nothing could break through the stand-off as the language distances stretched out further between us.

Our first rehearsal ended with no answers and it continued like this for days. The adventure was soon beginning to take a toll on my spirits and I eventually started to almost dread each morning's conflab, sensing a growing suspicion arising from their side too. After each session, we would retire to the kitchen and eat round the table with Patrick and his family. They would talk in Xhosa and I would not know what was going on unless I asked Vuyo to translate, which – as time went on – he appeared more reluctant to do. Afterwards, Vuyo would return Madosini by car to her concrete flat and through the afternoons I would then accompany him on his madcap dashes around the townships.

CHAPTER 36

TOWNSHIPS

Vuyo was born and raised in the township of Gugulethu. In Xhosa, it means Our Pride, and on these outings it was our most frequent destination. The people here on the whole lived in tenements which he called the native yards. Streets of identical concrete bungalows that ran for miles alongside each other in straight lines. Built by the establishment in the apartheid of the 1960s (after the neighbouring township of Langa became overcrowded). Gugulethu was raised to house the black people who commuted in and out of white Cape Town.

On the third or fourth day of my visit, I was for the first time invited by Vuyo to accompany him inside one of the native yards. It consisted of two pokey rooms made of breeze blocks. At the rear of the house was a washroom consisting of a metal toilet and an unconcealed copper pipe sticking out through the concrete to reveal a tap of cold water which drained away through a hole in the floor. The relatively larger room at the front acted as a living space where Vuyo introduced me to his friends. Tabza, Sipho, Lindiwe, and Tera. They sat around on threadbare furniture staring at a tiny black and white portable television set flickering away in the corner of the room. Ganga fumes hung in dusty, drooping clouds, while a few pot plants tumbled exhausted over the side of their brown plastic pots and headed straight downwards to the ground gasping for clean air. The men nodded in a friendly way but the girl did not look at me once and nobody asked questions. Their pensive faces remained glued to the tiny screen and their deep brown eyes appeared thoughtful over an American sitcom as it oozed toxicity out into the smoky room.

We went most afternoons to the native yards and Vuyo introduced me to many people. I began to make friends in particular with Tera. He was slightly older than the rest with a mellow smile and he always wore a navy-blue bucket hat pulled down over his eyebrows. Tera started to accompany Vuyo and myself in the car on our dashes. Wherever we went the small decrepit black and white TVs seemed to be spouting re-runs of trashy American soaps, which everybody turned to intently.

Even when commenting on the narratives and laughing with each other the dark eyes remained hooked to the screen. *The Bold And The Beautiful* with its array of fevered egos, back stabbing and two timing each other throughout every dreary cut price scene, appeared even more vulgar when viewed in the poverty of the native yards, and the aloof humour with which I might have watched in England seemed crass to me now. Afterwards outside, as we waited for Vuyo, I turned to Tera.

"Why do you always watch that shit, man," I asked.

He rose up out of himself and looked right back at me with his gentle eyes.

"Because we need to learn about life," he said.

"But that isn't life," I said. "It's bollocks. That isn't real."

"Life is life," he replied.

Suddenly confused, I searched for an insightful response but that brief exchange had left me silent with all sorts of questions racing around my brain and it was clear that this particular conversation was over now anyway.

****

Every person to whom I was introduced had a story about the European man and what he had done to them. Or indeed what he was still doing to them. Almost all the people I met, according to Vuyo, had never spoken to a white person before and as a result were seemingly even more determined to impart these tales to me. Intriguingly, there was no aggression in their eyes. They stood before me again and again to talk at length. Sometimes with a passionate energy or other times with a slower meditative sadness but most hauntingly it usually manifested in a calm resigned almost factual account with no obvious expression, forcing you to listen more clearly to the truth itself.

These stories focussed upon slave labour, beatings by the police, and the injustices of the poverty that the people endured now and in previous generations.

Patrick, an older man whose family had been torn apart through forced labour camps, was dressed in an Ipswich Town FC tracksuit and a baseball cap. We sat together on two wobbly chairs in his broken-down house and he hung his head, shaking it almost imperceptibly.

"They never even asked me about my father when he died. And he had given his whole life to them. He worked himself into the earth for 'their' money."

****

The sadness these stories invoked grew inside me as the days went by and there was nothing I could do or say but witness these narratives and soak them up. What must eventually have been 50 or so of these harrowing stories sent deep roots into my heartache as we travelled through the various townships of Cape Town, and I began in some small way to recognise the sheer scale of the pain. I was just one man meeting only a tiny percentage of people in this gargantuan tumbledown that stretched on and on. It was terribly uncomfortable at times to have to be there and be the one in the white skin.

Life was teaching me that I had to be quiet and listen without interruption and pass over my own discomfort, as much as I was able to. The pain I had suffered due to my own troubles, however meek in comparison, was the reason I was able to swallow this bitter lesson mouthful upon mouthful without trying to spit it out or somehow sugar coat it by pretending I could identify.

By the early evening, Vuyo would drive me back to his brother's house and then disappear, but not before politely enquiring whether this was OK. Every day I would reassure him but every evening he would ask again out of courtesy and slowly but surely a bond of friendship began to blossom between us.

In the house, it was relatively quiet in the evenings. On the first day, we'd all gone to a posh supermarket by the airport where they'd loaded a trolley to capacity. At the checkout, everybody, including the cashier, turned to look at me and that was the end of most of my spending money. So, after our evening meal the family would watch TV and I'd retire to my room in an attempt to try and process each day.

At first, I wondered whether I was serving some small purpose by 'being' white and listening with as open a heart as possible. But after a while it struck me one night as I lay in bed half asleep. They were telling me these stories for my benefit, not the other way round. That realisation hit me like a train and I noticed as I reflected upon each day my mind was often empty of its more familiar content. The ghosts of my usual preoccupations now appeared so flimsy in comparison to what was unravelling before my eyes that at times I could barely even look at myself in the dusty bathroom mirror.

One evening, whilst scribbling in a notebook, I watched the door of my room opening in slow, clumsy bursts and suddenly Yoneli, the youngest child aged six, stepped in. Peering at me through her brown eyes, she closed the door cautiously behind herself whilst searching for some kind of rebuke from me. She was dressed in bright orange pyjamas with a chubby face and an unruly Afro hairstyle. By her every gesture you could tell she'd been warned by her parents that on no account whatsoever was she to enter this room and bother me but her curiosity had finally won out. It was all you could do but to break out into a spontaneous smile and realising she was welcome she immediately jumped up on the bed beside me with a cheeky grin plastered across her face. However, she quickly recognised that the atmosphere of the room was not conducive to mucking around and with a child's inquisitiveness demanded in English,

"What's that music playing?"

"It's John Rutter," I replied, being a regular listener to his requiem at the time.

She looked directly at me without embarrassment and we both became quiet and immersed in the music. I watched her face move through a series of bewildered expressions as the choir sang through the darkness and light, sadness and hopefulness of the piece, wondering if she'd heard anything like it before.

We continued sitting together and listened to the second movement, *Out of the Deep*. In her witness, the cello's lament had never sounded so profoundly within me as the mournful choir arose. We were eventually interrupted by Yolanda who came in through the door to reprimand her sister. But before she took her out, we all sat on the bed together for a while longer and listened to the Rutter some more. Yoneli the younger one wore a serious and intense expression, whilst Yolanda embodied a dreamier countenance.

This first encounter was the beginning of what became regular visits from the girls, who as the days rolled by would knock on my door, hang out and listen to all kinds of music. I assured the mother Orianda it was cool and their enthusiasm towards me became a welcome respite from all the intensity. They asked a million questions that mostly centred around my family. Both girls were noticeably fascinated by my brother and sisters and nephews and nieces and couldn't get enough of the gossip, insisting I repeat the funny stories whilst collapsing in giggles.

Yolanda, entirely from memory, sketched out a complex family tree in order to show me how all their sprawling relations fitted together. Soon enough, they also had me playing guitar and my song *Refrigerator*, which I'd recently completed, was their immediate favourite. Two days after playing it to them, they'd managed to learn every single word and invent a hilarious dance to go along with it too.

CHAPTER 37

THE HEALER

One morning soon afterwards, Madosini and Vuyo were late for rehearsal. The girls jumped around dancing in the front room as I sat on the floor playing *Refrigerator* yet again. At the finale of the song from behind us came a joyous whooping!

"Ree-free-goo-hoo-ha-ya!"

Unbeknownst to me, Madosoni had come in and witnessed our performance and we all burst out laughing as she impersonated the final howl of the song.

As a result, for the first time our rehearsal began in a more easy-going atmosphere. Thanks to the smiling faces, I sensed Madosini lighten and some newfound hope entering the proceedings. Playful jams ensued with Vuyo showing off on the marimba and me no longer trying to reign him in.

****

Later on that evening, the relief of the morning focussed my thinking. Freed momentarily from anxiety I was finally able to reflect with some clarity. The harrowing stories I'd heard, the heart-breaking poverty I'd witnessed, the difficult rehearsals, the joy of the unexpected friendships with Yoneli and Yolanda and Madosini's strange charisma were spinning around in my head as I tried to make some sense of it all. After a while, however, my mind began to replay one particular incident.

A few days previously in the car with Vuyo, having just heard a few more troubling accounts, we were driving home together in silence. Suddenly, out of nowhere he'd turned on me, eyes flashing.

"The white people came here with mirrors," he said. "They used their mirrors to cheat us. Cheat us out of our land and our cattle and steal our minerals. They cheated us with mirrors, my brother. Before that we looked at ourselves in the river."

Unable to get those words out of my head, it suddenly hit me as I saw myself sitting on that child's bed.

I was looking to this situation to regain some kind of recognition; imagining if I could get the project to work, I could shake off the sense of failure that had haunted me since Strangelove split; imagining if I could please Madosini and Vuyo and somehow sort out these rehearsals and help create some interesting music then maybe people would believe in 'me' again. Maybe 'I' could get 'somewhere'.

I saw it clearly. How I wanted this association with Madosini to get me back on my way to the top, to enable me to appear somehow important in musical circles. In some ways, was I really so different from the people who first came here with mirrors to plunder resources? It wasn't easy or comfortable to have to sit with that until my imagination carried me deeper and showed me another memory. Madosini, playing the WOMAD festival on the day I'd first encountered her.

The image was still so bright and clear. On first witnessing her, before any of this happened, my heart had opened wide to Madosini. And I knew those tears were genuine and that in truth this was why I was here. Because I loved her music. That was the reason I was sitting in this tiny bedroom in the townships. My ambition and longing for some new musical direction might have stepped in and clouded things afterwards but at heart my love for Madosini had a purity that had arisen spontaneously and I knew I could trust that.

Out of this realisation, a decision began to arise. I would give up trying to control things and instead simply embody the part of me that loved Madosini. Relinquish all the responsibility of running rehearsals, which I'd somehow found myself pushed into, and as much as possible turn away from the anxiety that was present as a result of my hoping the collaboration would 'go somewhere'.

I lay on the bed with gunfire still occasionally ringing out in the distance as a sudden, fierce determination to change my role emerged. I would trust a more innocent impulse. Because we are all innocent until we start to feel guilty. It may get covered over by the way of the world and by our own desires but we all carry that innocence somewhere within us. We were all once just like Yoneli and Yolanda. In the recesses of our hearts and minds. And when that innocence shows itself again like it did when I'd first heard Madosini, it reminds us of who we really are underneath all our little plans and designs.

****

So, the next day at the start of rehearsals, I spoke to Vuyo.

"Today, I'm not going to play guitar, bro. I just want to listen to Madosini," and he translated those words to her.

She looked back at him with a studied concentration and as always repeated what he'd said in Xhosa to be sure.

One thing I'd learned about Madosini in the short time we'd spent together was that she loved, more than anything else, to play music. Kneeling on the floor in front of her – as I'd done on that first day in Reading – she held court without hesitation for the next three hours. I closed my eyes and started to drift away. Listening more deeply than ever before, the worries fading as I began to re-enter her dreamworld.

In my mind's eye, I witnessed Madosini leading a line of young people across the plains of Africa. A long snake of villagers, who danced and raised and lowered their arms and followed her as she played mouth-bow, out across the wilderness. I saw a huge red sun and V-shaped formations of flamingos flying to the horizon and I saw Madosini as a young girl running through her village as clear as if I were there myself. The darkness of the huts and the cool, deep wells and the mountain ranges of her homeland. All the while her trance-inducing music drew me further into these pictures and at the end of the three hours it was almost as if I'd been asleep. When I opened my eyes, she once again nodded and left.

This is how rehearsals proceeded from that day on. Explaining I was trying to listen with a greater clarity to Madosini, they both accepted this without question. Later, Vuyo and I would jam and the quality of our time together shifted. Madosini played and every day I listened till the reverence grew so strong you could almost hear the faraway mountains clapping their hands. I didn't know how the hell we would ever accomplish anything this way but at least we were building an atmosphere conducive to some kind of collaboration.

Madosini, as well as being unreachable in her seriousness, was now at times also capable of twinkling fun. She possessed a self-deprecating, playing-the-donkey side that suddenly began to emerge at the most unpredictable moments – limping around the room and waving her umrhubhe in the air, ranting about devil birds; screwing her face into strange contortions reminiscent of Yorkshire gurners and engaging in a series of comic dances that parodied different animals. The natural way in which the girls brought out that streak in her was enthusing our rehearsals with a much-needed level of playfulness.

****

Vuyo sat patiently and watched all this unfolding, and each day we drove Madosini home together. In the afternoons, we continued to cruise around in the car and as time went by he began to talk more openly about his life. Vuyo was involved in a number of projects in the townships aimed at nurturing young people's musical talent, and one morning when our daily rehearsals were postponed, because Madosini had to look after her grandchildren, he took me along on a hastily reorganised work excursion.

After 30 minutes riding through unfamiliar neighbourhoods, we arrived at a school which consisted of two mouldy prefabs covered in poorly executed graffiti and squatting in a concrete dip that looked like a one-time skateboard park gone to the dogs. However, the joyful cacophony that greeted your ears on stepping out of the car couldn't have been more of a contrast to these surroundings. Spread across the slanting concrete, about 50 kids aged around six years old were playing marimbas in unison. One boy in particular with close cropped curls, wearing a faded-blue Superman t-shirt, played with such abandon that it was impossible not to be taken aback by his deftness on such a ramshackle instrument. The teachers howled streams of instructions, turning the complex music this way and that through twists of ever-increasing tempo and intensity. A frantic, melodic, and yet pleasingly discordant racket that punched a hole through the grey sky and sent a vibrant black rainbow shooting out over the dirge of the townships. The pulse of Africa was pounding up through the surface of this playground and I laughed out loud at the power, registering deeply in my senses more clearly than ever before what music can accomplish: its power to transform. Roots spread out from my feet like veins through the crumbling pavement and reached their way down to the fire at the centre of the earth. In that pure moment, nothing could have told me that this was somehow not the most wonderful place in the world.

Later that morning, Vuyo drove me further to meet a band he managed whom he predicted would be hard at work in rehearsals. Four young women aged about 16, who played Kudu horns. The kudu being an antelope that lives out on the savanna. In a shabby, broken-down wooden shed, the girls danced around in circles blowing these cumbersome horns through cross rhythms that as always drew you into yet another trance.

Afterwards, Vuyo offered serious, lengthy feedback on their performance while the sun emerged from behind the clouds and began to shine in through the empty window frame that looked out over some dreary scrubland. Their eyes lit up with youthful concentration, soaking in his every word and responding to him with equal measures of laughter and reticence. You could sense that these young women thought the world of Vuyo and my own respect was growing for him too. The enthusiasm he transmitted was infectious and though it would have been easy to be cynical and see his efforts as primarily self-serving - and perhaps there was something like that about him - at the same time you could see he was making a real difference in people's lives. After what I'd already seen so far, this made it easy to admire him and I'd challenge anyone brought up in the conditions that Vuyo had known not to be in some way self-serving anyway.

He was full of knowledge about the townships and would often lecture me as we drove around. During the 1950s, the apartheid regime had tried to limit the number of black people who were pouring in looking for work. Eventually, no more Africans were permitted to settle permanently west of a line 1000 km away and women were entirely banned from seeking work in Cape Town. However, so many were desperate for employment that the government was unable to quell the tides. The townships became massively overcrowded and when people could no longer legally find accommodation, they set up the squatter camps. Makeshift homes of corrugated iron, cardboard, and plastic sheeting. Vuyo had already pointed out these camps to me many times. Miles and miles of derelict shelters.

****

One afternoon Vuyo suggested we pick up Tera and go on a wider tour of the townships and take a trip to the squatter camps too, because he knew an African healer whom he'd promised to introduce me to. I had earlier enquired of Vuyo whether we could meet a witch doctor as I wanted to learn more about the native spirituality first-hand. Vuyo said 'witch doctor' was not a term the Africans used because it was a white man's term and had a derogatory connotation and that I must be careful not to use this particular phrase. However, he would be happy, he said, to take me on a visit to the healer.

We drove further than ever before and reached a large covered area that acted as a marketplace. These structures had sprung up across the townships after the fall of apartheid. Built by Mandela for the people. They consisted of a broad concrete floor with a corrugated iron roof supported by rows of tall iron posts but without any enclosing walls. Here, under the shelter of the iron roof, on battered wooden tables, the stall owners sold sheep's lungs, livers, intestines, and the entire heads too.

"This is the food that the white man does not want to eat," said Tera, "So it comes here to these people."

In huge open ovens, they cooked the offal – and also in oil drums of water and fat, balanced on stilts, with open fires burning underneath. Tera removed the lid from one of these oil drums and the putrid steam rushed out hot into my face clearing away to reveal tightly-packed woolly heads bobbing in greasy water. The market was milling with people dressed in ill-fitting nylon suits, baseball caps, t-shirts, sweatshirts, or jeans that were often either too big or too small. You could only assume the result of packages of second-hand clothes delivered by charities and distributed to people who grabbed whatever they could.

We wandered on through the tables and I saw an old man eating a boiled sheep's head. The severed head was upright on the plate facing towards him with its face and eyes still intact. He sliced off a piece of the boiled ear smiling at me and lifting it upon a fork. Raising it in my direction in a joyful salute as I walked by, watching as he tucked in. From behind a wall of green tennis court wiring, a sad-looking young woman sold small jugs of sour milk through a flap.

Younger people played pool on a derelict table whilst argumentative older guys sat around watching, drinking illegally-brewed white liquor.

Tera took me to one side and showed me the oil drum fires that people took into the shacks.

"It is freezing out here at night, brother, and the people cannot sleep. They heat their homes with oil drum and paraffin fires and many of them will die from suffocation when they fall asleep and leave them on, but they will still take the risk because of the terrible cold and many times a man will stagger back drunk and forget to turn off his fire and his home will burn and many homes will burn and hundreds will die in the fires".

Tera had eyes which radiated the sense of a man who had been disappointed many, many times and yet still looked out into the world with a hope that the kindness of his own nature was not in vain and he always told his stories in a calm, measured voice.

Everybody was staring in my direction. Because as always, I was the only one and Vuyo said that my white face was a particularly rare occurrence in this area.

"What would happen to me if I was here without you?" I asked.

As was often the case when I posed a slightly worried question, his whole face burst into delight. By now I'd had to accept that upon many occasions regarding our exchanges they both considered me to be completely naive and found this insight endlessly hilarious.

"They would rob you. They would rob you and they would beat you to within an inch of your life or they might kill you. If you were not with us, my brother, you would be dead meat. You are a white man, Patrick. You are not an African."

He pointed out that final statement to me as if I were somehow oblivious to the fact.

"They see you are with us, my brother. Otherwise, they might kill you," he chortled again, playfully putting his arm around my neck.

Ambling through the large bustling crowd together as we made our way back to the car with Vuyo and Tera still laughing and talking to each other in African.

Their mood darkened however as we drove up to the squatter camps. This area was called Snake Park and the roads turned to mud and the wheels of our car slid around, recklessly close to the cardboard houses that wilted under tarpaulin rooftops and stretched on in all directions for miles. The streets of Snake Park could not make up their minds and twisted one way or another without reasoning.

We drove for a while, searching amongst the chaos of makeshift shelters for the Healer's shack, which eventually became recognisable to Vuyo by some special beads hanging outside to show who lived there.

Vuyo waited, stooping down and talking with his head hung. A low voice mumbled in ascent and in went Vuyo followed by Tera. It was dark inside as you bent down to enter the small room made entirely of layers of cardboard and wood lashed together with thick parcel tape. There were five men crammed inside, one of whom was coughing and wheezing with an alarming gusto for a man so old and thin.

On our arrival, these men were dismissed and we had to go back outside to allow them to depart. They filed past us emotionless and with a defeated air.

On re-entering, the eyes became accustomed and you were alerted to an agitated, rustling movement. A white cockerel with a red gizzard and a red beak showed itself in the gas light. The rooster flapped about but its wings and legs were apparently broken as it could not bring itself to stand and was tethered to the dirt floor.

The healer's name was Rasta and he gestured for us to kneel down. For a good while, nothing was said. His gaze transmitted a darkness that stretched far within himself and his eyes dipped and moved back and forth. Before him scattered across a moulding scrap of vinyl flooring were a dull array of potions, ointments, powders, and herbs – arranged in a jumble. He began moving his hands in a circular motion above these artefacts as if searching for inspiration and eventually selected a handful of a mountain brush which he abruptly set ablaze, sending up pungent clouds of smoke that filled the hut and provoked an itchiness over your face.

Under the influence of this thick, white smoke, Rasta started to mumble and hum to himself - slowly beginning to impart a vision that he said my spirit was inspiring within him. Suddenly, the pictures he offered became more vivid and his presence filled the shack with an increasing vitality as he spoke in what was finally a river of babbling sound. All conveyed in perfect English.

As the custom insists, I am sworn to secrecy regarding this vision and in fact Vuyo related to me sternly afterwards that I was not at liberty to share it with another person at any time for the rest of my life.

As Rasta's words trailed away, I opened my eyes to see a wide smiling face and twinkling eyes radiating in the shadows. A mad smile that seemed to reach out and take hold of me. The unease I'd experienced on entering his shack had completely disappeared and I was able to return his gaze without a glimmer of discomfort. We remained suspended in the half-light for a good few minutes smiling at each other. Until I thanked him and held on to his hand as he helped me up and rose to show us out.

Before leaving, I handed him some red berries taken from my hawthorn tree on the Downs in Bristol and he told me.

"Thank you, I will make something from these, my brother."

We stepped outside of the timelessness of his cardboard hut and into the great silence that was twilight over Snake Park. The wretched houses stretched out over the mud like the back end of some forgotten festival where the crowd had refused to go home, living on site way after the music had stopped and any sense of fun had long since packed up and deserted. The rain fell so gently that it was like some great trembling spirit full of love was crying with shame. The whole place appeared to me infused with a great mysticism that perched over every shack to the horizon. Snake park reached out and took a place in my heart forever. I was just a tiny part of a vast, collapsing world that I'd had no idea about.

****

The days spun by with more rehearsals and mad journeys. Sometimes, when we had to travel to townships further away, Vuyo would employ the ring roads that circumnavigate Cape Town. Faster dual carriageways that serve the suburbs of the city but also link up the townships that lie outside the boundaries of Cape Town (the tourist destination). On these roads, I began to notice an occasional solitary figure lurking on the hard shoulder in the blazing sunshine and there were enough of these men for me to recognise that they must represent some kind of phenomena.

"Who are these guys who hang out on the side of the roads here with the cars zooming by, man? What's the point?" I asked Vuyo, as we whizzed past another one.

The shadow men would stare at your car as you approached shuffling back and forth with furtiveness. Or like this latest one – with his arms by his sides facing towards us and offering the palms of his hands like a renunciation.

"These are bad men," Vuyo informed me.

"Why are they bad?" I disputed.

"They are bad people, Patrick, my brother. These men try to jump in front of cars."

"What? Why do they do that?"

"I will tell you why. Because these men are very poor. They have no money and they do not want to work. There is some money from the government for someone if they are disabled in a road accident. So, these men jump in front of the cars hoping that they will be disabled so that they can steal the money for that small grant from the government. It is not even that much, my brother."

We sped by another one of these hand-wringing figures. This one walked away from the car as we approached, his courage failing him. Or perhaps he was trying to make a judgement. Trying to win a disabling injury that would sustain him through his poverty without instead being killed on impact. Perhaps 'we' were travelling too fast.

Vuyo continued, his eyes blazing.

"I drove by a man the other day and he tried to jump in front of me, my brother. But I went round him and I tell you I drove back and I found him and I beat that man with a stick and if you were not here now, I would beat these men too."

Sometimes I was lost for words.

Vuyo did indeed carry a hefty stick in the car and as we sped on, he would not allow himself to listen when I attempted to offer my interpretation of the situation. He became irritated and dismissive of my suggestions and refused to allow himself any of the compassion that I insisted on. Only championing the point that these people would try to claim money that was not rightly theirs. So, we never spoke of it again. But the pensive shuffling men soon found their way into my dreams and became something of a preoccupation. Later in my room, buzzing in my ears, it would occur to me once again that the things that I most often worried about in comparison were embarrassing to admit to now. Even in front of myself. Because when I was aware enough to witness the trains of my more usual thought patterns, I knew that Africa was listening too and I couldn't be myself anymore.

****

One morning, a few days before I was due to depart, a couple in their 30s turned up unexpectedly towards the end of one of our rehearsals. Rouvanne and Lenni were white and they managed a well-known band called Amampondo, for whom Madosini occasionally guested; a percussion outfit from the township of Langa. Amampondo were one of the acts who'd played Nelson Mandela's 70th birthday party at Wembley Stadium and Rouvanne appeared keen to hear any music we'd created. Having noted his credentials, I immediately tried to talk my way out of this opportunity but wasn't successful because Vuyo was enthusiastic and kept furnishing us with suggestions of what we could perform. South Africa is not a place where you can justifiably surrender to weakness.

One of the concepts we were experimenting with was a version of my song *Evergreen* sung over an instrumental piece Madosini played on the umrhubhe. As yet, this was only worked out in an informal way and remained more of a loose idea. Nevertheless, we found ourselves playing it anyway with, in my case, palpitations.

Without ceremony, Rouvanne whipped out a hand-held camera to record this moment for posterity and at the time I assumed this was for his personal use. He came across as a true music enthusiast and I still had absolutely no sense of the internet and what was coming. That video found its way onto YouTube of course and when I saw myself years later it was an odd sensation of exposure. The world had changed forever and people could capture your performance and then broadcast it on a public platform even if it was just a rehearsal. But I didn't know about any of that yet.

He also recorded a spontaneous jam based around a marimba piece by Vuyo and a deranged theatre piece we'd only previously discussed, which involved Madosini and myself enacting an African fable where she rescued me from the Echingutu bird – a huge, black bird with a white collar.

After these 'recordings', the conversation moved on to gossip and general music trivia in Cape Town. Rouvanne and Lenni had come to pick up Madosini to take her to a beach where Amampondo were doing publicity shots and suggested that Vuyo and I should accompany them and get some photos with her too. In truth, I was fixated on getting back into my room as soon as possible but could again offer no plausible excuses.

We drove over to their house and offices in the white part of the city which I'd never seen before. After everything I'd witnessed since arriving in Africa, it was strange to finally experience some of the ivory grandeur of Cape Town, the European city, the affluence of the white areas and the fine homes surrounded by barbed wire. Even more unsettling, it was also a bit weird being around 'white people' again. They had a different feeling about them now.

****

We squeezed into a minibus with Amampondo and drove off to the photo session. There were so many members in the band that spaces were limited and I ended up by chance next to Madosini with the shock of recently having had to perform in front of the music managers still coursing through my veins.

The bus was a riot of bright colours because of the traditional costumes and the air was filled with the sound of happy, chattering African voices. All at once, a sense of comfort seemed to emanate from the warmth of Madosini's arm, which was pressed up against my own arm as we sat together on the cramped double seat. I was becoming accustomed to my silent self now. To the sense of being part of something and yet at the same time not part of something and suddenly the pressure of the weeks began to rise up in waves of exhaustion. As the minibus left the city behind, there beside Madosini I found myself laying my head upon her shoulder.

As the minutes passed neither of us pulled away and eventually, she took my head and cradled it in her arms. An expression of intimacy unlike anything which had passed between us before that moment. My eyes closed. My head on her shoulder in the bright sunshine. The warmth intensified. The sense of light grew stronger. This was not the sun that lives in the sky. It was another sun that rises from within us when the time is right. An inner sun that cannot shine as the result of any kind of demand but rises only as a gift that life delivers to us if it so chooses. A terrifying sense of the great reality that occurs when you are freed from thoughts and feelings and delivered into the imminent present.

****

They were gone for a while doing their photos whilst I sat on Table View Beach with its pale sands. Staring across the green sea to Table Mountain. The inner sun blazing on as a fine rain fell in the humid air and the breeze from the sea played over my face. That mad, twinkling smile from Snake Park reached out from the sands and took hold of me again. The clouds parted and the sky turned blue.

Rouvanne and the rest came bounding up and proceeded to take three hastily arranged photographs of Madosini, Vuyo, and I. However, just before Rouvanne snapped us – one of the members of Amampondo stepped in and popped an African headdress upon my head.

"The black feathers of a king," he laughed.

And they all laughed. Laughing at me again and I didn't know why. Their faces, alive with mischief. Something had shifted because I didn't care so much anymore – and I thought I knew for sure that there was no malice in it. They were just laughing – a laugh I'd never be able to understand.

****

My time in Cape Town was coming to an end and Vuyo drove us to meet his father. To me this was something of an honour, and I hoped an expression of our growing friendship, because Vuyo had already told me quite a lot about this man.

The hot sun was back out again and on the way there, Vuyo turned to me in the car, buoyant with anticipation.

"He's better at smiling and lying in his bed in the afternoons and letting God do the work," he laughed.

The old man lived in a shack in Gugulethu where sunlight shone in through a big whitewashed window that was perhaps once a shop front and into an empty looking room with a brown wooden slatted floor covered in dust. The ceiling slanted along to a lower wall adorned with simple Christian prayers and a poem written on paper by one of his grandchildren and stuck on with yellowing Sellotape.

"They will never be able to put you down, grandfather. Whatever they say about you or whatever they do to you, they will not succeed in breaking your spirit. They will never succeed in extinguishing the light from within you".

A few pieces of dusty old English furniture were scattered around the otherwise vacant room where he lay on a wooden bed. Vuyo's father had thick black rings under his eyes. They'd been given to him by the talons of an eagle when he was younger. A witch had stuck them around his eyes with the precision of an artist. The ritual's meaning had vanished into history and all that remained were the black rings like two black question marks under his eyes.

The old man fumbled in a plastic bag and pulled out some military badges that he wanted to show me, squabbling over them amongst himself in Xhosa, with Vuyo translating and explaining.

"He's lost the badge he once owned that came from the Boer war. That was given to him one day when he was still just a boy by an old drunk in the street. The drunk was dying"

Vuyo's father told stories from the past. One about a boy, whose face he'd just remembered that very morning, who'd stolen a polecat out of a cage in the old market of Gugulethu.

He spoke directly to me now in a hesitant broken English.

"We went in with the big sticks and beat them. We were beating the children too and he was one of them. That's when I remember his mother crying," he said.

"That boy," he continued, "ran away to the mountains after that - because there the sun brings you gifts of honey and soft margarine".

Just as quickly the old man went back to speaking in African with Vuyo translating again.

"He says he wants most of all to be on television with his grandchildren."

"He misses his white master. In those days, people knew where they were. He misses his place."

Vuyo would have never condoned such words but when translating for his father his voice remained measured and he offered no retort.

The old man continued mumbling, looking through the badges.

"He'll never say how much he loves his children and how much he hopes they will never see him die," Vuyo said.

"He beat his first wife when they were younger because she dropped money down at the drainage factory."

The old man handed me an envelope where he kept the hair of his granddaughter which was cut from her head on the day of her christening when she was three years old. Black curly hair in a faded yellow envelope.

He spoke again with a slow urgent passion. Vuyo patiently turned it all into English.

"In the mountains in Transky, there is a sheep farm where an old woman has a signet ring with the real blood of Jesus Christ in a tiny secret compartment.

"He knows now that in the end it doesn't matter how you live your life that matters. It's how you live your death that counts."

His face darkened as he clutched an old rosary and Vuyo continued competing with him in their opposing tongues.

"He abandoned some children down by the big river who were starving from lack of food. He had bread in his pocket for his own children."

"When the white's left, they took away their electric lights. He loved the electric lights and when they went you could see the stars but he was amazed by the electric lights."

We left him there fingering his way through the military badges and carefully returning them to the plastic bag. It felt to me an injustice to leave that old man on his own in that room. I wanted to kneel at his feet and weep.

****

To mark the occasion of my leaving South Africa, I searched out gifts for Yoneli and Yolanda and purchased some felt tips and colouring books from what Vuyo called the 'white man supermarket' by the airport.

Their joy had played a significant role in melting the ice frozen over our early rehearsals and I remained indebted to them. Their innocence in seeing me as something more than just the white man. They did not appear, as yet, to consciously bear the same wounds and as a result breathed fresher air into all our lives, which the rest of us were then able to breathe back in together.

One evening, as the sun cast an orange glow across the paving stones outside the house, I played guitar and stared up to Table Mountain whilst the girls skipped on the road. The outline of the mountain presided over many of the places I'd visited in Cape Town and its presence seemed to represent the patience of some ancient old man.

"Have you ever been up Table Mountain? Climbed it, I mean?" I said to Yolanda.

"No," they repeated together.

Yolanda and Yoneli stopped skipping and peered blinking up at the flat top of Table Mountain. At that moment, a handyman passed by staggering a crooked line, pushing a wheelbarrow brimming over with wooden planks. Flamingos were flying to the horizon in a flickering v shape.

The mountain coughed and cleared its throat, lit up its pipe, and puffs of white clouds rose up from out of its ears. Yolanda, who loved to read in English, rushed inside and reappeared to recite information concerning the mountain from her schoolbook.

Table Top listened back to his press release whilst regarding the white man and the two black girls who were staring back up at him from the front yard far away in Montana.

The following morning, accompanied by their mother, we travelled across town to the white district and took the cable car up. We looked out across the sea to Robben Island where Nelson Mandela had been captive for a number of his 27 years of imprisonment. Spontaneously baptising each other using water from rock pools that we discovered in the nooks and crannies - and at the very edge of one of the sheer drop promontories, we also discovered a perfect echo.

"Check out my refrigerator," screamed Yoneli.

"Check out my refrigerator," said the mountain.

"Wow!" said Yoneli.

"Wow!" said the mountain.

"Check out my refrigerator!" we all cried together.

"Check out my refrigerator!"

****

Later that afternoon, Vuyo took me out in the car once again. We drove aimlessly as he mused out loud about some of his favourite subjects. Car-jacking, Mandela, gumboot dancing, his girlfriend, his ex-girlfriends, his potential new girlfriends, who all had complicated stories attached to their exotic-sounding names. We roamed far and wide that day.

This was yet another part I'd never seen. Stopping the vehicle and winding down the window, Vuyo pointed out the dwelling place of a man who had persuaded Madosini into a recording studio a few years earlier to play a set of her songs.

"She was paid only seven rand, my brother," he said in a low voice.

"And Madosini knows nothing of recordings?" The wind was blowing over the tarpaulin that hung over the fence.

"She is from Transky. She doesn't know.

"He sold 10,000 copies of the CD to the whites and Madosini got nothing. Nothing, my brother."

Vuyo clicked his knuckles over the steering wheel.

People in this part of the townships lived in small prefabs and he showed me how the crooked producer had purchased all the prefabs around himself and turned them into a bigger interconnecting mini kingdom of prefabs on the proceeds of Madosini's recording.

Part of the old woman's serious and suspicious nature throughout the early part of our rehearsals began to make more sense to me.

Madosini lived in destitution and was forced many hours each day out on the street to hustle for cash to feed her grandchildren. Despite her musical genius she was cleaning and washing for people and trying to sell her handmade instruments.

"No. I told you already, my brother. She got nothing from him," said Vuyo, further annoyed.

The wind rustled around the little kingdom of prefabricated houses all barricaded together. All built on trickery and deceit and someone else's talent.

****

Further up the road, Vuyo spotted yet more of his vast army of acquaintances.

Everywhere we went, he seemed to know people. Quietly introducing me in mumbles again. I shook hands and looked into the drowsy eyes of six men who all appeared to be in their 40s and 50s but could have been younger, or older.

"Jose, Thousand, Oscar, Dizzyman, Spinach, and Mazaleni."

Vuyo readily accepted the reefa they were sharing and we stood together forming a rough circle at the corner of a quiet junction on a small square of scruffy brown grass surrounded by the rows of prefabs. Vuyo had grown far more relaxed regarding my presence and our days were completely unstructured now apart from the rehearsals. The men chatted on in slow, pensive African voices. No other cars passed by. They shrugged non-committedly as I refused the weed but still offered every time it came round to me again. Vuyo pulled his Mbira from the car and began to play. Even the wind seemed lazy. The humid air, like drapes over your shoulders.

Suddenly, the languid trance was broken.

"Mr White Man. You raped my mother!"

The loud, urgent voice was coming from a man in his early 30s with thick dreadlocks and a white sweatshirt and blue jeans, who'd rounded the corner and was striding towards us, shouting and pointing his finger at me.

"Mr White Man, you raped my sisters!"

A howl of great anguish. Vuyo remained on the floor with his Mbira and nobody else in the assembly moved either.

"You raped my country. You stole my Gods," he accused.

I could feel the heartbeat in my feet. Primal terror surging up through my body.

Vuyo stood up by my side and tried to interrupt the man who continued his tirade in African.

"You raped my mothers," he then shouted into my face.

"No I didn't," I replied looking into his wild eyes.

He remained inches from my face now.

"No, I didn't, no I didn't," I said again.

'This is it, he's going to kill me,' said the voice in my heart.

Vuyo barged in between us and spoke to him in Xhosa and the man remained quiet.

Then, Vuyo turned towards me laughing and said,

"He doesn't mean you, Patrick. He hates you because you are white."

Vuyo then spoke again in African. They argued for a minute or so more before the man retreated. Shouting, bounding away along the street. Still intoxicated by his own anger and turning back to gesticulate in my direction. Gradually, it began to hit home that I wasn't going to die or be beaten. Vuyo started to laugh again at my angry face saying I didn't understand.

"You are white, Patrick. Don't think that you are a black man."

The stoned circle shot me the same non-committal glance as before. The weed continued to circulate, and Vuyo went back to his Mbira.

I couldn't look at any of them. The truth was I would never truly understand what they had been through. A terrific gap seemed to stretch out between us, like the mouth of some great sadness that didn't know how to speak. The joint carried on going around and I wanted the ground to swallow me whole. From that moment onwards, the guilt I'd experienced since arriving in South Africa had a different aura around it. The terror I'd experienced in believing my life was coming to an end had dislodged some deep sense of survival. Finally, I recognised that I'd just have to believe in the hope of some kind of reconciliation but not by simply retreating into myself. The angry man with the dreadlocks had dragged that out of me.

****

The small group of men were still chatting away as I drifted back from my thoughts and Spinach turned and spoke to me in English. He was an ageing man with close cropped grey and black curly hair and one seriously bloodshot eye. A musician and, unlike most of the people I'd met in Cape Town, a man who'd had some experiences outside of the townships. Because of this, I sensed he felt some affinity towards me as an outsider.

"I saw a place called Barcelona once, man," he said.

"Oh yeah - I know," I replied.

"And it was a total fucking disgrace. I asked them why they called it Barcelona but nobody knew. Not one of them could tell me. What a disgrace that was. Ahhhh, brother," he shook his head at the ground and I nodded in agreement with no idea why I was agreeing. Just happy to have been included in something.

That evening, we met Tera in his yard and for the first time during my stay, they suggested we go out together. Vuyo drove us from the township and along the ring roads into Cape Town centre and then to an area with European architecture. Underneath a brown stone office building, down some steep stone steps, was a stone room illuminated by dark orange lamps. A small underground club with one central space surrounded by a few roughly hewn smaller rooms all of which were covered in African masks. In the larger room, on an obscurely lit stage, five African men performed a percussion improvisation using a variety of large drums. They moved nonchalantly back and forth on stage to the rhythm. The audience, who were entirely composed of white people, sat on plastic garden chairs facing the band. They were a mixture of young students and middle-aged New Agers and clusters of dreadlocked traveller-looking-types, who despite this wore expensive clothes and perfumes.

Together they played drums at the behest of a conductor, who raised and lowered his hands in time with the music and gesticulated rhythmical breaks with emphatic hand and mouth gestures. The white people in the audience stared at him and followed his every articulation. They were not always able to keep up with some of the more complicated phrases but none were slouches and the massive sound they created together in the echoing room was truly impressive.

The musicians on stage remained serious as the vibe began to build and their skill and perseverance in moving through the to and fro of the improvisation appeared faultless. Eventually, the music fully locked in and started to rise up through the foundations of the building and take possession of one and all. The deep pulse that beats through the landscape of Africa and belongs to no one.

****

After an hour or so, there was a break from this drumming, and in their usual relaxed manner Vuyo and Tera dragged me over to meet the band. Humphrey, the main man conductor, was tall with thick dreadlocks pouring down his back. He was wearing a white 70s suit and a fistful of charm bracelets hung down from around his neck. His face was pretty and he smelt strongly of whiskey and he insisted on offering me alcohol on several occasions in swift succession as I continued to refuse with a variety of increasingly unusual ripostes.

"If *I* drink alcohol, the police will have to come, Humphrey."

Or, "I would do, Humphrey, but they don't actually have enough booze in this whole place for me once I get started."

Confusing one-liners I'd used on other occasions to get people to back off who were encouraging me to drink. Humphrey however, instead of being taken aback, only chuckled at these jibes and as a result kept on offering and continuing to chuck whiskey down his own face. The black people and the white people had segregated into different parts of the club and as a result I didn't speak to a single white person all night. Instead, I sat with Vuyo, Tera and the band, plus their hangers on.

Humphrey eventually roused the band back on stage and the deep hypnotic rhythms broke in again. The audience returned to their chairs and started playing along with drums which they held between their knees. Humphrey was undoubtedly drunk and it was increasingly amusing to witness him play the fool whilst still looking cool as fuck.

"I like Humphrey," I shouted to Vuyo.

"He is a good man, but he drinks too much and I never knew anyone who's had so much trouble with women, my brother. Oh my God, my brother," Vuyo laughed, his gargantuan manic laugh shaking his head from side to side with his gold teeth flashing.

After two or three numbers, Humphrey grabbed the mic between songs.

"Tonight is a special occasion. We have a musician here with us in Cape Town, visiting from Britain. Land of hope and glory. He doesn't know it yet but he's coming up here with the brothers to help us out on this next number. Ladies and gents welcome to the stage, Patrick Duff!" He launched into my name with exaggerated long vowels whilst ushering me forwards with his hands.

I jumped up onto the stage to mercifully rousing applause and Humphrey passed me the thunder shaker. The band went into the next number and Humphrey continued to play the fool and conduct the audience through the rhythms.

Man, I was onstage in Cape Town with the brothers. On stage playing thunder. I kept my head down, joining in only occasionally as the thunder shaker made a real racket and I genuinely (maybe for the first time ever) didn't want to upstage anyone. Yet it was still one of the most uplifting experiences I'd ever had on a stage up to that point. The hypnotic charge and the relentless pounding of the beat and being a part of it. Standing next to Humphrey and feeling like I belonged. Our so-called song went on and on for about half an hour.

It wasn't till later that night as I lay in bed that I suddenly remembered. It was one of the many things the healer had prophesied on my behalf after he'd finished his vision. Just as I was leaving as we stood outside his shack in Snake Park, he'd whispered,

"And you will play on a stage before you leave South Africa, my brother."

The following morning was our final rehearsal and I would be returning to Bristol the next day. I could see no purpose in changing the strategy we'd developed which involved me simply listening to Madosini play.

Throughout all of our communications Madosini had never spoken directly to me and always looked at Vuyo as he translated my words and he in turn would look back in her direction as she replied. Her African dialect followed by his English interpretation, the pair of them seemingly in cahoots and me somewhat of a satellite. This last time however she noticeably faced more in my direction.

Her voice remained an incredible mystery to me. Dark, guttural, and full of the clicks of Xhosa.

"Madosini says this is the last day and you will go tomorrow. She wants to say she is happy you have come.

"Because of Madosini, you have come here to learn this music.

"Madosini says the young people from her village are not interested in her music. They have all gone away to the towns to look for work but you have come here from England to learn.

"Madosini says something has brought you here."

Her voice was suddenly rich and lilting as she began to speak for longer than I'd ever known her to.

"Madosini says this is the music of the grandmothers. Taught to her by her grandmother and from her grandmother to her grandmother back through from the ancestors to the beginning.

"This is our music, the gift of our people, which we pass on through the generations.

"Madosini says that she will now pass on to you what was passed on to her through her grandmother.

"Madosini says you must know you are the first white person and the first man who has received this gift from the ancestors."

She picked up the uhadi, turned her chair to fully face me and began to play a song. Slow and mournful and imparted with a great seriousness and concentration. Taken aback, I sat uncertain as to what was happening. Frozen to my seat. Then, astonishingly, Madosini raised her head and looked me in the eyes. She had never once held eye contact with me before. Never. Always avoiding my gaze until that moment.

Now she was looking right at me. Right into my eyes. As if a thick, dark hood which she had been wearing the whole time had suddenly been raised and thrown away. A sense of light appeared to arise from within her and then to surround her and then to occupy the space between us and then permeate through the whole room and the electricity began to pour through my body. The uhadi bow swayed back and forth, the tune turned inwards on itself, but gathering in intensity. Her garments pushed away from her left shoulder as the hollow gourd undulated across the flesh on the upper part of her breast to create the wah wah wah wah wah sound. My body began to twitch. The light she channelled reproduced a corresponding field of light in my imagination. A vast field of light stretching in all directions and a cool breeze blowing through with the ancient music.

It took all the strength of will I could muster within myself to remain still and experience the majesty of this woman who sat before me. Without attempting to defend myself against the intense power of her charisma, it seemed at one point that I was transforming. Becoming more of Madosini than I was of myself. Through the intensity of the passing moments, I kept repeating 'surrender, surrender' like a mantra within my head whenever the sense of vastness felt like it might overwhelm my own existence. Her brown eyes, my brown eyes. Her swooping voice, my swooping voice. Her body, my body. Her ancient spirit, my ancient spirit.

Once the song had ended the decorum of the room returned quickly and Madosini nodded once again with a profound seriousness. It had all happened so quickly and it was hard to assimilate but suddenly, in that moment, I believed I'd been transformed.

"Madosini says the project must continue now and she must come to

England and you, Patrick, must find a way to bring us there."

That night, I sat on the bedroom floor with Yoneli and Yolanda, who were miserable. Yoneli said I was her best friend in the whole world and they both drew me pictures with the felt tips I'd bought them.

The next day, before going to the airport, we drove to Gugulethu so I could say goodbye to Tera.

Tera, or Eric Lugano, had become my closest brother in Africa. He was sitting outside one of the native yards and sloped towards us as the car pulled over.

"I am sorry to see this day, my friend," he said.

We stood in the street.

"Your spirit is African, my brother Patrick. I have tried to show you something. You have seen a community but there is nothing to do here. Every day, my brother and I sit and wait, not knowing what to do. Time is long and hard. You are the first white person I have ever met in my life. You have done your people proud," he continued looking into my eyes.

"I have learned many lessons from you, Patrick. I will tell you honestly before meeting you I believed that all you white people were corrupt and that you were all evil, but you have shown me that this is not true."

He asked for my notebook and wrote away inside it as I stood before him. There was nothing any word could say that could express the admiration I experienced for this man.

He then told me about how he'd stood in the crowd the day Nelson Mandela was released from prison and how Mandela had spoken to the people. How the crowd's voice had risen up in an ecstatic victory wail. He said it was the greatest moment of his life as he clutched my hand,

"The greatest moment of my life, Patrick."

Tera walked away from us and back into his long, hard life in the township. A depression clouded over me and settled down in my mind and from somewhere deep in my heart I heard a voice from heaven crying black. I became even more troubled as Vuyo drove me to the airport. Once again, I simply didn't know who I was anymore.

CHAPTER 38

BRISTOL

In the turbulence of the plane, I opened my notebook to where Tera had written.

'Judge Me Not By The Colour Of My Skin'

'I met this white boy. He wants to know my name. I am black. I am not a man's man. I am God's son. He sees my expression. He is not happy.
Judge me not by the colour of my skin.

'His eyes are glittering. He shows me passion. He smiles at me. I smile back. I then tell him my name. He shows love. He looks caring.
Judge me not by the colour of my skin.

'We talk. We become instant friends. He is human just like me. He trust me. I trust him. I confide in him. He does the same. People are staring at us.
Judge me not by the colour of my skin.

'It is true you'll never know what you've got till it's gone. Is it not also true that you do not know what you've been missing until you meet it.
Judge me not.'

There were 6,000 miles still to fly.

****

When I arrived home, there was a dull, yellow light flickering in my kitchen. A mustard yellow. The walls were decaying and the lino came away under my feet and the armchair in the front room had been moved and was facing away from me as I entered from the landing. I went over to see if anyone was sitting in the chair and there was an old lady who looked like a shrunken head. Perhaps a thimbleful of life existed in her; perhaps she was dead.

The kitchen was warm and musty. My whole world was a kingdom of deterioration. In the rusty fridge, dripping with warm condensation, I found dead silver snakes and dead black fish and in the salad drawer there were dead tadpoles, but in my imagination I could see what they should have been. I could see the riverbed and the hazy water and the black fishes moving quickly. Then, the arms of the river were suddenly around me in an embrace.

I wanted to set fire to the flat. I held the dead tadpoles. The inert jelly, dead in my hands. The old woman with her chest caving inwards and her grey hair scraped back into a bun. The armchair a filthy dark purple and her brown face wrinkled with an estranged smile.

I wanted to torch the place. I could not conceive that a place could exist with such riches of decay. In the annex room, which was once a small toilet, there was now a mineshaft downwards. In an attempt to escape, I jumped into the hole. Down and down I fell, until I found myself on the top of a piston that rose and fell. The piston was part of a great machine that was part of a great factory that churned out people. People who looked like office workers, computer scientists, and county council chief executives.

I jumped off the piston and walked around the factory, lost and anxious, until a man came in with a torch. He was dressed in a purple suit. It was Jimi Hendrix. Jimi led me away from the factory with his torch through a series of dark corridors that lead to a backstage room. He handed me the feather from his brown hat and we walked out together onto a blacked-out stage where a spotlight searched over the audience's faces who were seated in silence on red velvet chairs. The spotlight eventually fell upon one particular person who wore a pig mask.

On stage, glass bottles were dancing around on a table, sliding in and out of each other like country dancing.

I told Jimi I didn't drink.

"It's not alcohol, man," he whispered back to me.

So, I tried one. It tasted of lime, lime green. Jimi told me to close my eyes and he showed me what green music sounded like. Then, the colours changed. Yellow music. Purple music. Black music.

He led me away from the stage and outside into the surrounding fields.

To a stately home, made of cubes, where each cube room was a different colour. Inside the cubes, the walls were like jelly and just for fun you could throw yourself against them and bounce back off and if you ran at them really fast you could run straight through the walls and into the next cube which was a different colour. Jimi and I decided to split ourselves into many different versions of ourselves so that we could occupy many compartments all at the same time. We became like hundreds of bees in a honeycomb but I still knew it was only me and Jimi really.

I watched one tiny me running around and I picked myself up and popped myself into my mouth. Experiencing within and without. Simultaneously being surrounded by myself 'and' surrounding myself. Like Russian dolls. The Russian dolls of myself.

We were in clear, deep water now.

Eventually, I came up out of the water. A snake's tongue licking at my face, flickering. I came up into a sunken garden. Waist deep in a stone pool. Something pink was coming into focus. It was a garland of pink flowers around the neck of a statue at the water's edge.

The feet and hands of this statue were alive and I knew that they were the feet and hands of Christ who was wearing a yellow and brown robe. I took hold of the hands and felt the warmth. The head and body of the statue remained stone. The stone head of a child king who leaned to one side with his stone crown. I kissed the stone face of the child king and he started to come back to life and then I saw the child king rise up and walk.

He led me out of the garden and into a market square where I saw the mediaeval ramparts that enclosed us. The scaffold and the gallows and the crowds. People were falling from the ramparts and the cobbles of the square were giving way. I watched people falling down into an underground river. The remaining crowd was waiting for an execution and rats were running away through the streets. I saw a man on the gallows hanging by his neck spinning on the rope and I watched him decaying down to a skeleton.

Then, I watched the flesh return to his bones. All his flesh grew back again and a strong handsome young man emerged. He raised up his arms and clutched the rope above his neck. He pulled himself upwards and eventually grabbed the top of the scaffold and released himself from the hanging rope. The crowd let out an almighty cheer and white horses ran into the square.

After several more days, I travelled out to Real World studios in Box to explain to Thomas we needed more time to write material. Anxious to see him again, all that worry was beside the point. He was nothing but encouraging regarding my suggestions and by juggling our budget was soon able to arrange for Madosini and Vuyo to stay in the U.K so we could continue our 'rehearsals'. In fact, as luck would have it, they were both playing with Amampondo at the WOMAD Reading festival that summer. So, after the gig we'd have three weeks together to sort out some music, he said.

Unfortunately, while unloading the gear in Reading, Vuyo dropped a giant bass marimba on his leg and was rushed to hospital. When I eventually met him again in the backstage hospitality tent, his wound was thickly bandaged but you could still see blots of blood seeping through the white linen.

****

Back in Bristol, rehearsals recommenced in the small back room of a house in Montpelier where Madosini and Vuyo were staying with a friend of Annie Menter's. On arrival, I had no idea how the process might unfold, but as soon as I walked into the room Madosini stopped playing and pointed to my guitar case. This was the first time she'd ever initiated action in a rehearsal and continued to gesture at the case, her head nodding. She started to play and then stopped. Again, to point at the guitar case with her reed. It appeared she was restless and eager to begin and so, reaching for the guitar, I moved a capo up and down the neck till I was roughly in tune with the unfretted string of her uhadi.

Madosini then began the same frantic song that had greeted me and despite all previous attempts, I found myself improvising lines over the top and staying in time - as well as staying in tune. Somehow, I just knew what to do now and the room began to pulsate with the rhythms as we locked in together for the first time. Once that music had taken root the three of us began to improvise melody lines with our voices, to create a trance-like round. Despite the fact that this was the first time we'd ever clicked, it sounded so natural and yet at the same time so unusual that by the end of the exploration we all began to laugh. This was one of the most extraordinary musical experiences of my lifetime. Our laughter grew and grew until it became almost hysterical and Madosini mimicked my laugh so that we all laughed some more – and somewhere in the midst of that laughter I got the feeling that the whole musical trial in Africa had been a test. Some kind of a strange test that they'd always known about.

But I couldn't be sure whether that was true or not. Or whether it really was the reason we were all laughing so much.

****

At the end of that three hour rehearsal, we'd written six songs. Six effortless songs that flowed spontaneously into the room. Finding myself improvising lyrics from my time in Cape Town and knowing we could have written six more if we'd wanted, because there was so much to say bubbling away inside me.

Thomas dropped in a few days later to listen. His presence and endorsement were an incredible source of strength to me at this time and after months of worrying I walked home that night with my head held high. I could finally breathe fresh air. Because something 'musical' had at last materialised and whatever obstacle had been blocking our collaboration seemed to have vanished.

However, the very next day all that pressure was straight back on again. We had a gig at Cropredy festival the following weekend. An event organised by Fairport Convention. Thomas had negotiated a slot on the bill so that we could get a taste of a live performance together, before embarking on our more rigorous PRS schedule.

****

Annie Menter drove us across to Oxfordshire where it quickly became apparent we'd been booked to play on the main stage. Our appearance had been hastily arranged and the organisers informed us that we had 15 minutes in between two of the scheduled acts, and that we'd be going on pretty much straight away.

As we waited at the side of the stage, I noticed my hands shaking. It was a hot, humid day and hairspray infused sweat began running into my eyes seconds before we were due to begin. There were hundreds of faces tilting up to listen and all our music was less than a week old.

However, before the compere had reached the end of his introductions and actually invited us on, Madosini broke rank. She limped awkwardly out from the wings and rudely cut over him and waved her umrhubhe mouth bow in the air screaming in Xhosa, pointing at the audience and gesticulating wildly, pacing back and forth along the front of the stage. A move that was not in our game plan whatsoever.

"What the fuck is she doing," I said to Vuyo through the side of my mouth.

He stood there unflustered. Ears slowly shifting out of his stoned reverie and attuning to the sound of her caterwauling. He sniffed the air and replied in the most casual manner,

"She is cursing them, my brother. This is the curse of her village. The curse of her people."

Madosini continued for a good minute shouting loudly and continuing to wave her arms. The compere had long since retired and all the faces waited in the sunshine staring up at her - uncertain as to what they were witnessing.

"What *is* she doing?" I mumbled once more. This time to myself.

Madosini began to play a quiet song on the umrhubhe. This wasn't in the game plan either. Stagehands ran round her with mics and a ghostly hush fell over the spectators. She held them suspended in a trance with the rumble of the rest of the festival still present but unattended to by anyone within her sway. An old woman with a mouth bow and hundreds, maybe even thousands, of people standing in a field in noonday silence.

Afterwards, rapturous applause broke out and the quality of that spontaneous reaction was thrilling to experience from the side of the stage. Like me, the audience had immediately taken her to their hearts –despite having been unknowingly cursed.

She then waved us on without even turning in our direction. My guitar was sliding wet in my hands but mercifully I had an incredibly simple part to play as we went into the first song we'd ever written together called, *My House Is Yours. Your House Is Mine*.

This number was a more rousing affair than the lament she'd just offered and I was the one who began the singing. A lonesome melody over uplifting African rhythms. Madosini had once told me that to see clear water in your dreams is a most auspicious sign and all the English lyrics were based around that image of clear dream water. She sang alongside me in the chorus in African as did Vuyo and we built up the hypnotic round to finish.

"My House is yours. Your House is mine. My House is yours. Your House is mine."

I never found out what they were actually saying.

This outro went on and on until I recognised that none of us were quite sure when it was supposed to stop as we'd never got around to writing an ending. Both Madosini and Vuyo had strayed a long way from anything we'd previously attempted in our rehearsals but I stuck to the plan and tried to maintain some kind of order by furnishing the music with a continuing reference.

Eventually, my sense of decorum grew stronger and I realised someone would have to do something. Knowing that the other two, intoxicated by the crowd's attention, would easily keep playing forever, I butted in musically and ended it in the most obvious way imaginable; by gradually slowing down and then doing a bleeding obvious rock 'n' roll bombastic final chord frantically strummed and intensified into one final series of stabs. Luckily, it seemed to work in a humorous kind of way because we were immediately hit by rounds of rowdy, fun-filled cheering.

****

The backstage team shouted our time was up. We'd managed to play just one song together but I walked off that stage like I was walking through the red dust on the planet Venus. Back in our dressing room, Madosini was woo-hooing to the top of the sky and outside I leant against the prefabricated hut. Despite everything I'd been through over the years, this was already the weirdest gig I'd ever done up to this point in my career.

****

Back in Bristol, rehearsals continued more slowly after our initial outpouring. Vuyo's leg was not healing and he was becoming increasingly convinced that this was because the English doctors had told him to keep it bandaged and covered in antiseptic ointments which up to this point he'd sceptically agreed to. It was a fearsome wound which he was utterly fascinated by and on countless occasions I was badgered into watching him undress the bandages to sit through another of his diagnoses. Where he'd lecture me on his opinions regarding the white man's medicine. One morning, with the healing still not advancing at a satisfactory pace as far as he was concerned, he pronounced the wound needed air and from that moment on each day we were greeted with the unappetising sight of it going septic. He would not listen to me imploring him to cover it up for his own sake and so I finally gave up.

CHAPTER 39

SINGAPORE

Our next engagement was a concert in Singapore at the WOMAD festival. On stepping off the plane, we were hit by a wall of tropical heat and even though it was past midnight, the sweat immediately began to pour down my face as we limped across the tarmac and into the air conditioning of passport control.

WOMAD had booked us into a luxurious hotel but jet lag soon had me wandering the nearby streets and at three a.m., a sudden rainstorm pelted showers of warm water onto the crown of my head. I was soaked through to the skin within seconds. Standing in the middle of the road with my head thrown back. The perfect antidote to the physical tyranny of a cramped plane and a tropical baptism to celebrate the longest journey I'd ever made in my life up to that point.

We still had five days until the concert and Madosini remained alone in her room whilst Vuyo chatted up women from the other WOMAD acts who were staying in the same hotel, leaving me at a loose end to explore Singapore. The Buddhist and Hindu temples and the endless shopping malls. All connected through to each other by long underground passages with air conditioning. And the Raffles Hotel Bar where little sparrows flew in through the open windows to take monkey nuts out of your fingers.

****

The night before our gig, Annie Menter invited Madosini, Vuyo, and I out to eat. Walking us from the hotel reception to a food hall in a nearby shopping mall where Madosini and Vuyo consumed more fried chicken than you would have believed possible.

Afterwards, we sat around the plastic table and Madosini appeared more relaxed than I'd ever seen her. This good naturedness encouraged me to ask a question I'd never felt able to before. Two of her fingers, one on each hand, were severed just below the knucklebone. I'd often wondered: Why was that? She didn't hesitate to respond and we were soon listening to the song of her voice and witnessing the expressive faces she pulled when telling stories about herself.

"Madosini says that when she was a young girl, the healer came because her mother and father were building a new hut for the family. The healer said that the house would need protection from evil spirits who live in the bush and who are always looking for a home. They will live anywhere they can, especially if there are young people. The healer said that they would need a powerful spell to ward off those spirits. So, he took Madosini's hands and chopped off two fingers and then later fixed them into the clay that is put into the central column at the ceiling. So that when the clay dried the knucklebones would stay up there and ward off the bush ghosts."

Madosini told this story with a surge of passion, waving her mutilated hands around to further emphasise the point. Uncharacteristically, her eyes caught mine on a number of occasions.

After this story, she relaxed still more and without prompting began to relate how she'd contracted polio. Madosini walked with a pronounced limp because one of her legs was permanently straight.

"Madosini says that the polio came when she was seven years old. She had to stay alone and could not play with the other children for a long time because she was so ill. She would never run again.

"Madosini went to live with her grandmother and this is when she was taught how to play the instruments. As a way of comforting her. Because she was the grandchild who was sick. This is when the music came and when her grandmother passed on the gifts of the ancestors.

"The first instrument Madosini learned was the uhadi. The metal string of that instrument is made from the bracelets of our grandmothers. When the grandmothers die, they take the bracelets that have been wound around their wrists for their whole lives and they hammer them straight again on railway sleepers. This is why the strings are crinkled and why they sound this way and why they are such a strong connection to our people.

"Once, when Madosini was younger, she led a line of children across the wilderness. Playing the mouth bow. The umrhubhe. Leading this line was the tradition of her village and a great honour. But it has all stopped now because the young people have moved away into the cities and the music of the ancestors is forgotten."

Madosini's face became grave as she continued and we sat around her in the food hall. In that moment, I suddenly recognised life had delivered me to a place far clearer than any I could ever have imagined for myself. The dreams I'd harboured for so long and which had caused me so much pain were being replaced by something simpler. The clear water that poured from this old African woman, who sat embodying a world so utterly different from my own. Suddenly, the strange wonder struck me. The fact that I'd ever even known her. The fact that I sat around a table with her now. The fact she knew me. That she knew my name. That we'd written songs together. That she'd shared such riches with me. And I honoured her now in a way I'd never known possible. Sitting before her half excited, half terrified, as she continued to recount the tale of the line of children that she'd once led through the wilderness with her mouth bow. Because I had already witnessed that scene in my imagination. I'd seen it clearly on the day back in Cape Town at rehearsals, when I'd first decided to stop trying to work out how to run the show and instead just listen to her play.

****

Although we'd already performed at Cropredy, this was our first full-length concert. WOMAD Singapore was held in Fort Canning Park. A series of gardens on the side of a hill where the ancient royalty of Singapore is believed to be buried. We were due to play on one of the smaller side stages on the outskirts of the festival.

In a humid canvas marquee that served as a backstage area, Madosini and Vuyo changed into their extravagant costumes and feather headdresses. Sitting before long mirrors, daubing dots of creamy paint onto their faces with their fingertips. Just before it was time to go on Madosini hung a mosaic of coloured beads around my neck and promised they were a blessing on me.

On stage, she sat in the middle whilst Vuyo and I flanked her on chairs, one either side. We proceeded to move through our newly born songs and the audience numbers increased as we played. Pulled to the stage by the eerie music that rose out into the warm, clear night. This time the sound was coming back through the monitors so pure and rich that I could fully hear the depths of the overtones she played with and how they added another layer of complexity to the overall sound and how Vuyo's percussion referenced those depths. The orange gourd of her bow burned brightly under the lights and I sat next to her in a state of awe; at times experiencing the strangest sensations, as if for brief flashing moments I was suddenly looking out of her eyes. For brief flashing moments suddenly seeing the faces of the audience from her point of view. And then just as suddenly being back behind my own eyes and finding myself playing guitar, and the shock of being me again not wanting to make any mistakes.

Madosini underwent a profound personality change onstage and I was quickly learning that she was capable of breaking away from any plan or set list to do whatever she felt if the mood took her. These interludes gave the concert a restless, spontaneous edge. She would start hopping around the stage shouting and whooping and pointing her finger at the audience or at the sky in a kind of mock accusation. These outbursts regularly drew clouds of spontaneous applause and delight from the audience which encouraged her to continue and go further.

I saw myself in a supportive role and was more than content to remain there. However, on a few nerve-racking occasions, the spotlight came upon me when I performed numbers which I'd written on her instruments. A song called *24 Hour Hard Shoulder Man*, about the sorry men who threw themselves in front of cars back in Cape Town. I launched into The Cramps-like riff on the uhadi whilst Madosini came in on backing vocals during the choruses and Vuyo accompanied me throughout with percussion which had changed every single time we'd ever played it – depending on what mood he was in or how stoned he was. That night in front of an audience, he went especially mad for it and I sensed a growing warmth coming from the crowd and searched for Thomas' face. There he was, smiling. I felt our friendship deepening in those days away, as my life opened up onto a narrow road of light that stretched out into the darkness.

Before leaving, Thomas also booked us into a recording studio in central Singapore so we could record some versions of our songs and get a sense of how they sounded on tape. However, on arrival Madosini's attitude shifted and she at once became suspicious and withdrawn. Because of her previous experience with recordings, she'd immediately recognised the environment. Through Vuyo, I implored her to understand that we would never take advantage of her, but seemingly she wasn't having it.

Annie, whom she trusted, repeated these sentiments but even with her assurances the old lady remained ruffled and petulant. The session was then conducted in a tension that would have given the mid period Rolling Stones a run for their money, and although Madosini did finally agree to play she offered nothing of her usual charisma. Vuyo and I argued about the song structures and all the progress we'd made and all the trust we'd developed amongst ourselves seemed to take a step back. The hood went down over her eyes again and we returned to the hotel in a silent taxi.

Next day, they flew to Cape Town and I returned to Bristol without even getting a chance to say goodbye.

****

After all the excitement and drama in Singapore, on getting home there was another sobering realisation. My now ex-girlfriend Sophie had left the flat and taken all the 'stuff' we possessed with her. Thinking about it, I do remember there was some talk regarding this, but on reflection I hadn't been listening properly. Anyway, there was no furniture left now. Even our bed was gone and the duvets and the plates and cutlery. Because in truth it was all hers anyway. Sophie was talented and clever and driven and she'd known how to make our house into a home. I sat on my amplifier eating dry muesli out of the box.

A few days later, I was interviewed by the *Independent* newspaper with a journalist coming up from London. In the paper he described it as my minimalist pad.

Behind the scenes in the bedroom, I was sleeping in a pop-up tent with coats thrown over it because she'd taken the curtains too – but thankfully I'd made sure he hadn't seen that.

Our next engagement was another WOMAD festival in the Canary Islands. First night there, lying on the bed in the hotel in Gran Canaria, I wrote the song *Thought Birds*, which 10 years later would appear on my album *Visions Of The Underworld*.

Here come the Thought Birds at the break of dawn
Singing out a chorus in the swaying corn
Carrying the cracked eggs of Einstein's disease
Whispering their dark names in the apple trees

And when they fly
They black out the sky
Standing in the shadows as the day goes by
And when they fly
They black out the sky
And when they fly
They black out the sky

Here come the Thought Birds scratching at the door
Ragged wings and kingdoms, Socrates with claws
On the horizon iron ships and blood
Twisted beaks and feathers fossilised in the mud

And when they fly
They black out the sky
Poisoning the shadows as the day goes by
And when they fly
They black out the sky
And when they fly
They black out the sky

****

Madosini arrived early the next afternoon and Vuyo called my room to say she wanted to see me. This was the first time we'd reconvened since the studio in Singapore and Madosini appeared to have remained agitated, mumbling to Vuyo that her straight leg was giving her pain after the aeroplane. She was in a room high up in our skyscraper hotel where it smelled strongly of the Vaseline that she often rubbed into her dry skin. From the window, you could look out across a jumble of roofs to the sea. Sunshine lit up her face as she sat awkwardly on the hotel chair, squinting and holding an uhadi in her right hand, which she waved about as she spoke.

"Madosini says she has given you a special gift, Patrick. She has passed on to you what has come from the ancestors. You must realise how great a gift this is. You have to be grateful to her. Madosini has made this uhadi for you. So that you can have your own instrument. She walked a long way in the hot sun to get the wood and the gourd.

"You must realise this is not easy for her. She is an old woman.

"Madosini has made this for you and you must pay her. You must pay 60 euros for this uhadi, Patrick. And you must pay her now. She will take the money from you straightaway."

These words were conveyed in an atmosphere that was impossible to read. A guardedness pervading the hotel room like the early days in Cape Town when Madosini had been robust and distant. I handed over the money and she nodded with her lips pursed in a sulky pout. Vuyo continued to enthuse about how much effort had gone into the making of my instrument even after I'd handed over the cash, which she methodically folded into her make do wallet, a small plastic bag she stuffed into a pouch worn around her waist.

I left the room uncertain again.

That night, alone I picked my way down to the edge of the sea, which was dark and wild due to strong westerly winds, and I watched the white foams chasing themselves up over the beach. Just out of reach of the waves, I drew a large circle in the sand and sat in the middle. Waiting for some inspiration. Waiting for some great thought to replace me. I wouldn't leave that circle until something came to my aid. But all you could hear was the sea calling back into your ears, and hours later I walked back up to the hotel through the sand. Nothing had happened and I'd have to face whatever was coming on my own.

I didn't see either Vuyo or Madosini over the next few days, and it wasn't until the night before our performance that we began to make plans. Once again, it was clear they expected me to come up with all the ideas. We had more time to fill at this festival and were on a larger stage further up the billing. My initial suggestion was that Madosini should go on alone and we could join her later on in the concert. She had a repertoire of hundreds of songs and could do anything she wanted.

"Madosini says we are all getting paid the same amount of money for this concert. We should all play for the same amount of time."

"OK, fair enough," I said, as we sat together in the Vaseline-smelling hotel room.

We had an hour-long set to deliver and lacked consistently strong material. It was then that another idea hit me.

"OK," I said, "We'll do the same set as Singapore, but I'll say some stuff about South Africa. I'll talk about my experiences in Cape Town"

****

The following evening, we took to the stage with a translator in tow. I'd ascertained that most of the audience would be Spanish speaking and wanted to be sure they'd understand. This time 'I' sat in the middle with Madosini and Vuyo on either side and to my far right towards the edge of the spacious outdoor stage stood the translator.

There had been torrential rain in the hours before our concert, but it had eased to a gentle drizzle. Going onstage, we were greeted by the sight of hundreds of black umbrellas and no sense of who was underneath them.

Although there were clear pictures in my mind, I hadn't exactly planned what to say between each of our songs and it was on that stage in Gran Canaria that it all started to unravel. The poverty, the squalor, the fires, the hard shoulder men, the squatter camps, the native yards, the fine white districts, the barbed wire. The same anger that had been cooking in me for some months began to rain down on all those umbrellas. Every time I turned to the translator and urged him to convey my stories, he became the focal point of the gig again. I'd dragged him in at the last minute and he stood there repeating the words, doubling the time it took. A nervous young man who had suddenly become the focus of a festival audience.

Madosini sat oblivious to proceedings, unable to understand a word either the translator or I spoke until she was roped into the next number which prompted the next diatribe of what was rapidly becoming a one man show. My one man show. On reflection, I could sense her sitting there unmoved in the corner of my eye but remained too wrapped up in myself to recognise the signs. Angry about what I'd seen in South Africa - I was getting carried away by that anger and by the sense of being judged by the audience for that anger - and the stage nerves further fuelling a growing sense of contempt.

John Lydon says that anger is an energy and I'm sure that's true but anger can be incredibly self-indulgent too. The charm, humour, and spirituality of Madosini's gigs that had inspired such awe in me were lost that night. Tera had said my spirit was African and I'd quite forgotten the fact that it was me under those umbrellas too. By the time I'd run out of steam, we walked off stage and Vuyo said,

"Let the old woman play".

She remained there and sang a mournful song that I'd never heard before. The strange beauty of her voice and the ancient vibration of the ancestors filled the damp night air. I stood at the side of the stage and immediately realised my mistake. I'd momentarily forgotten the hard lessons I'd learned in Cape Town. Still pumping with gig adrenaline, regret flooded my heart as she played on and I felt like sending a cry out into the darkness. But instead I stood listening to her and left the festival as soon as she'd finished. Back at the hotel, it was raining again and I stared out into the night with my forehead against the window and the sound of the air conditioning unravelling my soul.

****

The next afternoon we were booked to give an hour-long workshop. On arriving, it became clear that Madosini was going to tell stories and according to Annie Menter, there was nothing required from me but to listen. Hoping this workshop might be a chance for me to redeem myself, I'd been mistaken. A young African woman translated Madosini's words and I sat unable to comprehend either the Xhosa or the Spanish, listening until the final few minutes when everyone stood up together in the large, echoing warehouse.

Madosini had most likely been recounting tales of village life and customs to the sizable group of children accompanied by their parents.

For the finale of the workshop, with her mouth-bow between her lips, Madosini led the children in a line around the lengthy perimeter of the warehouse. It was the Xhosa tradition of her village coming alive before our eyes. The same ritual she had acted out as a young woman that had become denied to her because of the migration into cities and the young people's reticence regarding the music of their ancestors.

Hundreds of miles from her homestead, Madosini's eyes twinkled bright as she played the bow and the Spanish children snaked around the room behind her. They must have danced that large warehouse four or five times. She skipped and whistled and scraped and the children smiled and clapped along. I'd never seen Madosini so full of happiness as I stood there in the shadows with my head bowed, leaning against the corrugated iron wall; in my own way knowing just how much she had longed for this. Knowing how much it meant to her. Knowing that this moment was an expression of her most precious wish. Knowing that the ancestors were there too, weaving their strange magic on her behalf.

And it suddenly became clear this workshop was the real reason we had come to the Canary Islands.

****

We travelled back to the UK together in high spirits for two final engagements to honour our grant from the PRS. A gig at the Eden Project and a gig at the Bristol Folk House. Vuyo's leg was healing. Amazingly, it appeared he was right to have removed the bandages, and his wound was returning to a more palatable colour. We took the stage for the last time at The Folk House with the scars beginning to dry.

Our final concert blossomed into a celebration. I was back in my role of supporting. Many people had shown up and the response was uplifting and full of the specific kind of warmth you get at a hometown concert when it goes well. Afterwards we all hugged again in the dressing room and smiled and joked around and laughed, watching Madosini playing the fool backstage for the final time.

The project was over, and the following day I walked down to Montpelier to say my farewells.

CHAPTER 40

ROOFTOPS

Vuyo strutted out to greet me dressed in my favourite leather jacket. Having at first asked to borrow it, he'd recently begun to imply he wanted it, because of how much he would appreciate it – and because of the hardship of the townships – and because of what his friends back home would say if they ever saw him in a jacket like this one.

"That was so thin, like a shirt."

He could express himself with an almost childlike appeal when requesting people donate their possessions to him - and I'd watched him accomplish these steals on numerous occasions since his arrival in the UK. During his stay, he had accumulated stereo equipment complete with speakers, tape deck, turntable and amplifier, two ghetto blasters, an assortment of clothes and tablecloths. Incense burners, packs of cards, piles of cassette tapes, scented candles, plates, knives and forks and a key ring in the shape of a miniature formula one motor tyre with the word 'Michelin' impressed upon it. All now wrapped up in a series of bedsheets. But even with all that knowledge before my eyes he was still able to magpie my jacket away too.

However, Vuyo was sulking that particular morning, having just discovered that he was bringing home only a tiny fraction of his treasure trove. WOMAD insisting they were not prepared to pay the hundreds of pounds it would cost due to extra weight in the aircraft. Mercifully, 'our' budget was completely spent.

He moaned for a further few minutes and then seeing the futility in it and recognising this was our moment to say goodbye he snapped himself back, smoothing down the arms of my once leather jacket and sticking out his neck a couple of times.

"We don't say I love you to a man from where I come from," he said. "We say: I believe in you."

He looked at me straight with his strong brown eyes. "I believe in *you*, my brother," he said.

"I believe in *you*, my brother," I said straight back.

We gave each other a long hug and slapped each other on the back many times - and then he stood once more on the street in front of me in my leather jacket. As was often the case, laughing. I laughed too this time because I was pretty sure for once I knew what the joke was about. We both knew he'd pulled a fast one with that jacket and I didn't have what it took to ask for it back. Because I was white.

****

Madosini emerged from the house on York Road and into the cloudy street. Dressed in her casual clothes. A scruffy oversized dark-purple T-shirt with a wilting neckline and a brown travel blanket wrapped around her waist into a makeshift skirt. One more time shoving her precious instruments, carefully bound in bubble wrap and Sellotape, into a cab. Cars were parked either side of the thin street so that the stationary taxi blocked the road. She turned away from the boot and looked at me.

"Madosini says that she will now say something for you, Patrick."

She frowned a little in the summertime cloudiness, sweat glistening on her brow. Lopsided on her straight leg, rocking backwards and forwards on the tarmac.

"Madosini says that before you came to Africa, she'd returned to her village in Transky and it was a terrible sight in her eyes. The storms had come and blown the roof of her hut away. The hurricane had destroyed almost everything. There was nothing she could do but to bring the grandchildren to her son's apartment in Cape Town.

"When you came to Africa, Patrick, she did not know you. She had never even thought of a person like you. But the money we have generated from this project has given her enough to pay for the roof to be rebuilt. She is happy and she is saying that she is grateful to you. For your smile and for your love – and for your curiosity for the music and for the ancestors. This has put the roof back on her house again. They have been building and the work will be finished when she arrives home."

She looked me in the eyes now, smiling. A clear, natural smile that lit me up and lit up the streets around us.

"I… love… you," she suddenly said in broken English.

"I… love… you," she said once again in a voice that sounded so strange, coming from a mouth I'd never heard speak English before.

"I love you, Paaatriiick," she said, enjoying the unfamiliar sound of the words on her own lips, gesturing for me to approach in a manner that mockingly scolded me for not having approached already.

She threw her arms around my neck and I threw my arms around her and in the warmth of our embrace I spoke into her ear,

"I love you, Madosini. I love you, I really do."

"I love you Madosini."

"I… love… you," she said once more, and laughed.

Vuyo laughed too and we all laughed together and she began to dance in the middle of York Road, clapping her hands and spinning around on her straight leg and stamping her good leg into the ground and whooping loudly. She leant her head back and yowled and yelped and yodelled into the great, grey, gloomy sky of Montpellier. A grandmother on a warm, cloudy day with sweat dripping from her face until the heavens collapsed down upon us.

We stood there in the rain and tears came into my eyes again as they jumped into the taxi. She waved manically, smiling through the rear window as I waved back. There was a light in her eyes. Freedom, and mischief, indescribable sadness, and indescribable dignity.

A Black Madonna from a remote village in Transky on the Eastern Cape who'd one day witnessed a whole new world driving towards her in a motor car. An 81-year-old little girl whose eyes stretched back to the beginning of time.

Vuyo sat up front of the car, already engaged with the driver in an oration of his township life that would continue all the way to Heathrow. Madosini was going home to her beloved grandchildren. Watching as they drove away along the very same road where years before just 10 doors up I'd lived with Elin and her mum.

Madosini continued to wave out the back window until the end of the street where she turned away and leant her head against the window. She would mumble quiet songs to herself for the whole of that journey home. The taxi disappeared and the rain stopped and a couple of junkies walked by half engaged in an anxious conversation. Madosini was gone and I stood for a while with my feet stuck to the road. Because I really didn't know which way I was supposed to go anymore.

****

I walked back home and in the weeks and months that followed found myself writing songs once more. Which, in truth, was all I'd ever known how to do. Still not knowing what was going to happen to me.

These songs didn't suddenly sound African and on the surface nothing much seemed to have changed. It was the same kind of song I'd always written until I recognised the place from within me where that music came from was singing so much more closely in my ears now. Because as the dust began to settle at the end of all those experiences, I woke up one morning and just knew it in my bloodstream. She was a songwriter and I was a songwriter and no one would ever be able to take that away from us. Madosini had left me with the certain knowledge of the greatest gift of my lifetime.

Meeting and writing music with an old woman who'd played for 79 years on top of a mountain to no one but sheep before experiencing any kind of recognition whatsoever – and then falling in love with her – had given me a glimpse into a different world.

Madosini didn't even know who Elvis was. She didn't know that Brian had died in the swimming pool. That Kurt had shot himself. That McCartney was still here attempting to perfect his legacy.

She showed me simply and without words – another world. A world that had always been closer to me than the one I'd been living in and one I was finally able to truly recognise by her living example.

Because somewhere along the way, I'd lost my way. Homeless and apparently rootless and then signed to EMI in a haze of drugs and alcohol and then coming out of those wasted years surrounded by successful contemporaries and suddenly realising I wanted to be successful myself.

Desperate to prove something. Desperate to prove to everybody that I was somebody just at the same time that it was all taken away.

Deep down I'd seen myself as a failure ever since.

My head was still full of those hopes and fears. I'd been floating in a void for years. Living a kind of improvisation in which I tried to hide or master these anxieties and preoccupations. Difficulties within myself which in truth I'd always battled with – but which the 90s in Britain had helped to further develop in a specific way - and that were even now still continuing to shape-shift through my life. Because I was never going to change completely. I'd always be somehow part of the scene. A western musician in a sea of other western musicians all competing for survival. I knew that. I'd never be able to totally walk away from all my hopes and fears. Africa had shown me that. Because by travelling to Cape Town I'd finally started being able to accept myself. The way I actually was. And not by pretending I was someone else who was deeper and beyond it all.

Because at the same time as all those dreams there was something else and it really, really, really wasn't the consolation prize. It was something richer and more mysterious than anything any rock 'n' roll dream of mine would ever be able to deliver. A spirit I'd always sensed was present in the silence when the music was over. In the silence when the music was playing. A spirit that had visited me on occasions. A spirit that had revealed itself to me as a little boy. A spirit I'd once sensed in the Albert Hall. A spirit that had saved me from addiction. A spirit that had spoken to me on the hillsides of Carmarthenshire. A spirit that had led me to Africa and carried me through every triumph and mistake I'd ever known.

I was part of a living tradition that stretches back into the mists of time. My little history was connected to a greater history. A greater history that made sense of all the pain and all the joy of my own little life. A greater history that connected me through to the ghosts of my own ancestors.

Because after Madosini left that's what began to happen. My ancestors came to me over and over again in dreams and visions. Irish and Welsh ghosts who, despite being dead, still had things that they wanted to say to the world. Things left unsaid which I turned into songs for them. And they queued up to talk to me.

Through the crucible of my own life, and then by her sudden presence, Madosini had crystalised what my dad had unknowingly been trying to teach me all those years before. On Saturday nights when he'd play the songs my grandfather had taught him. That music is a spirit that gets passed down through the generations. And that spirit needs music to stay alive. And that this is my job. To keep that spirit alive. And to write songs that arise from that place. Because there is a place for me. The place where all dreams end.

I needed someone from a faraway world to show me that.

Life is simple. Simpler than I'd ever realised.

Danny Freeman
My name is Danny Freeman
From the fighting town of Cork
I learned to drink Malt Whiskey
Before I could even talk
I'm the man who stole your wife
Let me tell you to your face
My name is Danny Freeman
And I'm back in the race.
They said that I was washed up
That I had lost my spine
Cause I squandered my inheritance
On devil drinking wine
Come sit beside me brother
And I'll plainly state my case
There was never a state that I was in
That was not a state of grace
My name is Danny Freeman
And I'm back in the race
So saddle up that old grey goose
It's another New Year's Day
And everything I ever owned
Was the price I had to pay
My name is Danny Freeman
And I'm riding high today
So listen up you gentlemen
With all your precious gold
The day will come and you'll all bow down
To a treasure that can't be sold
And everything you've sailed for
Will be sunk without a trace
And all your precious words and deeds
Will be spat in your face
My name is Danny Freeman
And I'm back in the race

Patrick Duff

LOVE IS STRANGE

My life was only just beginning and that story continues in another book I've already written and soon to be published which describes the path that materialised at my feet after meeting Madosini. A path I could never have planned. Because I was to walk further out into the darkness I'd seen on the Downs in the weeks after Strangelove had ended. A path that took me all around the world.

I wrote this book for you. Not for me. I wrote it for every person who's ever struggled and messed up and who is trying to stay alive and stay true to themselves and who senses that they do have something beautiful to say despite everything. This is part of my contribution to that. I hope that it helps you to keep on keeping on.

I've never written a book before and I did it by myself as the spirit watched over me. One afternoon, I got back into bed, closed my eyes and waited. The first thing I saw in my imagination was that tour bus.

Perhaps you'll come and see me at one of my concerts one day – I hope so. And I truly hope you'll hear the spirit in the music I play and I hope you'll stay till the end. To say hello.

INDEX

Oh as i was young and easy
in the mercy of his means,
Time held me green and dying
Though i sang in my chains like the sea

Dylan Thomas